About Island Press

Since 1984, the nonprofit Island Press has been stimulating, shaping, and communicating the ideas that are essential for solving environmental problems worldwide. With more than 800 titles in print and some 40 new releases each year, we are the nation's leading publisher on environmental issues. We identify innovative thinkers and emerging trends in the environmental field. We work with world-renowned experts and authors to develop cross-disciplinary solutions to environmental challenges.

Island Press designs and implements coordinated book publication campaigns in order to communicate our critical messages in print, in person, and online using the latest technologies, programs, and the media. Our goal: to reach targeted audiences—scientists, policymakers, environmental advocates, the media, and concerned citizens—who can and will take action to protect the plants and animals that enrich our world, the ecosystems we need to survive, the water we drink, and the air we breathe.

Island Press gratefully acknowledges the support of its work by the Agua Fund, Inc., The Margaret A. Cargill Foundation, Betsy and Jesse Fink Foundation, The William and Flora Hewlett Foundation, The Kresge Foundation, The Forrest and Frances Lattner Foundation, The Andrew W. Mellon Foundation, The Curtis and Edith Munson Foundation, The Overbrook Foundation, The David and Lucile Packard Foundation, The Summit Foundation, Trust for Architectural Easements, The Winslow Foundation, and other generous donors.

The opinions expressed in this book are those of the author(s) and do not necessarily reflect the views of our donors.

SUSTAINABILITY IN AMERICA'S CITIES

Sustainability in America's Cities

Creating the Green Metropolis

Edited by Matthew I. Slavin

 **ISLAND**PRESS

Washington | Covelo | London

Library of Congress Cataloging-in-Publication Data

Sustainability in America's cities : creating the green metropolis / edited by Matthew I. Slavin.
    p. cm.
  Includes bibliographical references and index.
  ISBN-13: 978-1-59726-741-0 (cloth : alk. paper)
  ISBN-10: 1-59726-741-4 (cloth : alk. paper)
  ISBN-13: 978-1-59726-742-7 (pbk. : alk. paper)
  ISBN-10: 1-59726-742-2 (pbk. : alk. paper) 1. Urban ecology (Sociology)—United States. 2. Urban
policy—United States. 3. City planning—Environmental aspects—United States. 4. Urban ecology
(Sociology)—United States—Case studies. 5. Sustainable development—United States. I. Slavin,
Matthew I.
  HT243.U6S87 2011
  307.760973–dc22

                                                                                    2010044184

Printed using Electra

Text design by Karen Wenk
Typesetting by Karen Wenk
Printed by

Printed on recycled, acid-free paper

Manufactured in the United States of America
10 9 8 7 6 5 4 3 2 1

Keywords: Bicycle infrastructure, brownfield remediation, car share, climate action planning, green building,
green economy, Honolulu, LEED, Milwaukee, mobility, New York, ocean wave energy, Philadelphia,
Phoenix, Portland (OR), renewable energy, San Francisco, stormwater management, sustainable city, triple
bottom line, urban agriculture, urban forestry, urban planning, urban policy, Washington, DC

CONTENTS

H ow things have changed. It wasn't too many years ago that the idea of a sustainable city in the United States or elsewhere was held to great ridicule as impossible to define and unrealistic to attain. Although these issues are still debated, there is today a much deeper understanding of sustainability in cities than ever before. What seemed to some like a fad just ten or fifteen years ago seems like serious and enduring public policy today.

Although cities' interest in the pursuit of sustainability has waxed and waned, there are today no fewer than fifty major U.S. cities that have come to the realization that the pursuit of some aspect of sustainability warrants explicit attention as a matter of local public policy. Some cities have looked to sustainability policies as a mechanism to achieve greater social and environmental equity (Agyeman 2005; Pearsall and Pierce 2010). Others have seen sustainability as a way of making a measurable contribution to fighting climate change in the face of Washington, D.C., political institutions unwilling to take on this issue (Betsill and Bulkeley 2006). Still others have come to realize that sustainability (especially "green" and "smart growth") approaches to local economic development may well offer pathways to livability where traditional approaches to economic development now fail (Fitzgerald 2010; O'Connell 2009). Washington, D.C., has even seemed at times to be moderately willing to be supportive, particularly through the Obama administration's dual focus on "green jobs" and the economic stimulus of 2009, although congressional elections in late 2010 cast doubt upon the durability of this support. Still, cities sometimes have responded by recognizing that they can get more federal aid for economic development when they propose to create green jobs. Regardless of the specific motivation, sustainability in cities seems alive and well, here to stay.

Early city efforts were largely grounded in defining sustainable indicators projects. The activities of Sustainable Seattle, Inc., in the late 1980s were focused on creating an indicators project (AtKisson 1996), and many other cities followed suit. Sometimes alternatively referred to as indicators of livability or indicators of progress, these projects seemed to percolate from the grassroots. They rarely originated in city government, but rather got their impetus from resident groups and organizations. They appeared motivated by the dual assumption that developing an indicators project, which specified measures of important sustainability variables and monitored them over time, would necessarily produce greater sustainability, and measurement of progress would push reluctant or resistant city governments into appreciating the pursuit of sustainability (Brugmann 1997).

Today, city governments themselves have taken up the charge, often incorporating the work of resident and nonprofit organizations and sometimes defining a need where resident organizations have not (Portney and Berry 2010; Portney and Cuttler 2010). Such city efforts, along with those originally spearheaded by grassroots and neighborhood organizations, focus on specific public policies that are thought to be consistent with trying to become more sustainable (Jepson 2004; Zeemering 2009). Cities have adopted and implemented policies and programs that convert their vehicle fleets to alternative fuels and hybrids; they encourage or require green building, especially greater energy efficiency; they provide funding for homeowners to retrofit their buildings for energy efficiency; they adopt policies to protect and improve the quality and accessibility of their water; they try to reduce the amount of carbon and other air emissions originating in their boundaries; they change the way they practice land use management through zoning to emphasize highest and best environmental and ecological uses rather than highest and best economic uses; they practice mixed use development and urban in-fill housing to encourage greater density and decreased energy consumption; they offer alternative food sources through sustainable agriculture, food policy systems, and community gardens; they try to get residents out of the personal motor vehicles and to look for more efficient alternatives, including public transit; they try to clean up hazardous brownfield sites, and to limit their residents' exposures to known hazardous materials; they sometimes even work with other metropolitan and regional municipalities to deal with externalities that are often ignored, such as sprawl; they protect open spaces and parklands; they engage in strategic economic development to encourage more green jobs—employment that is not associated with environmental degradation; and many other activities and programs. These programs have actually been adopted and implemented. And they do these programs in order to grow their local economies, not to limit them. This is not pie-in-the-sky wishful thinking.

With all the activities going on in cities to work toward becoming more sustainable, perhaps the most surprising fact is that the empirical analysis of those activities is still in its infancy. While increasing numbers of cities have bought into the idea that they can become more sustainable places, and into the idea that there are good and valid reasons for doing so, much of the written work on sustainable cities takes the form of outright advocacy, almost at times preaching a pure gospel rather than making clear empirical arguments concerning what works and what doesn't in cities' actual experiences. This is beginning to change. Rather than being told what could be done or what should be done, research is starting to address the direct issues of what kinds of programs and policies have been tried, which have worked, how they have worked, and why they might work (or not work) better in some contexts and cities than others.

There is a real thirst among city leaders to learn what other cities are doing, to understand what some refer to as "best practices." Yet research on sustainability in U.S. cities has certainly not advanced to the point that such best practices can readily be identified. There are many works that describe programs that cities could pursue, but fewer works that give detailed accounts of how cities actually develop such programs. Cities' practices can be identified, but without some assessment of how well these practices work in different settings, prescriptions seem premature at best. And so, as described below, this book jumps into the void, providing detailed information heretofore not readily available. But more on this later.

There is much research that needs to be accomplished in the realm of sustainable cities. There are many empirical questions that need to be addressed, and this book takes us down the path of starting to fill some of those gaps. There are very basic questions: How can sustainability policies be designed to ensure that they do not cost more than unsustainable alternatives? How can local

officials be convinced that making longer-term investments in sustainable alternatives saves money in the long run? Which specific policies and programs seem
to work best? Are there more (or less) effective ways of implementing sustainability programs? Are there ways to effectively influence local officials to cooperate and coordinate with surrounding municipalities? Can sustainability be pursued, as a matter of local public policy, in ways that definitively support both
short-term and long-term economic growth? To what extent, and in what ways,
do local policies contribute, in some measurable way, to making cities and metropolitan areas more sustainable? There is much common wisdom about most
of these issues, but there is surprisingly little systematic research on these and a
whole host of related issues.

An important part of moving sustainable cities research along requires in-
depth analysis of specific issues, cases, and cities. That's what this book does.
Each chapter in this book provides a city-specific look at a program or initiative
that addresses a particular aspect of local sustainability. Each chapter situates its
analysis in a particular line of inquiry, helping the reader understand why this
"case" is important, effective, and potentially transferable. I also have some
thoughts about how to situate these cases, and how to relate them to other research and pressing questions.

In chapter 2, Matthew Slavin and Kent Snyder present an analysis of the policies and programs that the city of Portland has developed to address climate protection through reducing greenhouse gas emissions across the city. This case
study is important for several reasons. Portland has probably done more, to
greater effect, than any other city in the United States. To understand what a city
can do, in a comprehensive and integrated way, this chapter provides a level of
detail that should help inform similar efforts elsewhere. Contrary to much common wisdom, it also provides evidence that when cities choose to address air
emissions problems, they can be pretty successful. In chapter 3, Christopher
DeSousa provides a firsthand account of sustainable redevelopment that has
been done in Milwaukee. With the demise of much of its manufacturing employment base, and the abandoned buildings and properties that came with this
demise, Milwaukee embarked on an effort to redefine the design and development of a large section of the city in ways that are consistent with the pursuit of
sustainability. For those who do not have a vision of what such redevelopment
might look like, this chapter is must reading. In chapter 4, Jonathan Fink examines efforts to develop green technology industries as a major strategic part of

the local economy in Phoenix. He makes the case that such strategic efforts do not guarantee success in terms of economic development. Economic development is difficult under any circumstance, and building a green economy is neither easy nor necessarily more successful than more traditional economic development.

In chapter 5, Gerrit Knaap and colleagues at the University of Maryland take a focused look at LEED-certified green building in the nation's capital. They point to Washington, D.C., and its environs as being at the forefront of the movement to plan and develop LEED buildings, and how the green building movement is the product of a convergence between public sector policy makers and private sector property developers. While the progress in constructing LEED buildings has been significant, the authors suggest that the greatest benefit in terms of creating sustainable cities in the future may be extending the principles underlying LEED more broadly to the design and development of area-wide patterns of land use, density, and transportation and urban infrastructure.

Chapter 6, by Aaron Golub and Jason Henderson, addresses the very important issue of what can be done to get people to be less dependent on their personal motor vehicles, as illustrated in the case of San Francisco. Unfortunately, many cities concede that this challenge is impossible to address. Particularly because of the link between motor vehicle use and air emissions, finding alternative ways for people to be geographically mobile is of great importance. This chapter provides a wealth of possibilities for cities contemplating their alternatives. Just as motor vehicles represent major contributors to air emissions, so too does the production of energy (especially electricity). Chapter 7, authored by Matthew Slavin, Doug Codiga, and Jason Zeller, focuses on what Honolulu has accomplished in its effort to become energy-independent through developing renewable energy sources.

Philadelphia, in its larger metropolitan context, provides a platform for Lynn Mandarano to present in chapter 8 the excellent case of what has been done to manage storm water in a sustainable way. Philadelphia represents an important case study of sustainability broadly, particularly because it has come such a long way in a relatively short period of time. Largely since the election of Michael Nutter as mayor, the city has taken on tough management and policy issues related to sustainability, including watershed, wastewater, and storm water management. Like Philadelphia, New York City has made incredible strides in its effort to try to become more sustainable. Anchored by its PlaNYC strategic plan, with strong support from Mayor Michael Bloomberg, New York has arguably done more to achieve sustainability results than any city in North America. It is fitting that two chapters should be devoted to specific elements of this effort. In Chapter 9, P. Timon McPherson provides a case study of what that city has done to protect and improve urban green space through urban forest restoration. And in chapter 10, Nevin Cohenn and Jennifer Obadia take a close look at how New York has sought to address food security and sustainable food systems through greening the food supply.

Individually, these chapters represent important, in-depth analyses of specific cities' programs. Taken together, they build a rich picture of the great opportunities have to affect their sustainability and livability. City leaders should find these contributions to be very helpful as they contemplate whether, and how to, address sustainability in their own places and contexts.

—Kent E. Portney, Tufts University

ACKNOWLEDGMENTS

Publishing an edited volume is never easy. This is particularly true when addressing a subject as wide-ranging, multidisciplinary, and rapidly evolving as urban sustainability. Reflecting this, this book brings together a number of scholars and practicing professionals who have drawn upon their expertise to contribute original, previously unpublished empirical studies of how large cities in America are working to make themselves more sustainable. Above all, I want to thank the contributors to this book for their enthusiasm and their willingness to share their accumulated knowledge.

I want to thank Island Press for recognizing the need for a book that can help both educate students, policy makers, and professionals in the practice of developing more sustainable cities. Both Island Press Senior Editor Heather Boyer and Assistant Editor Courtney Lix demonstrated the level of professionalism and commitment that has established Island Press as a global leader in stimulating and communicating ideas for creating a more sustainable future in the United States and globally. I want to express my most heartfelt appreciation to Heather and Courtney as well as everyone else at Island who has worked to bring this book to fruition.

Last, I want to thank Sy Adler, Professor of Urban Studies and Planning at Portland State University. It was during a discussion with Sy that I mentioned the need for a book that would empirically examine the issue of urban sustainability in a broader context across a range of American cities. Sy suggested that I expand my work into a book. The results can be found in the pages that follow.

Chapter 1

The Rise of the Urban Sustainability Movement in America

MATTHEW I. SLAVIN

> It remains to be seen how U.S. cities will act to reduce their carbon emis-
> sions in coming years . . . given that most cities . . . have already been built
> and it is becoming crucial to find ways in which to make them function
> sustainably.
>
> —Herbert Girardet, World Future Council, 2008

In searching for a tipping point at which sustainability became mainstream
in America, one might look to 2005. In that year website SustainLane.com
began issuing annual rankings of the fifty most populous cities in the United
States. SustainLane is not the only rating system that uses quantitative scoring to
rank U.S. cities in terms of how green they are, but it has become the most highly
visible and widely referenced source for comparatively assessing sustainability
in urban America. Its annual rankings have been reported by broadcast media
networks National Public Radio, CNN, NBC, CBS, and ABC, posted on a wide
range of social networking Internet sites, and received coverage in the *New York
Times*, *Wall Street Journal*, *Los Angeles Times*, and *USA Today*. Mayors Michael
Bloomberg of New York, Richard Daley of Chicago, and Gavin Newsom of San
Francisco have all publicly praised the website and the high rankings accorded

their city's greening initiatives.[1] In the age of the Internet, SustainLane is perhaps the most visible sign of the rise of sustainability to the top of public policy agendas in the urban milieu in which nearly 80 percent of Americans now live and work.

Defining the Sustainable City

The word *sustainability* has come into such common usage that it sometimes seems ubiquitous. At the outset, this leads to the need to answer two principal questions with regard to the sustainable cities movement. First, what is a sustainable city? And second, why is it important that cities become sustainable? In answering these questions, it is useful to draw a distinction between sustainability and sustainable development. Sustainability in its broadest sense is the capacity of natural systems to endure, to remain diverse and productive over time. Sustainable development is the practice of humans arriving at a level of economic and social development that does not inevitably alter ecological balance.[2]

Sustainable cities are those that design and manage their form of governance, economies, built environment, transportation systems, energy and water use, food production, and waste in a manner that imposes the smallest possible footprint upon the environment. They strive to transport themselves using means that minimize fuel consumption and pollution and greenhouse gas emissions and build and operate buildings that conserve energy and water and provide healthful living and working conditions. They feed themselves with locally produced agriculture and utilize renewable energy. They have economies that seek to benefit from emerging growth technologies and job sectors that minimize environmental externalities and embrace long-term commitments to an inclusive range of workers. They strive to reuse brownfields and recycle, re-manufacture, and otherwise divert materials from landfills and incinerators. Sustainable cities couple top-down visionary governance with bottom-up involvement. They embrace a collaborative and consensual approach to policymaking among governments, businesses, and environmentalists that aims to proactively and cost-effectively eliminate or reduce the loss of biodiversity and forestall potential ecological calamity. The sustainable cities movement signals a departure from the kinds of trade-offs and antagonisms between economic development and the environment that have traditionally characterized urban development in the United States.[3]

The Rise of the Sustainable Cities Movement

As to why cities globally are acting to make themselves more sustainable, three principal reasons present themselves. First, urbanization has created increasingly unavoidable conflicts between development and local environmental carrying capacity. At the same time, the limits of traditional infrastructure and other technological approaches to maintaining a balance between development and the environment are becoming unavoidably clear. Cities have embraced sustainability in an effort to find alternative, low-impact solutions to meeting their public infrastructure, health, and community livability obligations. Second, economic development is a primary function of municipal governance. In their sustainability initiatives, cities seek to capture the benefits of emerging green economy opportunities. Third, global warming is perhaps the predominant imperative confronting the world in the twenty-first century. The threat it poses to America's cities is significant. Cities have embraced sustainable development as a means to mitigate and adapt to climate change. How cities are responding to these challenges though their sustainability initiatives is the major theme of this book.

Today 80 percent of Americans reside in urban areas. The nation's cities are home to preponderant concentrations of America's economic resources and industry. An overwhelming majority of the nation's 71 billion square feet of commercial office, apartment, and industrial buildings and 128 million housing units are in cities, which together consume 40 percent of the nation's energy and produce an equivalent amount of total U.S. greenhouse gas emissions. Feeding the 244 million Americans who live in urban areas is highly energy intensive. So is transporting urban America; transportation accounts for 29 percent of U.S. energy use and generates an equivalent share of U.S. greenhouse gas emissions. In 2007, the United States generated approximately 254 million tons of municipal solid waste, mostly from cities.[4]

Sprawl has been perhaps the most defining characteristic of urban America over the past 60 years. Sprawl and attending automobile dependence and decentralization of industry have had a number of deleterious consequences including air and water pollution, congestion, and disintegration of once-vibrant central city neighborhoods. Sprawl has led to encroachment upon wildlife habitats and destruction of wetland resources critical to controlling floods and protecting drinking water supplies and increased public service and infrastructure costs.

Urban sprawl has been linked to increased public health risks arising from poor nutrition, increased obesity and hypertension, and heightened incidences of traffic fatalities.[5]

That urban infrastructure is under pressure is clear. A widely cited 2007 study by consulting firm Booz Allen Hamilton placed the price tag of repairing urban water, power, sewer, and transportation infrastructure in the United States over the following 25 years at $6.5 trillion.[6] Retrenchment by the federal government from financial assistance to cities that began in the late 1980s placed greater burdens on local governments. The generally growing economy of the 1990s and first half decade of the twenty-first century bolstered city finances. However, the recession that settled upon the United States in December of 2007 has struck city finances hard. Overall city revenues dropped in 2009 for the first time since 2002, providing for the worst fiscal outlook for U.S. cities in twenty-four years. With the *Wall Street Journal* reporting that American cities "have the worst ahead of them," they are unlikely to be able to fund the investments needed to construct new infrastructure and repair deficiencies on their own in the foreseeable future.[7] To the degree that urban sustainability initiatives can reduce the cost of these investments while addressing environmental carrying capacity concerns, cities will be better able to meet their public infrastructure needs in the future.

Highly public spectacles have brought home the risks of neglecting environmental carrying capacity and the limits of reliance on traditional infrastructure solutions to problems urban America faces. In 1987, the nation's TV viewers were treated to nightly reports of a garbage barge that sailed from New York City and was repeatedly turned away from discharging its cargo at ports along the eastern seaboard and Gulf coast before it foundered at sea, heightening the realization that landfill space is a finite resource. On August 1, 2007, an interstate bridge spanning the Mississippi River collapsed during rush hour in Minneapolis, killing 13 and injuring 145. In 1998, the Loma Prieta earthquake collapsed a section of the San Francisco–Oakland Bay Bridge while tens of millions of Americans watched the 1989 World Series. Above all, the destruction of much of New Orleans in 2005 after flood barriers constructed by the U.S. Army Corps of Engineers failed during Hurricane Katrina provided evidence of the risk of relying upon technological solutions alone in the face of the vicissitudes of Mother Nature. Technology failed again spectacularly in April 2010 when British Petroleum's Deepwater Horizon drilling platform exploded and collapsed into the

Gulf of Mexico. With more than 4.9 million barrels of oil having spewed into the Gulf—twenty times what was discharged into Prince William Sound by the Exxon Valdez—Deepwater is "the worst oil spill in United States history."[8] Queuing at gas stations during the oil crises of the 1970s brought home the vulnerabilities of an urban energy infrastructure dependent upon imported oil in an unavoidably personal way to almost every city dweller. Herbert Girardet points to this as the moment when the urban sustainability revolution started.[9]

While the federal government has enacted important laws that address threats to our water and air, these efforts have often been piecemeal, approved only after pressing problems reached such potentially catastrophic levels that the need to act was unavoidable. This left pressing problems such as the recycling of household waste unaddressed.[10] It can be argued that earlier action would have forestalled or at least mitigated the worst environmental excesses and that the cost would have been lower if action was taken earlier. These realizations have played a significant role in prompting the leaders of America's cities to search for more sustainable, cost-effective, and low-impact solutions to meeting the infrastructure, health, and environmental management needs of their communities.

The economic development needs of urban areas provide another impetus to the sustainable cities movement. Studies prepared by the Pew Charitable Trust and by consulting firm Global Insight for the U.S. Conference of Mayors (USCM) help highlight this. The Pew report showed that green economy jobs grew at almost two and a half times the rate of overall U.S. job growth in the period between 1998 and 2007. The USCM study estimated there to be a total of 750,000 green jobs in the United States in 2006. Approximately 85 percent of these jobs were located in metropolitan areas with more than half in the high-paying science and engineering, legal, research, and consulting sectors. The nation's ten largest metropolitan areas accounted for almost 25 percent of the total. The USCM report projected that up to 4.2 million new green economy jobs could be created in the United States between now and 2038, with the majority in America's large cities.[11]

Green collar jobs in manufacturing offer the potential to revitalize the economies of hard-hit industrial areas. The doors to a number of shuttered manufacturing plants have already been reopened for the production of wind turbines and solar energy panels. In 2009, the state of Michigan and General Electric announced plans to reopen a former General Motors manufacturing plant in the economically devastated Detroit area for research and development of electric vehicle batteries; that facility is expected to employ up to 1,200. The plant began operations in January 2010, using fuel cells manufactured in South Korea to supply batteries for GM's new Chevy Volt plug-in hybrid electric vehicle.[12]

The growth potential of the green economy offers tremendous opportunities to re-employ displaced low- and semi-skilled workers in vocations such as installing rooftop solar energy cells, weatherization, and other retrofits that increase the energy efficiency of commercial buildings and homes. The green economy offers the greatest opportunity for creating jobs and wealth since the commercialization of the microprocessor and personal computer. Given the important place economic development occupies on the agendas of the leaders of America's cities, the potential to capture growth in green economy business formation and job creation is a central driver in urban sustainability initiatives.

The third main factor in the rise of sustainability to the top of urban agendas in the United States is global warming. If SustainLane's rankings highlight the degree to which sustainability has become mainstream in America's cities, a look at how sustainability has taken root in an institutional manner helps demonstrate the instrumental role played by climate change.

The point at which sustainability began to assume an institutional character can be traced to 1983 and issuance of a report by the World Commission on Environment and Development. Commonly known as the Brundtland Commission in acknowledgment of its chair, former Norwegian Prime Minister Gro Harlem Brundtland, the United Nations convened the group to develop policies to promote economic and social development in the face of accelerating global depletion of natural resources. The Commission's report offered what has become the most widely accepted definition of sustainable development in use today: "Sustainable development is development that meets the needs of the present without compromising the ability of future generations to meet their own needs."[13]

A framework for development of sustainable cities followed in 1991 with the establishment of ICLEI, the International Council for Local Environmental Initiatives, when more than 200 local governments from forty-three countries convened at the first World Congress of Local Governments for a Sustainable Future at the United Nations in New York. The Congress was a prelude to the U.N.'s summit on sustainability in Rio de Janeiro, Brazil. The Brundtland Commission had noted that cities in industrialized nations have a special responsibility for fostering sustainable development because they "account for a high share of the world's resource use, energy consumption, and environmental pollution."[14] Agenda 21, the U.N. development program to promote sustainability that emerged from Rio, gave further attention to this point in that:

> So many of the problems and solutions being addressed by Agenda 21 have their roots in local activities, the participation of local authorities will be a determining factor in fulfilling its objectives. Local authorities construct, operate, and maintain economic, social, and environmental infrastructure, oversee planning processes, establish environmental infrastructure, and assist in implementing national and sub national environmental policies.[15]

In 1993, the same year that environmentalists, architects, planners, and property developers began discussions on what would emerge as the LEED green building rating system, Portland, Oregon, adopted the first comprehensive local government plan in the nation aimed at reducing CO_2 emissions. The goals of Portland's Local Action Plan on Global Warming were ambitious: a 20 percent reduction from 1990 CO_2 levels by 2010, exceeding what was later prescribed by the Kyoto protocols. These goals were to be pursued through six strategies: land-use planning, transportation, energy efficiency, renewable energy, solid waste recycling, and urban forestry. As an instrument of urban policy, Portland's climate plan demonstrated the city to be taking an approach to sustainability through a range of instruments, providing an essential link in bonding the concept of ecological carrying capacity to the city's development process. Other cities followed, including San Francisco, where a citizen-led movement that began in 1995 resulted in the city adolpting a comprehensive citywide sustainability plan in 1997.

Another important step in the institutionalization of sustainability occurred in 1994 when British management consultant John Elkington coined the phrase "the triple bottom line." Elkington employed the principles outlined in the Brundtland Commission's report to describe a methodology for managing, measuring, and reporting government and business activities within the context of an interlocking relationship among environmental health, social well-being, and economic performance. This relationship is often depicted in terms of a Venn diagram of three interlocking circles, each circle representing respectively planet, people, and prosperity.[16] Elkington laid the groundwork for cities to begin developing indicators to measure their performance in sustainable development. In

2007, the triple bottom line was adopted by the United Nations and ICLEI as a standard for public sector full-cost accounting of the societal, economic, and ecological costs and benefits of sustainable development.

Between 1996 and 2002, the number of cities participating in ICLEI rose from 47 to 127, a number that would grow to 600 in 2009. Cities were developing sustainability policies, plans, and initiatives aimed at addressing climate change and ozone depletion, agriculture, biodiversity, air and water quality, energy, food, education, procurement contracting, local economic performance, equity and equality, and environmental justice.[17] Responding to growing interest among its own membership, in 1999 the U.S. Conference of Mayors created the National Council for Resource Conservation to craft a strategy for conserving energy and natural resources because "resource conservation today means sustainable growth tomorrow."[18]

The growing commitment by America's cities to sustainability and the fight against global warming served to highlight a divergence between priorities at local and federal levels of government. In 2001 President Bush withdrew U.S. support of the then-pending Kyoto Protocol, refusing to send it to the Senate for ratification. Administration officials charged the treaty was too costly and "an unrealistic and ever tightening straightjacket.[19] In 2002, the Environmental Protection Agency concluded that global warming was most likely due to human activities. President Bush dismissed the EPA's report and administration officials spent much of their eight years in office questioning the science underlying anthropogenic climate change. October 2009 would see the administration of President Obama release an EPA "endangerment finding" that greenhouse gas emissions posed a significant threat to the country. It recommended that the federal government begin emissions regulation. EPA had actually issued the finding in 2007, but the Bush administration had suppressed its release for two years.[20] This book is not about federalism per se, but it is clear that for America's urban sustainability movement, "a key spur for local action was the perception that the federal government was dithering on climate change and energy conservation."[21]

In 2005, the same year that the Kyoto accords went into effect committing major industrialized countries—but not the United States—to reducing their greenhouse gas emissions, the Conference of Mayors founded its Climate Protection Agreement. Leading the initiative was Seattle Mayor Greg Nickels, who had become concerned about the threat that melting glaciers posed to his city's drinking water supply. Other cities were equally concerned. A 1995 heat wave in

Chicago that killed as many as 750 had impressed upon the people of that city what a future dominated by atmospheric warming might look like. Maps were developed showing that a not-improbable-warming-induced 1-meter rise in sea level would inundate much of the coastal metropolitan belt of 5.4 million people between Palm Beach and Miami, possibly flood the site at which the World Trade Center once stood in Manhattan, and threaten New York City's subway and sanitation systems. Arid areas of the Southwest would become drier, further imperiling the water supply; pestilence would threaten agricultural production that cities rely on for food.[22] The cost of replacing infrastructure vulnerable to warming-induced storms and sea level rise in Houston and Galveston would be placed at $12 billion.[23]

The Mayors' Climate Protection Agreement committed signatories to the goal of meeting or exceeding Kyoto accord targets of a 7 percent reduction in CO_2 emissions in their own communities by 2012. The signatories also committed to urging the federal government to adopt the Kyoto targets and enact a cap-and-trade greenhouse gas emissions trading system. Initially, the mayors of 141 cities signed the agreement. Mesa, Arizona, became a signatory in 2009, bringing the number of cities participating in the Mayors' climate agreement to 1,000, a number that has since grown.

Where Sustainability Stands Now

A 2007 survey of 132 cities conducted by the mayors' conference found that 92 percent considered their efforts to reduce greenhouse gas emissions (GHG) as part of broader sustainability efforts to improve air quality and public health.[24] A 2009 study by ICLEI concluded that the steps cities were taking to reduce their environmental footprints were promising, but "given the most recent estimates by scientists that emissions need to be reduced by 80 percent by 2050, continued aggressive action is necessary over the next forty years to meet the scale of the challenge."[25] In fact, in 2009, only a single American city is known to have actually reduced its overall CO_2 emissions from the 1990 baseline levels called for under Kyoto, ICLEI, and the conference of mayors agreement. This is Portland, Oregon, where, as discussed in chapter 2, progress in GHG emissions reductions is primarily attributable to the city's aggressive development of bus and light rail public transportation, energy efficiency initiatives undertaken by the city's electric utility, and the presence in Portland of more LEED green buildings per capita than in any other city in the nation.[26]

The 2007 survey also revealed continued tension between local leaders and federal government over sustainable development. Only 5 percent of the surveyed cities said that they had found the federal government helpful in their greening efforts. Forty-one percent said the federal government had not been helpful at all. Relations between America's cities and the federal government certainly improved with the election of Barrack Obama as president. One sign is the $2.8 billion in federal funding that was approved for the Energy Efficiency Block Grant program as part of the American Recovery and Reinvestment Act economic stimulus package Obama signed in February 2009. The mayors' conference had lobbied heavily for this. Also, in September 2009, the Environmental Protection Agency, acting under authority granted it by the Supreme Court to regulate GHG emissions, issued new rules to increase automobile fuel efficiency standards and limit CO_2 emissions from automobiles.[27] The following month saw the Obama administration finally release the EPA endangerment finding that had been sequestered by the Bush administration. However, these moves fall short of the promise Obama made during his presidential campaign to obtain congressional approval of comprehensive federal climate and energy legislation to address GHG emissions. In mid-2009, the House of Representatives passed a bill that would institute a nationwide cap-and-trade system to reduce emissions. However, amid the most severe economic recession since the Great Depression, and in the face of strong opposition from a coalition made up of the coal and oil industries, states and electric utilities heavily dependant upon coal for their electricity supply, the U.S. Chamber of Commerce, the National Farmers Union, and others, the Senate failed to act similarly. The website Tree-Hugger.com followed up on the Senate's failure with the headline "It's official: The climate bill is dead."[28]

So it seems that at least for a while longer, it may continue to fall upon cities to take the lead in devising and putting into practice sustainability initiatives for reducing atmospheric warming emissions. The balance of this book is composed of case studies of how eight of America's largest cities are endeavoring to do this and similarly address other related environmental, economic, and social needs.

Organization of the Book

This book examines sustainability initiatives in select large cities: Portland, Oregon; Milwaukee; Phoenix; San Francisco; Honolulu; Philadelphia; New York

City; and Washington, D.C. Selection of these cities for inclusion as case studies reflects several considerations. Most important, they all demonstrate innovative approaches to addressing the theme of this book: how cities are finding sustainable, environmentally friendly solutions to meeting their community health and infrastructure needs; striving to create green economies; and mitigating and adapting to climate change. All of these cities rank among the fifty most populous in the United States. It is by and large America's most populous cities that were the first to embrace sustainability as a priority. They typically have the most significant resources available for greening themselves and also the most pressing challenges to and motivation for doing so. An examination of large cities is therefore particularly instructive in offering lessons on how to formulate and implement urban sustainability initiatives. Regional diversity is important to capture the varied ecological influences that come into play in the sustainability movement. The cities featured here span the geographical divide from the Northeast and mid-Atlantic to the industrial Midwest, Pacific Northwest, and the Southwest. With the inclusion of Honolulu, we add the largest American city most distant from the continental U.S. mainland and the only large American city surrounded entirely by water.

Last and always, a key consideration in assembling an edited volume is the need for contributors who posses both expertise and enthusiasm for a book's purpose and can dedicate the time and energy needed to ensure that a well-researched and -written work is published in a timely manner. In this, the editor feels fortunate to have been able to collaborate with a group of scholars and professional practitioners who are very well informed on the sustainability initiatives of the cities featured herein and who have contributed the following chapters.

Strategic Climate Planning in Portland, Oregon

According to website SustainLane.com, Portland, Oregon, is the most sustainable city in America. It is the only large American city to have actually reduced both overall and per-capita CO_2 emissions in the period since 1990. In the second chapter of this book Kent Snyder and I examine the evolution of strategic climate planning in Portland and the policies and programs the city has adopted to reduce its carbon emissions. These include development of one of the most extensive light rail and streetcar systems in the nation and an ambitious LEED green building program. Portland's success is also tied very closely to city initiatives to realign local economic development efforts and establish Portland as a center of sustainable business. We find that a key to the city's success has been its strong local environmental culture, its tradition of activist government, and a willingness to innovate by realigning local institutions to more effectively focus resources upon attainment of city sustainable climate and other environmental goals.

Brownfields to Greenfields in Milwaukee

Milwaukee's efforts to transform the Menomonee Valley from one of the most blighted industrial districts in the Midwestern United States into a center of sustainable employment are addressed by Chris DeSousa in chapter 3. Visions of a sustainable urban future don't often include conventional manufacturing, given that it is blamed for causing many of our urban environmental ills in the first place. Beginning with an introduction to the area's rich industrial history, the valley's cleanup and ongoing redevelopment are chronicled in terms of how key stakeholders forged a new and more sustainable vision for the valley and the plans, policies, programs, actions, and funding mechanisms adopted to overcome the barriers to redevelopment that have enhanced industrial employment through sustainable design, green infrastructure, transportation improvements, family-sustaining wage planning, and community involvement. Intrinsic to Milwaukee's approach was a focus upon integrating the triple bottom line concept of people, planet, and prosperity into the area's redevelopment strategy.

Creating a Regional Green Economy in Phoenix

In chapter 4, Jonathan Fink highlights some of the unique events and characters responsible for helping to bring metro Phoenix, and Arizona more broadly, into the "green economy." Critical factors included early success in coordinating high-tech development across the state through the establishment of economic clusters; an emphasis on leveraging Arizona-specific assets, like semiconductor expertise and the potential for academic partnerships to promote solar manufacturing; and the ability of academic leadership to persuade a spectrum of legislators to view public research universities as entrepreneurial enterprises worthy of temporary but large investments rather than as government agencies entitled to steadily increasing, recurrent budgets. Yet, recent episodes in the metro Phoenix story also reveal the degree to which transition to a green economy can be contingent upon the vicissitudes of electoral politics and short-term economic cycles. The underlying question for Phoenix and for any city that is plotting its way to a greener future is how quickly and long-lastingly transformation can occur through technological and political means if the culture is not yet sufficiently receptive.

LEED Green Building in Washington, D.C.

Chapter 5 points to Washington, D.C., and its metropolitan region as national leaders in the development and implementation of the United States Green Building Council's Leadership in Energy and Environmental Design (LEED) rating system. According to SustainLane.com, Washington, D.C., ranks second in the nation in terms of the number of LEED certified buildings among the nation's fifty largest cities. In this chapter, Ralph Bennett, Amy Gardner, Gerrit Knaap, Madlen Simon, and Cari Varner provide a policy and planning perspective on how LEED standards have been implemented in Washington, D.C., and in selected counties in the D.C. metropolitan region. There is a discussion of how public and private interests converged in the transformative effect of LEED standards in the area and case studies examine in depth the application of LEED in Washington and its metropolitan region. Finally, the chapter makes a case for the significance of LEED to the future of sustainable development in the region.

Greening Transportation in San Francisco

San Francisco has witnessed a flurry of interest in alternative transportation during the last fifteen years. In chapter 6, Aaron Golub and Jason Henderson examine how this has translated into the launching of two successful green mobility initiatives: the expansion of the city's bicycle transportation program and the launching of a citywide car-sharing service. These initiatives have been inspired by grassroots movements to envision a new kind of city and act on that vision to foster a "politics of possibility." From a simple idea, persistent advocacy by well-informed, passionate, and at times savvy advocates have transformed biking and car share into very mainstream tools for planners, developers, and city residents. The impacts of these initiatives have been profound, affecting travel, saving money, and reducing parking, automobile ownership, and greenhouse gas emissions; they have resulted in changes to the planning code of the city of San Francisco. These developments point to the important role mobilization by grassroots activists and social entrepreneurship played as prime movers behind San Francisco's green transportation initiatives.

Green-Tech Energy in Honolulu

Honolulu depends upon imported oil to generate electricity thirty times as much as the average across America and the threat posed to the city by climate change is significant. Doug Codiga, Jason Zeller, and I examine plans to transform Honolulu, Hawaii's largest municipality, into one powered primarily by renewable energy in chapter 7. Discussion focuses upon how Honolulu came to be heavily dependent upon oil for electricity generation and how the Hawaii Clean Energy Initiative emerged during the first decade of the twenty-first century as a response to this overdependence. The initiative amounts to nothing less than a paradigm shift that would enable Honolulu to drastically reduce its dependence on imported oil and rely primarily on renewable energy sources such as wind, solar, and other clean energy resources, including electric vehicles. If various obstacles can be overcome, the Hawaii Clean Energy Initiative affords an opportunity to transform Honolulu into perhaps the most energy-independent municipality in the nation.

Sustainable Stormwater Solutions in Philadelphia

The city of Philadelphia has historically been among the leaders in urban water management in the United States and abroad. In chapter 8, Lynn Mandarano looks at Philadelphia's efforts to protect drinking water supply and address infrastructure capacity issues by investing in sustainable storm water management. Highlighted is the key role that regional collaboration has played in building a consortium of environmental organizations, community groups, government agencies, school districts, businesses, and area residents needed to implement integrated watershed management planning. Philadelphia's initiative signals an effort to break with a traditional "end of pipe" treatment approach to managing urban storm water flows and embrace fewer intrusive and capital-intensive practices in favor of those that are more environmentally friendly. The low-impact infrastructure development technologies being employed by Philadelphia are up to ten times less costly than traditional gray infrastructure investments projects such as large-scale storage tunnels. Philadelphia's Green City Clean Waters approach holds promise for other cities seeking environmentally friendly infrastructure solutions to meet their public service goals.

Urban Forestry and Carbon Offsets in New York City

On Earth Day 2007, New York City's mayor, Michael Bloomberg, announced a long-term vision for making New York City more sustainable by 2030. PlaNYC creates a long-term mission for NYC that has sustainability at its core. P. Timon McPhearson examines MillionTreesNYC, one of the city's most visible initiatives, in chapter 9. The campaign aims to add 1 million trees to city streets, parks, and private land by 2017 to expand the city's urban forest to offset locally generated greenhouse gas emissions. Discussion describes how unprecedented public response to a movement led by environmental activists has resulted in the planting of more than 174,000 new trees in the city. However, young urban trees have extremely high mortality rates due to heat, salt, and pollution, and can also suffer from lack of individual care during their early years. This chapter evaluates whether the city's urban forestry initiative can reliably function at an acceptable level and offers recommendations for additional research to determine how urban forestry campaigns aimed at offsetting greenhouse gas emissions can best be managed in the future.

Greening the Food Supply through Urban Agriculture in New York

Sustainable farm and food initiatives in New York City are the subjects Nevin Cohen and Jennifer Obadia address in chapter 10. Superficially, the system that feeds New Yorkers appears to work wonderfully. Yet, the city's food system is based on an inherently unsustainable and vulnerable foundation. It is rife with inefficiencies that increase costs, cause environmental problems, and inequitably distribute food and nutritional resources. The chapter assesses how New York City is moving beyond past practices to stimulate urban agriculture, improve food access in low-income neighborhoods, enact regulations to encourage healthier eating, expand farmers' markets, and put into place public procurement policies to support peri-urban food production. Questions are raised about whether these efforts will be sufficient and whether adaption of more comprehensive policies including a citywide food charter may be needed to meet future food and nutrition needs in a city whose population is projected to grow by a million new residents by 2030.

Current Trends and Future Prospects

In the concluding chapter, I summarize what can be learned from the urban sustainability initiatives featured in the aforementioned chapters. America's cities appear to be subsuming traditional activities and tackling old problems under the sustainability rubric and, at the same time, extending their reach to new areas of involvement that are beyond traditional mandates. They are often acting through new, innovative partnerships, both intergovernmental as well as in conjunction with the private sector and nonprofit and educational institutions. These cities are responding to coalitions that bring together an unusual convergence between business and environmental interests and are sometimes the product of spontaneous grassroots movements. They are embracing new technologies and ways of operating and can avail themselves of new methodologies and sustainability reporting frameworks including the triple bottom line for planning and problem solving. At the same time, this concluding chapter points to the need to do more if the challenges of addressing the impacts of urban development upon environmental carrying capacity are to be met, cities are to mitigate and adapt to climate change, and benefits from the potential of the green economy are to be captured. The lessons learned from the case studies presented in this book can play an important role in forging the strategies that are certain to follow in addressing these imperatives.

Notes

1. See www.sustainlane.com for a complete list of criteria used for city rankings. Other ratings include "America's 50 Greenest Cities" by *Popular Science*, the Natural Resources Defense Council's "Smarter Cities" rankings, *Country Home Magazine*'s "Best Green Cities in America," and GreenGuide.com's "Top 25 Green Cities in the U.S." See also "The 25 Least Wasteful Cities in the United States," retrieved October 24, 2009, at www.fastcompany .com/blog/ariel-schwartz/sustainability/nalgenes-top-25-least-wasteful-us-cities. For a discussion of how city livability rankings influence urban policymaking, see E. McCann, "Best Places: Interurban Competition, Quality of Life and Popular Media Discourse," *Urban Studies* 41, no. 10 (2008): 1909–29.

2. For discussion on the relationship between sustainability and sustainable development, see J. D Marshall and M. W. Toffler, "Framing the Elusive Concept of Sustainability: A Sustainability Hierarchy," *Environmental & Scientific Technology* 39, no. 3 (2005): 673–82; and Michael Redclift, "Sustainable Development (1987–2005): An Oxymoron Comes of Age." *Sustainable Development* 13, no. 4 (2005): 212–27.

3. See Herbert Girardet, "Creating Livable and Sustainable Cities," in *Surviving the Century: Facing Climate Chaos and Other Global Challenges*, ed. Herbert Girardet, (London: Earthscan, 2007), 103–26; Herbert Girardet, "The Metabolism of Cities," in *The Sustainable Urban Development Reader*, ed. Stephen Wheeler and Timothy Beatley (New York: Routledge, 2004), 125; David C. Gibbs, *Local Development and the Environment* (London: Routledge, 2002); Richard Register,. *Ecocities: Rebuilding Cities in Balance with Nature* (Gabriola Island, B.C.: New Society Publishers, 2006); Mark Raco, "Spatial Policy, Sustainability and State Restructuring: A Reassessment of State Sustainable Community Building in England," in *The Sustainable Development Paradox*, ed. Rob Krueger and David Gibbs (New York: Guilford Press, 2007), 214–37; Peter Newman, Timothy Beatley, and Heather Boyer, *Resilient Cities: Responding to Peak Oil and Climate Change* (Washington, D.C.: Island Press, 2009); and Kent Portney, *Taking Sustainability Seriously: Economic Development, the Environment, and Quality of Life in American Cities* (Cambridge: MIT Press, 2003), 9.

4. On the urban share of America's population, see U.S. Census Bureau, www.census.gov/population/censusdata/urpop0090.txt (accessed August 12, 2009). For building energy consumption and greenhouse gas emissions, see Lawrence Berkeley National Laboratory, June 2, 2009, U.S. Department of Energy, at http://newscenter.lbl.gov/feature-stories/2009/06/02/working-toward-the-very-low-energy-consumption-building-of-the-future/ (accessed October 26, 2009). On transportation and greenhouse gas emissions, see U.S. Environmental Protection Agency, www.epa.gov/oms/climate/index.htm (accessed October 2, 2009). On municipal waste production, see Environmental Protection Agency, *Solid Waste in the United States: Facts and Figures*, United States Environmental Protection Agency Office of Solid Waste (5306P), EPA530-R-08-010, November 2008.

5. Russ Lopez, "Urban Sprawl and Risk for Being Overweight or Obese," *American Journal of Public Health* 94, no. 9 (September, 2004): 1574–79; Barbara A. McCann and Reid Ludwig. "Measuring the Health Effects of Sprawl: A National Analysis of Physical Activity, Obesity, and Chronic Disease," Smart Growth America Surface Transportation Policy Project, September 2003; David Frumkin, "Urban Sprawl and Public Health." Department of Environmental and Occupational Health, Emory University, December 2001, www.publichealthgrandrounds.unc.edu/urban/frumkin.pdf (accessed October 17, 2009).

6. Association for Pure Water, "Infrastructure Needs Are Stretching Resources," 2009, www.americansforpurewater.com/i4a/pages/Index.cfm?pageID=3388 (accessed October 17, 2009).

7. Leslie Eaton, 2009. "Cities Braced for a Prolonged Bout of Declining Tax Revenues," *Wall Street Journal*, September 1, 2009, http://online.wsj.com/article/SB125177344884874971.html.html (accessed September 2, 2009).

8. Jason DeParle, "Mineral Service Had Mandate to Produce Results," New York Times, August 7, 2010, www.nytimes.com/2010/08/08/us/08mms.html?ref=us.

9. Herbert Giradet, 2007. "Creating Livable and Sustainable Cities," 109.

10. See Tom Daniels, 2008. "Taking the Initiative: Why Cities Are Greening Now," in *Growing Greener Cities*, ed. Eugenie Birch and Susan Wachter (Philadelphia: University of Pennsylvania Press, 2008). Enactment of the first federal clean air protections, the Air Pollution Control Act of 1955, followed an industrial smog that settled upon the Pittsburg-area town of Donora, Pennsylvania, in 1948 that killed 20 and sickened 7,000. The hazards of neglect surfaced again in 1969 when oil from a blown offshore rig contaminated beaches in Santa Barbara, California, and chemicals polluting the Cuyahoga River in Cleveland caused sections of the river to catch fire. The Santa Barbara spill and Cuyahoga River fire were instrumental in creation of the Environmental Protection Agency in 1970 and passage of the Federal Water Pollution Control Amendments of 1972.

11. The Pew Charitable Trusts, "The Clean Energy Economy: Repowering Jobs, Businesses and Investments Across America," June 2009, www.pewtrusts.org/news_room_detail.aspx?id=53254 (accessed July 28, 2009); and U.S. Conference of Mayors and the Mayors Climate Protection Center, "Current and Potential Green Jobs in the U.S. Economy," 2008, www.usmayors.org/climateprotection/surveys.htm (accessed December 8, 2008). See also Clean Edge Inc., "Clean Tech Jobs Report 2009," www.cleanedge.com/reports/reports-jobtrends2009.php (accessed October 15, 2009).

12. John Sterlicchi, "GM to Power Up Michigan Volt Battery Plant," *Business Green*, January 6, 2010, www.businessgreen.com/business-green/news/2255661/gm-power-volt-battery-plant.

13. World Commission on Environment and Development, *Our Common Future: Report of the World Commission on Environment and Development* (New York: Oxford University Press, 1987). Published as Annex to General Assembly document A/42/427, Development and International Co-operation: Environment, August 2, 1987.

14. World Commission on Environment and Development, *Our Common Future*: 242.

15. United Nations Environmental Program, Agenda 21: Section 28, Local Authorities (New York: United Nations, 2000).

16. John Elkington, "Towards the Sustainable Corporation: Win-Win-Win Business Strategies for Sustainable Development," *California Management Review* 36, no. 2 (1994): 90–100. See also John Elkington, *Cannibals with Forks: The Triple Bottom Line of 21st Century Business* (Springer: Netherlands, 1999).

17. Kent Portney, *Taking Sustainability Seriously: Economic Development, the Environment, and Quality of Life in American Cities* (Cambridge: MIT Press, 2003): 23. Kent's book is one of the earliest scholarly attempts at evaluating urban sustainability initiatives in the United States. Among his findings was that cities that took sustainability most seriously were those that had adopted indicators that went beyond measuring what it simply required by federal law.

18. U.S. Conference of Mayors quoting USCM president and Salt Lake City Mayor Deedee Corradini, retrieved August 12, 2009 at http://usmayors.org/pressreleases/documents/ncrc.htm.

19. Christopher Plumb, "U.S. Blasts Kyoto Pact as Straightjacket," Reuters, 2003, www.commondreams.org/headlines03/1201-01.htm (accessed May 6, 2009).

20. Dina Capiello, "EPA Releases '07 Climate Document Rejected by Bush Team,"

Washington Post, October 13, 2009, www.washingtonpost.com/wp-.dyn/content/article/2009 /10/13/AR2009101303897.html (accessed October 14, 2009).

21. Jonathan D. Weiss, "Local Government and Sustainability: Major Progress, Significant Challenges," in *Stumbling Toward Sustainability*, ed. John Dernbach (Washington, D.C.: Environmental Law Institute, 2002): 45.

22. Kristin Dow and Thomas E. Downing, *The Atlas of Climate Change: Mapping the World's Greatest Challenge* (Berkeley: University of California Press, 2006).

23. Environmental Defense Fund, "Climate Change Hitting Home, Galveston and Houston Residents on Notice," June 9, 2009, http://blogs.edf.org/climate411/2009/06/09 /climate-change-hitting-home-galveston-and-houston-residents-on-notice/ (accessed July 7, 2009).

24. See U.S. Conference of Mayors and the Mayors Climate Protection Center, "Current and Potential Green Jobs in the U.S. Economy, 2008, http://usmayors.org /climateprotection/surveys.htm, (accessed October 12, 2009).

25. ICLEI, "Report Shows the Power of U.S. Cities to Mitigate Climate Change," n.d., www.icleiusa.org/news-events/press-room/press-releases/report-shows-the-power-of-u-s-cities -to-mitigate-climate-change2014and-the-steps-they-need-to-take-to-adapt (accessed August 10, 2009).

26. City of Portland Bureau of Planning and Sustainability, "Climate Action Plan 2009," City of Portland, Oregon.

27. Josh Vorhees, 2009. "EPA Unveils New Emissions Standards for Cars," *Scientific American*, September 15, 2009, www.scientificamerican.com/article.cfm?id=auto-standards -cafe-rules-greenhouse-gas-epa (accessed March 12, 2009). Darren Samuelsohn and Robin Bravender, 2009. "EPA Releases Bush-Era Endangerment Document," *New York Times*, October 13, 2009, www.nytimes.com/gwire/2009/10/13/13greenwire-epa-releases-bush-era -endangerment-document-47439.html (accessed March 12, 2009).

28. Merchant, Brian, 2010. "It's Official: The Climate Bill Is Dead," *Tree Hugger*, July 22, www.treehugger.com/files/2010/07/its-official-climate-bill-is-dead.php.

Chapter 2

Strategic Climate Action Planning in Portland

MATTHEW I. SLAVIN AND KENT SNYDER

Climate change is the defining challenge of the twenty-first century.
—City of Portland and Multnomah County Climate Action Plan, 2009

Perhaps no American city has taken up the challenge of combating rising green house gas emissions as diligently as Portland, Oregon. Portland adopted the first municipal climate action plan of any city in the nation in 1993, with plan updates following in 2001 and 2009. Portland is also the only large city in America to have reduced both its per capita and overall CO_2 emissions during this period.

A climate action plan is similar to a municipal master, general, or comprehensive plan that employs analytical methodologies to identify community challenges, sets forth goals and identifies strategies and actions by which these goals are to be attained, and establishes benchmarks or other sorts of measures that can be used to assess the degree to which progress in meeting these goals is being made. In the case of climate action planning, the objective of the planning process is to mitigate generation of CO_2 and other globally warming emissions and position the locality to adapt to a warming planet. In this chapter, we examine the antecedents that paved the way for Portland's engagement with climate action planning and the key features that characterized the climate planning process in Portland.

Antecedents to Climate Change Planning in Portland

Portland's engagement with climate action planning follows a long history of local government and civic efforts to increase the city's livability and enhance the local environment. An early sign of this can be seen in creation of the Portland Development Commission as the city's urban renewal agency in 1956. The commission embarked on a program of rebuilding the city's downtown. Its first project involved creation of the auditorium district, whereby an "old stopover neighborhood on the southern edge of downtown Portland was leveled and designated for reuse by offices and business services."[1] As with many similar urban renewal agencies, the commission has largely been dominated by the city's business establishment. It has also been the subject of controversy and criticism at times due to the perception that it overlooked the city's neighborhoods to the benefit of downtown in making investments. Still, during the last fifty years, Portland has received frequent acknowledgment for its success in creating one of the most livable downtowns of any major American city. Among the reasons are the city's creation of a number of highly accessible downtown public parks, plazas, and fountains and development of one of the nation's most extensive regional light rail public transit systems. Removal of Harbor Drive, a freeway separating the city center from the Willamette River waterfront to create 36-acre Tom McCall Park also added prominently to the city's success. The park was named after the state's governor between 1967 through 1975 who, as will be seen, played a central role in injecting a strong environmental ethic into statewide and city of Portland planning regimes.

Describing Portland during the 1950s, Neal Peirce, an astute observer of urban America, wrote of a "town of quiet old wealth, discrete culture, and cautious politics" with a "monopoly on propriety and an anxiousness to 'keep things as they are.'"[2] In fact, the decade was a period of stagnation for the city. Portland experienced no population growth during the 1950s and ended the decade with slightly fewer residents than when the decade started. This all began to change in the 1960s, due in large part to growing in-migration to Portland of new residents from other parts of the country. Between 1965 and 1970, in-migration added 65,000 to the population of the Portland metropolitan area. In-migration would continue to grow in the following decades, accounting for an average of 40,000 new residents to metropolitan Portland annually between 1970 and 2000. Many settled within the city of Portland itself; between 1960 and 2000, the city's population grew from 372,000 to 529,000. Evidence also suggests that younger people between the ages of 20 and 35 comprised many of the new arrivals.[3]

A principle reason people moved to Portland was jobs. This was particularly so after technology giant Intel Corporation chose Portland's west side suburbs as the location for its first silicon chip fabrication plant built outside of California's Silicon Valley. The plant opened in 1976. Almost ten years later Intel built a second plant adjacent to the first, becoming the world's largest chip manufacturing plant at that time. Numerous other technology firms followed in Intel's footsteps.[4] Between 1976 and 2000, employment in the Portland area's technology manufacturing sector grew by almost 2.5 times, to more than 36,000, reaching such a concentration that the area came to be known as the "Silicon Forest." In fact, these numbers significantly understate the true magnitude of the impact the technology sector had in transforming the Portland area's economy.[5] The decision by Nike to build its global headquarters in the Portland region furthered the area's growing reputation as a "new economy" center.

Traditionally, Portland served as the business center of the state's forest products industry. However, concomitant with the emergence of the region's new economy Portland's forestry products sector entered a period of decline. This was particularly precipitous during the 1981–1983 recession, when the state's forest products sector all but collapsed in the face of high interest rates and a resulting decline in new housing construction. Epitomizing this decline was the decision by Georgia Pacific Corporation, one of the world's leading forest products companies, to abandon Portland as its international headquarters and relocate to Atlanta in 1982.[6]

There is anecdotal evidence that in addition to jobs, many of those who moved to Portland were attracted by the reputation the city was earning for livability and a high level of environmental awareness. More exacting evidence of this can be found in a report published in 1988.[7] It found that local technology executives in particular saw maintenance of a high quality of life and clean environment as an important factor in their ability to attract the highly skilled workforce they demanded.

In 1971, Oregon Governor Tom McCall was famously quoted as saying "We want you to visit our state of excitement often. Come again and again. But for heavens sake, don't move here to live. Or if you do have to move here to live, don't tell any of your neighbors where you are going."[8] McCall was responding to increasing concern that growing in-migration was causing conflicts in established communities, particular in terms of land use. Population growth was generating sprawl and traffic congestion, encroaching upon agricultural lands and impacting the availability of land for future industrial development. This was particularly so in the Portland area. The upshot of surging in-migration and emerging economic restructuring was increasing environmental activism by Oregonians.

One sign of growing environmental awareness was the state's adoption, shortly after the first Earth Day in 1971, of the nation's first law mandating refundable deposits on plastic, glass, and aluminum soft drink and beer containers.[9] Also in 1971, the state legislature opened the gas tax-financed highway fund to bicycle projects. A response to the rise of an increasingly vocal bicycle-commuting constituency in Portland, this made Oregon the first state in the nation to allow highway funding to be used for bicycles. It can be seen as a clear sign of the desire of Portland residents to combat air pollution emissions and a precursor to the efforts to combat global warming that would follow.

More far reaching was creation of the state's landmark growth management system by the Oregon state legislature in 1973. Aimed at reducing urban sprawl, the growth management law led to establishment of urban growth boundaries around metropolitan Portland and the state's other urbanized areas. Also delineated under the growth management regime were a number of goals and guidelines pertaining to land use, transportation, public facilities, air and water quality, and other development issues. Local jurisdictions were mandated or advised to consider these goals and guidelines in drafting and updating their comprehensive plans. Under Oregon's system, the comprehensive plan emerged as the primary instrument for guiding Portland's major initiatives in efficient land use and transportation and other local policy concerns amid what was generally a period of growth and prosperity during the decades that followed.

At the same time, there occurred a change in Portland's political leadership, marked by the 1972 election of Neil Goldschmidt as the city's mayor. At thirty-two, he became the youngest mayor of any major American city. Much of his electoral support came from the city's neighborhoods and Portland's newly minted arrivals. Reflecting this, while Goldschmidt continued to promote downtown revitalization, he also placed heavy emphasis upon livability citywide. A key part of his agenda was to strengthen the city's citizen planning commission to offset the preponderant influence yielded by the Development Commission over the shape and content of urban form. To expand citizen input into local government decision making, Goldschmidt also refashioned the city's planning bureau and created a new city Office of Neighborhood Associations. He was also instrumental in melding together the metropolitan area's bus system centered upon a newly founded transit mall in the city's downtown, generating momentum that resulted in development of Portland's highly vaunted light rail transit system, the Metropolitan Area Express (MAX), which began service in 1986.

Goldschmidt was also active in shaping the state's new growth management system. During discussions leading to establishment of Oregon's comprehensive goal-driven system of planning, advocates fought for inclusion of an explicit environmental carrying capacity goal. Such an explicit goal did not survive the need to strike a fine balance between the development and environmental interests that negotiated the growth management regime. But the concept was thematically incorporated into other goal methodologies including the energy goal component of the state growth management planning system. In a decade marked by two major national oil crises, Portland's mayor was instrumental in having an energy goal adopted, testifying before the state's growth management system goal setting commission that he was "compelled . . . to recommend and request that the Commission include—as part of the goals for land-use planning—energy conservation as a major subject."[10] At city hall, he created the Portland Energy Office and a citizen Energy Commission in 1979, the same year in which Portland became the first city in the nation to adopt a municipal energy policy.

Other influences played out in Portland during the 1980s. The port of Portland emerged as a depot for Asian car imports to supplant its traditional grain and timber shipping operations, and Portland International Airport commenced direct international air service to Asia to meet the needs of the region's increasingly globally minded companies. Concerns arose regarding the capacity of the Columbia River's hydropower dam system to meet rising electricity demand fueled by growth and about the effect the dam's operations were having in depleting the river's salmon stocks. This led to the creation of the Northwest Power and Conservation Planning Council. Headquartered in Portland, the federal agency's mission includes increasing the efficient use of electricity by the region's household, commercial, and industrial electricity consumers. Public concern in the aftermath of the 1986 Chernobyl disaster fueled an activist campaign that would culminate in 1993 with closure of the Trojan commercial nuclear generating station, operated on the city's outskirts by the state's leading electric utility, the Portland General Electric Company.[11]

Looking back, the period between 1960 and 1990 was one of population growth fueled by in-migration and economic restructuring. These changes were accompanied by a shift in the city's polity from what Neal Peirce characterized as "anxious to keep things as they are" to a city with a reputation as highly progressive with a worldly view and enthusiasm for acting to protect livability and environmental quality. These circumstances played an important role in Portland's embrace in the early 1990s of climate action planning as a key city priority.

Portland's First Climate Plan

In 1979, Neil Goldschmidt resigned as Portland's mayor to become transportation secretary in the Carter administration. His resignation triggered realignment on the city council. Following a short interlude councilman Frank Ivancie was elected in 1980 for a full four-year term in the mayor's office. A conservative democrat with strong ties to the business community, Ivancie was the lone dissenter in the 1974 decision by the Portland City Council to abandon development of the highly controversial Mount Hood Freeway, strongly opposed in Portland's eastside neighborhoods. He also opposed development of Portland's popular Pioneer Courthouse Square in downtown on the grounds the square would become a gathering place for transients. His conservative politics and probusiness positions were frequently at odds with an increasingly liberal and progressive electorate. In 1985, Ivancie was defeated in his reelection bid by J. E. "Bud" Clark. A tavern owner and liberal populist who occupied the mayor's office until 1992, Clark championed the arts and created a nationally recognized plan for the homeless. He also was a strong proponent for the MAX light rail system.[12] Clark's defeat of Ivancie can in many ways be seen as the culmination of the transition of Portland's polity from a politics of caution to one defined by pragmatic entrepreneurialism.

Goldschmidt's resignation also opened up a vacancy on the city council. In 1979, Goldschmidt's former city planning director, Mike Lindberg, was appointed to fill the open seat. Subsequently winning election to a full four-year term, Lindberg had strong desire to establish himself in a leadership position and found a conduit at the National League of Cities (NLC). Shortly after taking his seat on the Portland City Council, he was appointed to the NLC's energy and environment committee, rising by mid-decade to become the committee's vice-chairman and then chairman. Portland's 1979 energy policy had served as the blueprint for other cities to develop their own energy plans, and Lindberg himself attributed his somewhat rapid rise to the committee leadership to his role as having overseen development of Portland's energy policy as planning director.[13]

Lindberg's elevation to leadership of the NLC energy and environment committee paralleled the emergence of global warming as a concern among far-sighted leaders concerned about maintaining balance between development and consumption of the earth's natural resources. As discussed in the preceding chapter, in 1983 the Brundtland Commission issued its report that gave definition to the term *sustainable development* and cast special responsibility upon cities to ensure that they developed in ways that meet "the needs of the present without compromising the ability of future generations to meet their own needs."[14] It was also during this period, in 1988, that the United Nations Environmental Program established the IPCC, the Intergovernmental Panel on Climate Change. Domestically, local government leaders frustrated with inaction by the Reagan administration in the face of the threat posed by depletion of the earth's ozone layer were beginning to catalyze around a movement that would culminate in 1991 with the creation of ICLEI, the International Council for Local Environmental Initiatives, and its Climate Protection Agreement committing cities to reduce their greenhouse gas emissions. As chair of the NLC committee, Lindberg took an increasing interest in climate change. He was introduced to leading authorities on energy and environmental issues including Amory Lovins, author of the 1976 book *Soft Energy Paths* and founder of the Rocky Mountain Institute in Snowmass Colorado.[15]

While Lindberg was exploring climate change and energy issues globally, his growing interest had local roots as well. Alone among America's large cities, Portland operates under a commission form of government. In addition to having legislative responsibilities, city council members act as head administrators of individual city bureaus.[16] This gives them wide latitude in deploying city staff and budget resources toward issues of their own particular concern. Following almost a decade of turmoil set off by the 1973 Arab oil embargo, oil prices declined during the 1980s along with public concern in the United States over energy supply. This was less the case in the Portland. Forecasts by the Northwest Power

Planning Council pointed to population and economic growth outstripping available electricity supply in the region. Growing opposition to the Trojan nuclear plant portended the possible elimination of 12 percent of the region's electrical generating capacity. As city commissioner, Lindberg oversaw the Portland energy office whose attention he began to focus upon the threat posed by climate change. He received encouragement from other council members, including Earl Blumenauer. Elected to city council in 1986 after serving on the governing body of Multnomah County, in which Portland is located, Blumenauer would be elected to Congress in 1996 where ten years later he would become vice-chair of the U.S. House of Representatives Committee on Energy Independence and Global Warming. Working closely with the city energy office, Lindberg convened a public workshop on climate change shortly after release of the first IPCC assessment report in 1990 demonstrating a rise in global atmospheric temperatures and projecting impacts of the greenhouse gas effect.[17] Included among workshop participants that expressed support for efforts to reduce the city's greenhouse gas emissions was the recently founded Bicycle Transportation Alliance of Portland. In ensuing years the BTA would grow into one of the most powerful lobbies in a city where "bike helmets compete with school kids as the leading prop in political candidates' campaign literature."[18] Support also came from 1000 Friends of Oregon, cofounded in 1975 by Governor Tom McCall as an independent watchdog over implementation of the state's growth management act.

In 1990, the Portland City Council adopted an update of its energy policy. The 1979 policy had largely focused upon weatherization of residential buildings and acquiring basic data about energy use in the city. The 1990 policy cast its net much more widely. Its overall goal was to reduce energy use by 10 percent throughout the city—not just in residences but also in city operations, commercial buildings, industrial facilities, transportation, telecommunications, energy supply, and waste reduction—while also promoting new renewable energy resources.[19] In 1991, Portland joined thirteen other Canadian, European, and American cities as founding members of ICLEI's Urban CO_2 Reduction Initiative.[20] In 1993, Portland became the first city in the nation to adopt a municipal climate action plan.

The goal of the 1993 Carbon Dioxide Reduction Strategy was ambitious: a 20 percent reduction from 1990 CO_2 levels by 2010, exceeding what would later be prescribed in 1997 by the Kyoto protocols. The plan set out goals for emissions reduction in a number of areas including transportation, energy efficiency, renewable energy and cogeneration, recycling, urban forestry, and advocacy for federal actions. In this, as much as being seen as comprising an initiative in its own right, Portland's first CO_2 reduction plan can be seen largely as an extension of the city's comprehensive planning process and energy policy. The plan spoke to the many benefits that could derive from an effective global warming strategy. These included "reducing air pollution; providing cost-effective electric power and natural gas service; increasing reliance on renewable resources; reducing energy bills for businesses and families; expanding recycling; preventing urban sprawl and traffic congestion, and promoting tree planting." Pointing to a link between its emissions reduction strategy and other city priorities, the plan argued, "all of these benefits promote economic and environmental goals and enhance city livability."[21] Commenting on how the city's first climate plan came into force, Susan Anderson, then director of the city's energy office who wrote much of the CO_2 reduction plan, said "back then, we didn't talk about global warming because people would've thought we were wacky . . . we talked about making changes for the cost-saving benefits."[22] While Portland was the first U.S. city to adopt a plan to address global warming, climate consciousness in the city was still not a prevalent enough feature of public concern to stand on its own and needed to be tied to other priorities popular with the public like economic development and reducing the cost of government. Still, Portland was ambitious, as demonstrated in the city council's adoption in 1994 of a set of operating principles to create "a stable, diverse and equitable economy, protect and conserve air, water, land and other natural resources, native vegetation, fish, wildlife habitat and other ecosystems, and minimize human impacts on local and worldwide ecosystems."[23] If the words carrying capacity did not appear in the new principals annunciated by the city, the concept could certainly be inferred.

By 1997, Portland was able to claim a 3 percent per-capita reduction below 1990 CO_2 levels and a 7 percent per-capita decline in 2000.[24] This was attributed to two primary factors. One was the urban growth boundary's concentration of development. A second was a 30 percent ridership increase on the region's publicly owned and operated light rail and bus transit system. Together, these reduced emissions from auto generated sources.

A third contributing factor was that during the 1990s the region's regulated electric utility, Portland General Electric (PGE), commenced an aggressive initiative that included providing incentives to both household and industrial electricity consumers to increase the efficient use of energy. PGE would later become one of the first utilities in the nation to acknowledge the role electricity generation plays in global climate change and come out publicly on record as favoring establishment of a federal cap and trade system to reduce GHG emissions. Although the company is not without its critics, in its instrumental role as the region's electric utility, PGE can be very much seen as a constructive ally in the city's emission reduction efforts, much more so than utilities in many other regions of the country.[25]

Other companies began to express support for Portland's GHG emissions reduction goals. By the mid-1990s, the area's ski and wine industries had become climate conscious, seeing rising atmospheric temperatures as a threat to their ongoing business viability. In 2001, Nike joined the Climate Savers Agreement established by the World Wildlife Fund, committing to offset its CO_2 emissions by 13 percent from 1998 levels by 2005 by increasing the energy efficiency of its operations, retooling business travel practices, and purchasing renewable energy. The same year saw Portland-based The Collins Companies commit to reducing its emissions by 15 percent by 2010. In doing so, Collins became perhaps the first U.S. forest products company to make a commitment to reducing its global warming emissions. In both cases, the companies were seeking to both demonstrate their climate consciousness and at the same time save millions of dollars and increase their profitability.[26]

In 2000, the city released an updated evaluation of its progress in climate planning. Attention was called to the fact that the 1993 plan had set CO_2 reduction goals higher than those called for in Kyoto and that although per capita emissions had fallen, overall CO_2 emissions had actually increased since 1990 due to population growth. This cast doubt upon the city's ability to attain its overall emissions reduction target by 2010. The evaluation concluded that "although achievements in energy efficiency, transportation, recycling, and tree planting have helped achieve a reduction in per-capita emissions . . . today, seven years into the plan, we have far to go."[27] Reviewing Portland's carbon emissions strategy, the Progressive Policy Institute remarked, "while Portland's efforts to apply smart growth strategies to curb GHG emissions are working, they remain the exception to the rule," and called for the city to embrace "a broader array of tools . . . in the fight against climate change."[28]

Portland's Second Climate Plan

Increasingly, Portland was coming to be seen both nationally and globally as being in the forefront of municipal efforts to reduce greenhouse gas emissions. In

1996 Lindberg retired from the city council, being not only acknowledged as the architect of the city's entry into the battle against global warming but also as the longest-serving city council member in Portland's history. However this did not mean that the effort to mitigate and adapt to global warming was deprived of leadership. In 1998, former Multnomah County Commissioner Dan Saltzman was elected to the city council. Possessing degrees in civil and environmental engineering from Cornell and MIT, Saltzman was given responsibility for overseeing the city's Bureau of Environmental Services. In 2000 he combined the city's energy office, department of solid waste management, and cable franchise management operations to create an Office of Sustainable Development. He also capitalized upon his eight years of service as a county commissioner to bring in Multnomah County as a partner with the city in efforts to enhance regional sustainability. The partnership was confirmed through execution of an intergovernmental agreement in 2002 that created the Sustainable Development Commission of Portland and Multnomah County (SDC). The SDC was an outgrowth of the Sustainable Portland Commission. Whereas the latter's focus was primarily on internal city operations, the mission of the new SDC was cast wider. In addition to "greening up" internal government operations such as procurement, the SDC was charged with promoting sustainable building, heightening public awareness of sustainability principles and practices, and examining other opportunities to further promote sustainability practices across governmental boundaries. With the execution of the agreement, Multnomah County became a full partner with the city in seeking to mitigate and adapt to a warming climate.

In 2001, the city produced an update of its climate plan. When also adapted by the county, it became the joint city-county *Local Action Plan on Global Warming*. The new plan contained six elements: transportation; energy efficiency; renewable resources; waste management; forestry and carbon offsets; and policy, research, and education. Recognizing the difficulty in reaching the 1993 plan's target CO_2 reduction of 20 percent below 1990 levels by 2010, the plan reduced the emissions goal to 10 percent below 1990 levels by 2010. The new plan identified more than 100 short- and long-term actions to reduce greenhouse gas emissions in much greater detail than provided for in the original 1993 city plan.[29] Importantly, the plan sought to extend city and county climate initiatives beyond governmental institutions alone to the wider community. For each action in the plan, activities were identified as either government actions or community initiatives. Whereas government actions comprised steps the city and county could take internally to green themselves, community initiatives reflected local government's role as a partner, advocate, or catalyst for steps to be taken by community groups, individuals, and businesses. Plan actions were broken down into those to be accomplished by 2003 and those by 2010. The plan called for GHG emissions to be inventoried annually and progress reports to be provided to the city council and county board of commissioners every two years.[30]

Chief among complimentary initiatives that accompanied the new climate plan were city and county green building policies. Commercial, residential, and industrial buildings account for 40 percent of all energy consumed in the United States and produce an equivalent amount of the nation's CO_2 emissions.[31] The need to attenuate GHG emissions generated from the nation's building sector had been recognized in 1993 when the Natural Resources Defense Council brought together government agencies, architects and engineers, property developers and managers, and construction materials manufacturers to develop guidelines for what emerged as the United State's Green Building Council's LEED green building certification system. The LEED system was released to the public in 2000. It has been estimated that the average building designed to LEED standards can emit 33 percent less CO_2 than a conventionally constructed building, as well as reduce building water use and energy use and improve workplace health and safety.[32] With public release of LEED, the city and county adopted policies requiring that all new local government facilities be built to LEED standards. Buildings built by the private sector or nonprofit entities that received financial support from the city through redevelopment incentives such as tax increment financing or property tax abatements granted by the Portland Development Commission were also required to be LEED certified.

Excluding the government buildings, the new city and county green building policies targeted construction of at least 600 new housing units and 3 million square feet of commercial development within its first two years of operation. In practice, more than 1,300 units of housing and 3.5 million square feet were built or improved during this period.[33] A Green Investment Fund was also created, which, by 2003, distributed more than $800,000 to support construction of sixty-nine affordable housing, residential, and commercial development projects.[34] A number of the new projects would be located in the Pearl District, which may be home to the highest concentration of LEED-certified buildings to be found anywhere. A former rail yard district populated by decrepit warehouse buildings just north of the city's downtown business center, the Pearl had long been designated

FIGURE 2.1. Portland streetcar in front of the Brewery Blocks, developed by Gerding Edlen Development, Inc.

for redevelopment by the city. In 1999, the city commenced construction of a streetcar line through the Pearl District connecting Northwest Portland's residential neighborhoods to MAX light rail and Portland State University in downtown with its terminus at the Southwest Waterfront, another industrial area targeted for redevelopment (see figure 2.1). Portland is now home to more LEED certified buildings per capita than any other city in the United States.[35]

The Economic Imperative to Climate Planning

Portland's success in LEED construction points to a close link between the city's climate planning and economic development strategies. Climate planning in Portland did not take place in a vacuum. The burst of the dot.com bubble in 1999 hit the Portland area hard at the very time the city was beginning work on its second climate plan. Metropolitan area unemployment, at 5 percent in January 2000, rose to 8 percent in January 2001 and 9 percent in 2005. The imperative in Portland became how best to manage its climate change activities while at the same time reinvigorating the regional economy. Portland mayor Vera Katz summed up the city's approach in the introduction to the 2001 Local Action Plan. Katz wrote:

> We know that cutting CO_2 emissions is not only smart for the environment, it's great for business. If we reduce our CO_2 emissions, we also reduce local air pollution, plant more trees, lower energy bills for residents and business, use more solar and wind power, and create a more livable, walkable, community-oriented city for all of us.[36]

A certain air of ambivalence surrounded the Oregon's business community's attitude during development of the state's comprehensive planning system during the 1970s. According to Sy Adler, Professor of Urban Studies and Planning at Portland State University, "there was resigned acceptance among the builders, as well as the real estate brokers, that there was going to be a (growth management) boundary goal."[37] For the most part Oregon businesses did not oppose the growth management regime outright although there was opposition to selected provisions seen as particularly damaging to business interests including the carrying capacity concept. A similar air of ambivalence has characterized business attitudes toward climate planning. For example, the region's chamber of commerce, the Portland Business Alliance, has not publicly opposed the climate planning initiatives, although it has fought against certain provisions. As an example, the alliance successfully opposed a proposal by the city to require that all homes and commercial buildings produce an energy audit available for review by the public and potential property purchasers.[38]

Businesses were more concerned with stimulating the local and regional economy than in climate plans. The SDC also shared a strong interest in stimulating economic development, through promotion of a sustainable business sector in Portland. In 2002, the city council directed the PDC to prepare what emerged as the *Strategy for Economic Vitality—Portland 2002*. At the urging of the SDC, the end product included mention of sustainable industries as a business cluster worthy of attention and development.[39] However it was one of ten business clusters targeted by the PDC and not called out as a primary economic driver for the region's future.

In practice, many in the traditional economic development profession had difficulty understanding how a business could be "sustainable" and how to define a sustainable business in terms of the U.S. Department of Commerce SIC or NAICS definitions the PDC used to select companies for targeted economic development support. In 2003 the SDC began discussions about transitioning away from dependence upon fossil fuels, asking the question, "what will be required to move Multnomah County and Portland to a 100 percent renewable energy economy by the year 2040?"[40] Among the SDC's recommendations were that the state's electric utilities be required to generate a share of their electricity from renewable energy resources and that an economic development marketing campaign should be developed branding Portland as a national leader in sustainability. It was not until 2006, when at the urging of the SDC, the PDC made an explicit commitment to fostering climate friendly businesses in the form of an agreement with the city's Office of Sustainable Development to collaborate in promoting sustainable industry. By then, the state had joined in seeking to give impetus to an economic development strategy tied to sustainability and mitigation and adaptation to climate change.

In 2002, government and business leaders came together to create the Oregon Business Plan. Updated in 2006, the plan identified twelve business clusters toward which state economic development efforts were to be targeted. The main focus was upon such traditional foundations of Oregon's economy as forest products, computers and software, farming, tourism, and manufacturing. Although the Portland area economy suffered during the first half of the decade, there had been growth in one segment of the regional economy in the form of sustainably oriented businesses. Many of these businesses were small and not well represented among the area's traditional business leadership, but they were growing both in size and prominence. One was Clean Edge, founded in 2000 as perhaps the nation's first business research and publishing firms devoted to the cleantech energy sector. LEED green building consultants Brightworks and Green Building Services were gaining recognition. Converting a 100-year-old brewery into the mixed-use Brewery Blocks in the Pearl District, Portland-based developer Gerding-Edlen transformed itself from a builder of prosaic commercial properties to a winner of awards from the U.S. Green Building Council (see figure 2.2). Well respected Portland area winery Sokol-Blosser gained prominence for adopting sustainable viniculture methods, and consultants PECI and Ecos were establishing themselves as leaders in the field of energy conservation. Founded in 1997 outside of Portland in the small town of Ilwaco, Washington,

FIGURE 2.2. The wind turbines atop Indigo @ Twelve West, developed by Gerding-Edlen Development, Inc., will generate 9,000 kilowatt hours of electricity annually.

Shorebank Pacific emerged to pioneer socially responsible lending to businesses involved in green building, sustainable agriculture, renewable energy, and manufacturing of sustainable products.

Following the lead of Portland and Multnomah County, the state was also developing its own climate strategy that reflected a close tie between mitigation and adaptation to climate change and economic development. In 2004, the state issued its first *Greenhouse Gas Reduction Strategy*. According to the report:

> Many actions proposed in this report carry price tags, but they are generally in the nature of investments that can generate net economic returns to us over time. . . . . Many companies here have built prosperous business lines in energy efficiency products and consulting practices, in developing renewable energy technologies and adapting the power system for optimal use. We believe Oregon's entrepreneurs . . . can prosper by positioning themselves at the leading edge of change.[41]

In a highly publicized January 2006 visit to Portland to assess Oregon's economic development strategy, Professor Michael Porter of the Institute for Strategy and Competitiveness at Harvard University argued that with limited re-sources, the state and its economic regions needed to more effectively focus their economic development efforts. He pointed to the emerging sustainable busi-nesses as an area where the state and Portland were developing a competitive advantage. In early 2007, the Oregon State Legislature took several steps that helped cement the link between sustainability, climate planning, and economic development. Two stand out in particular. One was enactment of the Oregon Renewable Energy Act of 2007. It established the statewide renewable energy standard (RES) called for by the SDC under which Portland General Electric and Pacificorp, the other large utility serving the Portland area, would need to procure 20 percent of the electricity they sell to consumers from renewable en-ergy resources by 2020.[42] The legislature also revised the state's Business Energy Tax Credit (BETC). Created in 1979 at the same time that the city adopted its first energy policy, BETC provides tax incentives to promote investment in en-ergy efficient building and renewable energy. The 2007 revisions increased to 50 percent from 35 percent the proportion of a renewable energy project develop-ment costs that could be credited against the Oregon state tax liability of a busi-ness or individual holding the tradable tax credits. The change in BETC and adoption of the RES had a significant impact. Installation of new wind genera-tion in Oregon jumped from 438 to 885 megawatts (MW) between 2006 and 2007. By 2008, Oregon was one of only seven states to have more than 1,000 MW of installed wind generation, an amount equivalent to the generating ca-pacity of the Bonneville hydroelectric dam on the Columbia River.[43] Success in tying climate planning to sustainable economic development was demonstrated in 2008 when global renewable energy leader Vestas of Denmark announced that it would anchor its North American headquarters in Portland with plans to construct a new 500,000 square foot LEED Platinum headquarters building that would employ up to 1,200.[44] The same year saw Solar World open the nation's largest solar cell manufacturing facility in the Portland west side suburbs. Global renewable energy leaders Iberdrola of Spain and Horizon Wind Energy, the American arm of Portugal's Energias de Portugal, also established their conti-nental headquarters in Portland. These successes only heightened Portland's in-terest in moving assertively to strengthen its climate planning credentials as a tool for business development. This became clear in 2009 when the city adopted a new five-year economic development strategy with the stated goal that the city would "build the most sustainable economy in the world."[45] The same year also saw Portland and Multnomah County unveil a new iteration of a climate planning strategy.

The 2009 Plan

The question of whether global oil production has "peaked" is often the subject of vituperative debate. In May 2006, Portland City Council established a Peak Oil Task Force and charged it with examining the potential economic and social consequences should world oil prices rise in the face of declining oil stocks. The task force recommended decreasing total fossil fuel consumption by more than 50 percent over twenty-five years through a variety of measures including increases in energy efficiency, changes in transportation choices, and renewable energy development.[46] The following year the IPCC released its Fourth Assessment Report projecting potentially catastrophic consequences of a globally warming atmosphere. With the findings of these reports supported by evidence of the economic development benefits to be gained by creating a sustainable business sector, the city council and county commission passed resolutions in 2007 directing that a new joint climate strategy be developed. Evaluation of performance under the regional climate planning partnership showed that the city and county had continued to reduce their per-capita CO_2 emissions and had even succeeded in reducing overall emissions by 1 percent from 1990 levels.[47] However, that reduction was a far cry from the 10 percent goal established in the 2001 plan. The view that more needed to be done was widely shared and reflected in the decision to add an additional goal to the intergovernmental climate plan—reduce overall CO_2 emissions to 80 percent below 1990 levels by 2050.

In late 2007, a steering committee commenced its deliberations, composed of representatives from the SDC, the Peak Oil Task Force, and staff from eight local government agencies. First meeting with a group of scientists to help define the challenges and gaps in the current plan and to form a framework for a new plan, the committee continued to meet through March 2009. Other technical working groups explored possible actions to address energy use in buildings, land use, and mobility, and city and county staff worked on options around urban forestry and natural systems, food, waste reduction, and recycling. A draft plan was released for public comment in April 2009 and eight town hall meetings were held to discuss the plan with residents, businesses, and community organizations. More than 2,600 comments and suggestions were received and were incorporated into the final plan, which was formally adopted by the city and county in October 2009.[48]

In addition to the goal of reducing overall emissions by 80 percent in 2050 from 1990 levels, the 2009 *Climate Action Plan* set an interim goal of a 40 percent reduction by 2030. The plan identified more than 100 actions to be taken in eight categories: buildings and energy; urban form and mobility; consumption and solid waste; urban forestry and natural systems; food and agriculture; community engagement; climate change preparation; and local government operations. The plan is designed to be iterative, incorporating and building on lessons learned as follows: (1) every year there is a community inventory and report on local emission trends, fossil fuel use, and progress on implementing actions in the plan; (2) every three years the actions in the plan are revised and new ones are to be identified to be implemented in the subsequent three years; and (3) in 2020 a new plan will be developed to keep the city and county on the path to achieve the 80 percent reduction goal and to meet any challenges of adaptation to a changing climate.

The mechanics of the plan are driven by quantitative metrics where possible and demonstrate a complex and concerted approach to emissions reduction. The actions are prioritized based on a filter of three criteria: (1) emission reductions, (2) sphere of influence, and (3) community benefits. The purpose of the filter is to screen out those actions that may lead to short- or medium-term reductions but are unlikely to achieve necessary long-term reductions. Where possible, quantitative measures are used for prioritization. The plan focuses on those measures that the city and county are positioned to carry out. Sphere of influence filters were also used to screen out actions beyond the control of local government. Additionally, the plan identifies actions that create ancillary community benefits in terms of job creation, neighborhood support, and healthful living.

The Climate Action Plan was adopted in 2009 so, at the time of this writing, it is too early to evaluate how efficaciously it will work in practice. It is noteworthy, however, that projections call for the Portland area to grow by an additional 1 million residents by 2030.[49] While the plan does appear to have joined Portland and Multnomah County "at the hip" in the fight against global warming, most of the future growth is projected to take place in the suburban ring that surrounds Portland and Multnomah in counties and cities that are not party to the emissions reduction strategy. It is clear that Portland and Multnomah County have made a serious investment in their climate planning initiatives. Whether these surrounding jurisdictions will join the city and county in embracing a wider regional approach to climate planning remains an open question mark.

Anomaly or Aspiration

When preparing to write this chapter, one of the authors called up a former graduate school instructor who no longer resides in the Portland area. Told the subject of the chapter, the author received a response that, to paraphrase, "people are tired of hearing about Portland. . . . Portland's an anomaly." There is in fact debate as to whether, during the last fifty years, Portland has developed a cultural and political bias that makes it unusually well suited to the type of collective initiatives that characterize its efforts at climate action planning and whether the conditions that have made Portland so well suited can be replicated elsewhere. The aim here is not to resolve this debate. What is clear is that in Portland, climate planning emerged from a long tradition of environmental and planning activism guided by strong leadership. At the same time, the city fashioned new institutional arrangements that give force to the climate change agenda. Portland's experience offers promise as cities seek an effective vehicle for advancing a convergence between effective action to address climate change and promote local and regional economic development. To the degree to which other American cities can learn from Portland, we may be hopeful that progress can be made in addressing the threat that global climate change poses to the environment and economic well-being of the American people.

Notes

1. Carl Abbott, *Portland: Planning, Politics and Growth in a Twentieth Century City.* (Lincoln, NE: University of Nebraska Press, 1983), 171.
2. Carl Abbott, *Portland: Planning, Politics and Growth in a Twentieth Century City*, 173.
3. Population Research Center, Portland State University, 2009; Wikipedia, "Portland, Oregon," http://en.wikipedia.org/wiki/Portland,_Oregon (accessed March 11, 2009); Howard Weinberg, *Do All Trails Lead to Oregon? An Analysis of the Characteristics of People Moving to and from Oregon 1985–1990* (Center for Population Research and Census, Portland State University, June 3, 1995). In-migration to Oregon, mainly the Portland area, between 1985 and 1990 was highest among twenty- to twenty-nine-year-olds. Another analysis developed by

the reference in note 4 of in-migration to Portland from the city of Phoenix showed in-migration to be highest among those in the twenty-to-forty age group.

4. While large-scale growth in Portland's technology sector is primarily traceable to Intel's decision to build its first plant in the Portland suburb of Aloha, the area already had a technology presence in the form of Tektronix Corporation. Founded in east Portland in 1946, the company relocated to what would become the "Silicon Forest" in 1956. By 1976, Tektronix had grown to 10,000 employees and was the state's largest employer and the world's largest manufacturer of oscilloscopes and other electronic measuring devices. For this reason, it is Tektronix, and not Intel, that is sometimes credited as providing the initial impetus to development of Portland's technology sector.

5. See Oregon Employment Department, *Oregon Labor Market System* (Salem, Oregon). The job numbers presented for growth in the Portland area's technology sector actually understate the true magnitude of the technology sector's growth since they are based on federal SIC codes, which accounted only for manufacturing of electronic and electronics and electronic equipment and instruments and related products and did not account for growth in ancillary business services such as software design and development, Internet operators, and telecommunications. Data for this sector became available in 2001 with the replacement of SIC codes by the NAICS system, which in 2001 showed there to be almost 45,000 jobs in information technology and professional, telecommunications, scientific, and technical services to complement 42,000 electronics manufacturing jobs. By 2001, technology-related manufacturing and services account for more than 10 percent of total employment in the Portland metropolitan region. In contrast, wood products accounted for only about 5,000 jobs in metropolitan Portland in 2001.

6. Further reflecting the declining importance of forestry products to the Portland economy, in 2003 Louisiana Pacific, another global forest products company, relocated its headquarters from Portland to Nashville, Tennessee.

7. Matthew I. Slavin, *Washington County Economic Base and Labor Market Analysis* (Hillsboro, Oregon: Washington County, Oregon, Department of Land Use and Planning, 1988).

8. In something of an irony, Clay Meyers, who was Oregon secretary of state at the time when McCall made his comment, claimed that it was he who first used the "visit but don't stay" line as a joke during a presentation. Meyers mentioned the laughs he got to McCall, who then picked it up. Many business firms took the comment seriously however, as a sign that new business investment was not welcome in Oregon. Included was Intel. Intel was leaning against locating its facilities in Oregon but ultimately decided to move ahead with constructing its fabrication plant in the Portland area.

9. Earth Day founder Dennis Hayes grew up in Camas, Washington, just across the Columbia River from Portland.

10. Sy Adler, "Oregon Plans: The Making of an Unquiet Land Use Revolution" (unpublished manuscript).

11. Trojan accounted for more than 12 percent of Oregon's electricity generating capacity. Decommissioning and demolition began in 1993 and was completed in 2006. The plant operated for only sixteen years, twenty years less than its licensed design lifetime.

12. Clark is also perhaps Portland's most colorful mayor ever, having gained widespread publicity as the raincoat-wearing model for a poster titled "Expose Yourself to Art" in which he appeared to expose himself to a nude female public statue in downtown Portland.

13. Mike Lindberg, interview, March 23, 2010.

14. World Commission on Environment and Development, *Our Common Future: Report of the World Commission on Environment and Development* (published as Annex to General Assembly document A/42/427, *Development and International Co-operation: Environment*, August 2, 1987).

15. See chapter 1 for a discussion of ICLEI's role in the establishment of the sustainable cities movement in the United States. The IPCC was established in 1988.

16. The commission form of government gained favor as a reformist measure during the early part of the twentieth century. By the end of the century, all of America's fifty largest cities had abandoned the commission, however, in favor of either the city manager or strong mayor form of government. The exception is Portland.

17. IPCC, *First Assessment Report* (Geneva: International Panel on Climate Change, World Meteorological Institute, 1990).

18. Nigel Jaquiss, 2010. "Power to the Pedal," *Willamette Week*, February 17, 2010, http://wweek.com/editorial/3615/13701/.

19. See www.portlandonline.com/bps/index.cfm?a=116779&c=41462 (accessed March 21, 2010). The policy included the goal of cutting city government energy bills by $1 million within ten years. By 1999, city energy bills had been reduced by $1.1 million annually for a total reduction of more than $7 million.

20. See chapter 1 for a discussion of the role ICLEI and the U.S. Conference of Mayors have played in fostering local action on sustainability and climate change in the United States.

21. City of Portland, *Carbon Dioxide Reduction Strategy*, November 10, 1993.

22. Hari M. Osofsky and Janet Koven Levit, "The Scale of Networks: Local Climate Change Coalitions," *Chicago Journal of International Law* 8, no.2 (winter 2008): 409.

23. See "Sustainable City Principles" at www.portlandonline.com/bps/index.cfm?c=41482&a=111759. These principles were reaffirmed in the city's recent five-year Economic Development Strategy adopted in December 2009.

24. Whatcomcounts.org, "Portland's Local Action Plan to Reduce Carbon Dioxide Emissions," 2009, www.whatcomcounts.org/whatcom/modules.php?op=modload&name=PromisePractice&file=promisePractice&pid=155.

25. Portland General Electric, *The Electricity Sector's Role in Oregon Carbon Emissions* (Portland, Oregon, February 2009). PGE's progressive approach to climate change reflects in large part its electrical generating resource mix. It obtains more than 20 percent of its electricity from hydropower and only about a quarter from coal. These are 2009 figures, and coal's share was higher during the 1990s, particularly after Trojan shut down. But PGE has never been overwhelmingly reliant on coal, in contrast to many other electric utilities whose reliance on coal makes them steadfast opponents of federal limits on GHG emissions. For example, as a share of its total fuel mix, PacifiCorp, the utility that supplies electricity to much of Oregon outside the Portland area as well as Northern California, Utah, Wyoming, and Idaho, derives as much as three times more of its base load power generation from coal as does PGE. PGE's aggressive entry into energy efficiency was warranted in part by the closure

of Trojan, leaving the company only limited other options for quickly adding new generating capacity needed to meet the demand of the growing customer base it is mandated by law to serve. Having closed Trojan, Oregonians were not about to allow construction of a second coal plant in their state.

26. See World Wildlife Fund, "Nike Partners with WWF and Center for Energy and Climate Solutions to Reduce Greenhouse Gas Emissions," October 2, 2001, www.world wildlife.org/who/media/press/2001/WWFPresitem10798.html (accessed March 23, 2010). Also Osofsky and Levit, "The Scale of Networks," All Business, www.allbusiness.com /government/government-bodies-offices/8897056-1.html (accessed March 16, 2010).

27. Portland Energy Office, *Carbon Dioxide Reduction Strategy: Success and Setbacks*, (Portland, Oregon, June 2000).

28. Progressive Policy Institute, "Driving Down Carbon Dioxide" (Washington, D.C., November 24, 2003) www.ppionline.org/ppi_ci.cfm?knlgAreaID=116&subsecID= 900039&ccontentID=252224.

29. The 2001 climate plan is no longer available for viewing online. However, the 2009 climate plan may be viewed at the city of Portland's website at www.portlandonline.com /bps/index.cfm?c=49989&.

30. A summary of progress made in implementing the 2001 climate plan is presented in the 2009 climate plan referenced in footnote 29.

31. National Institute of Building Sciences, *Whole Building Design Guide*, 2009, www .wbdg.org/design/minimize_consumption.php.

32. U.S. Green Building Council, "Green Building Facts," n.d., www.usgbc.org /DisplayPage.aspx?cmspageID=1718.

33. City of Portland, Office of Sustainable Development, *ReThinking Development: Portland's Strategic Investment in Green Building Progress Report: FY 2000–2002* (Portland, Oregon) www.portlandonline.com/shared/cfm/image.cfm?id=118349.

34. See City of Portland, *ReThinking Development*.

35. Monica Lee Hawthorne, "Commentary: LEED Versus Passive House: What's the Difference?" *Daily Journal of Commerce*, February 24, 2010, http://findarticles.com/p /articles/mi_qn4184/is_20100224/ai_n50447587/.

36. City of Portland. *Local Action Plan on Global Warming*. Portland, OR: City of Portland and Multnomah County, 2001, p. 3.

37. Sy Adler, personal communication to Matthew Slavin, July 13, 2010.

38. Jim Redden, "Views Mixed on Climate Change Strategy," *Portland Tribune*, July 9, 2009, www.thetribonline.org/sustainable/print_story.php?story_id=124699156820032200.

39. See Portland Development Commission, www.pdc.us/pubs/inv_detail.asp?id= 347&ty=46.

40. Portland Sustainable Development Commission, "Summary of Energy Efficiency and Renewable Energy Committee Research and Recommendation to Adopt the Goal to Achieve a 100 Percent Renewable Energy Economy by 2040," January 18, 2005.

41. Governor's Advisory Group on Global Warming, "Oregon's Strategy for Greenhouse Gas Reductions," *Oregon.gov* (Salem, Oregon), ii–iii.

42. The standard also applied to other smaller utilities in the state with the RES goal being contingent upon utility size.

43. See U.S. Department of Energy, Office of Energy Efficiency and Renewable Energy, "Wind Powering America," 2010, www.windpoweringamerica.gov/wind_installed_capacity .asp. This website offers an excellent animated depiction of how installed wind capacity has grown over the years in the various U.S. states. See also American Wind Energy Association, "Wind Energy Grows by Record 8,300 MW in 2008," January 27, 2009, www.awea.org /newsroom/releases/wind_energy_growth2008_27Jan09.html.

44. Construction of the new Vestas headquarters building has been put on hold as a result of the economic downturn that began in late 2007.

45. See Portland Development Commission, *Economic Development Strategy: A Five-Year Plan for Promoting Job Creation and Economic Growth* (Portland, Oregon, n.d.), www .pdxeconomicdevelopment.com/docs/Portland-Ec-Dev-Strategy.pdf (accessed June 26, 2010).

46. City of Portland, *Report of the City of Portland Peak Oil Task Force* (Portland, Oregon, March 2007), www.portlandonline.com/bps/index.cfm?c=42894&a=145732.

47. See note 30.

48. See City of Portland, Bureau of Planning and Sustainability, *Climate Action Plan 2009* (Portland, Oregon), www.portlandonline.com/bps/index.cfm?c=49989& (accessed June 26, 2010).

49. METRO, *Regional Population and Employment Range Forecasts* (Metropolitan Service District, Portland, Oregon) March 2009 draft, http://library.oregonmetro.gov/files/20-50 _range_forecast.pdf.

Chapter 3

Greening the Industrial District: Transforming Milwaukee's Menomonee Valley from a Blighted Brownfield into a Sustainable Place to Work and Play

CHRISTOPHER DE SOUSA

All the forces in the world are not so powerful as an idea whose time has come.

—Victor Hugo

Visions of a sustainable urban future don't often include conventional manufacturing, given that it is blamed for causing many of our urban environmental ills in the first place. Decades of deindustrialization have resulted in poverty, joblessness, contamination, and visual blight, leading to a general sense that "rusty" old industry is a thing of the past, not the face of a city's modern future. So it is common for local governments to reenvision a "greener" future for their brownfield districts that typically include parks, condos, retail shops, research centers, and white-collar office jobs, particularly in those locations near the downtown core that are ripe for "higher and better uses."[1] It would seem strange to some then that the city of Milwaukee chose to reindustrialize the Menomonee Valley, a 1,400-acre district of prime land located directly in the heart of the city and visible to all who drive over it on the main interstate. Even more surprising to some was the desire of many stakeholders to make this project a model of sustainability.

This chapter examines Milwaukee's efforts to transform the Menomonee Valley from one of the most blighted industrial districts in the Midwestern United States into a vibrant employment center that has established Milwaukee as a leader in sustainable urban economic development. It begins with an introduction to the area's rich industrial history and its gradual decline into Wisconsin's largest brownfield district, and then describes how key stakeholders forged a new and more sustainable future for the valley. The valley's cleanup and ongoing redevelopment are chronicled in terms of key visions, plans, policies, programs, actions, and funding mechanisms to illustrate how stakeholders have steadily overcome the barriers to redevelopment and have enhanced industrial employment through sustainable design, green infrastructure, transportation improvements, family-sustaining wage planning, and community involvement. Intrinsic to Milwaukee's approach was a focus upon integrating the triple bottom line concept of people, planet, and prosperity into the area's redevelopment strategy. Lessons learned are spelled out to provide insight into how other cities can learn from Milwaukee's experience and recycle their brownfields into more sustainable places to work and play.

Gateway to the City

The Menomonee River Valley lies in the heart of the city of Milwaukee and has always played a pivotal role in the economic life of the region. The 1,400-acre valley spans almost 1 kilometer north to south and 5 kilometers east to west. Flowing through it is the Menomonee River, whose abundant fish and waterfowl provided the necessities of life for early Native American populations. In addition to providing a canoe route from Lake Michigan into the interior, the wild rice harvested in the valley was a vital source of food and even gave the valley its name, Menomonee being derived from the Algonquin word for wild rice.[2]

As European settlement increased in the late 1800s, the valley's accessibility to railways, Lake Michigan, and local river systems made it a prime location for industrial activity. In 1869, a group of business leaders supported by local authorities planned a network of canals and slips in the valley that were surrounded by parcels of land for industrial use. The project took a decade to complete and required vast quantities of material to fill in the marsh, including dredge spoil, gravel, and municipal and industrial wastes. As the renowned Milwaukee historian John Gurda aptly observed, "lumber yards, coal yards and sash and door factories sprouted in the eastern end of the valley even before the muck was dry."[3]

Larger industrial complexes, including tanneries, breweries, stockyards, and railroad shops dotted the entire valley by the late 1800s. The transformation of the valley from a natural system to an industrialized one is the feature that has most epitomized Milwaukee's evolution and, unfortunately, highlights the un-sustainable model of past industrialization efforts. To quote an 1882 newspaper article:

> Nothing, perhaps, more strikingly exhibits the rapidity and solidarity of Milwaukee's growth than the march of improvement in the Menomonee Valley. The bogs and marshes in that locality are being converted into firm ground, and the waters which formerly spread themselves thinly over a large surface are being confined to an artificial channel and made navigable for great ships. The vast tract, which but a few years ago was the home of the wild duck and the resort of the sportsman with his gun, is now partially converted, and soon will be entirely so, to the seat of manufacturing and commercial enterprises, which take rank among the first of their kind in the entire Northwest.[4]

By the end of the nineteenth century, residential communities had spread extensively along the valley's bluffs, producing some of the most densely populated neighborhoods in Wisconsin. Industry prospered well into the 1920s and only the Great Depression of the 1930s could curtail its growth, which quickly picked up again with the onset of World War II.

The industrial engine of the valley began to decelerate in the decades following the war. Highway construction made it possible for people to live further away from their workplace and for manufacturers to use roads to transport goods instead of rail and water. Although the opening of the Milwaukee County Stadium in 1953 and the Valley Power Plant in 1969 did breathe some life into the district, it was still suffering the same fate as many industrial districts in the Rust-belt. Indeed, the valley witnessed employment drop from more than 50,000 jobs in the 1920s to approximately 20,000 jobs in the mid-1970s to barely 7,095 jobs by 1997.[5] With its economic decline, a host of problems ensued in both the valley and surrounding neighborhoods, including unemployment, a reduced tax base, and pollution.

The city did make a few efforts to revitalize the valley in the late 1970s. These included rebuilding several roads, clearing blight, acquiring land, and locating a handful of city facilities in the area.[6] More attention, however, was devoted to renewing the valley when Mayor John Norquist, currently president and CEO of the Congress for New Urbanism, took office in 1988. As Gurda notes, "a series of public and private initiatives, not all of them coordinated, raised expectations for an area that had become one of the most underused in central Milwaukee."[7]

While several longstanding manufacturers continued to operate in the valley, there also emerged a new desire for amenities to reconnect it with the community. A number of amenities were added or planned for the valley in the early 1990s, including Marquette University's Valley Fields athletic complex, the Potawatomi Bingo and Casino, a new stadium for the Milwaukee Brewers, and the Hank Aaron State Greenway Trail. These developments, along with the rapid conversion of warehouse and industrial property into residential lofts and retail shops just east of the valley in the so called Historic Third Ward District, made it necessary for the city and affected stakeholders to come to a decision on the future of this historically industrial district. Fortunately, Milwaukee's Department of City Development, local businesses, and key stakeholders in the surrounding community could agree on one thing: the area needed to be revitalized and provide "family supporting" jobs.

Identifying Baseline Conditions and Preliminary Expectations

A vital step in the valley's revitalization occurred in 1998 when the city of Milwaukee coordinated and prepared a plan for the valley entitled *Market Study, Engineering, and Land Use Plan for the Menomonee Valley*.[8] An important component of this plan was a preliminary analysis of the state of the valley as it related to stakeholder desires, real estate market conditions, engineering infrastructure, and environmental pollution.

Public outreach and stakeholder participation efforts including workshops, interviews, and surveys revealed that many wished to see industry remain and expand in the valley. However, manufacturers were concerned about whether the haphazard mixing of entertainment and other uses would affect its long-term viability for heavy manufacturing uses. Market research revealed the importance of existing manufacturing employment to the area. The valley's central location, access to freeways, proximity to downtown, and access to labor also continue to be important attributes for manufacturers. The successful office conversion of a large tannery complex in the eastern end of valley also pointed to the potential for growth in that sector and raised the possibility that office might act as a buffer against escalating residential and retail encroachment from the east. While the plan found that additional recreational space was not required to serve local residents, there was support for passive green space to enhance the image of the district and to serve as functional infrastructure for flood protection, biking, and walking. Research and public outreach also revealed that there was no appetite for retail activity in the valley given that it would compete with struggling retail in surrounding neighborhoods and emerging retail in the Historic Third Ward.

The engineering analysis for the city's plan revealed that access to rail and water was a strength of the valley, but that access and circulation for vehicles, transit, and pedestrians needed significant upgrading. As for environmental conditions, very little comprehensive information about soil and groundwater contamination could be pulled together for the plan, but the information that did exist pointed to a high likelihood of problems resulting from more than a century of heavy manufacturing and land filling throughout the area.

In all, the plan recommended that the valley be upgraded and revitalized to retain and strengthen viable and existing industries, attract new industry to the western and central areas of the valley and promote "compatible" mixed-use development, largely in the eastern valley, and maintain and protect adjacent neighborhoods and business areas. On the basis of preliminary research and consultation, the plan recommended several "Implementation Agenda Action Items" to move the project forward:[9]

1. A public/private partnership should be formed to implement the Land Use Plan.
2. The city of Milwaukee zoning ordinance should be amended to facilitate implementation of the Land Use Plan.
3. Environmental and soil analyses should be undertaken at all sites suitable for redevelopment in the priority areas.
4. Financing for environmental remediation and site improvements should be made available.
5. A partnership and other official representatives of the city should take the leadership role in promoting redevelopment within the valley.

6. Land uses that degrade the environment or impede redevelopment should be eliminated.
7. Roadway reconstruction projects to support redevelopment in the valley should be undertaken.
8. The appearance of the Menomonee Valley should be enhanced through the creation of green space and other visual amenities.

Forging Meaningful and Equitable Partnerships

Although the city produced the plan in consultation with many stakeholders, its first and most important action item was to formalize the emerging public/private partnership by establishing Menomonee Valley Partners (MVP) in November of 1999. Supported initially with $200,000 in funding from a U.S. EPA Brownfields Redevelopment Pilot Grant received by the city in 1998, the MVP became a 501(c)(3) nonprofit organization that would act as a public-private partnership to facilitate business, neighborhood, and public partners in efforts to revitalize the Valley. MVP hired its first staff person in 2000 and grew gradually to 2.5 staff in 2003, 3.5 staff in 2006, to its current number of 4 full-time staff.

Since its inception, MVP has been advised by a board of directors of more than twenty stakeholders committed to and affected by the valley's future. The board has representatives from business and community groups as well as state and local government. Through this partnership approach, stakeholders are essentially required to work together to develop and implement the action agenda items in a manner that respects the interests of the different members. At the same time, the individual members indirectly commit to ensuring that their own activities contribute to moving the vision of the partnership forward. It is important to note that while MVP was a new entity, members of the MVP board represented longstanding and respected businesses, nonprofits, and civic organizations that had been operating in the local community well before the 1990s. This structure also helped formalizing the role of stakeholders in the partnership, balance power among participants, and enhance the credibility of individual members.

It should also be noted that in addition to MVP, there were several key stakeholder groups who played pivotal roles in developing and implementing the valley vision. Chief public partners included the city of Milwaukee's Department of City Development, Department of Public Works, the Wisconsin Department of Natural Resources, and the Wisconsin Department of Transportation. Business partners in the valley, whose efforts were further coordinated in 1999 with the establishment of the Menomonee Valley Business Improvement District, were also vital. The Sixteenth Street Community Health Center, a local nonprofit operating in the neighborhood south of the valley since the late 1960s, also led the charge for a vision that incorporated sustainability principles. All in all, the participation of an array of committed stakeholders representing broad interests under the coordination of the MVP resulted in the partnerships broad mission for the valley:

> Menomonee Valley Partners envision a redeveloped valley that is as central to the city as it was in the past:
>
> - Geographically central, with new ties to the surrounding neighborhoods;
> - Economically central, with strong companies that provide jobs near workers' homes;
> - Ecologically central, with healthy waterways and greenspace; and
> - Culturally central, with recreational facilities for the community.

Overcoming Key Physical Barriers

Early on, those involved in the valley's redevelopment knew that it was necessary to address two key barriers. The first was the negative stigma associated with what had become the state's most notorious brownfield. The second was poor accessibility to auto, truck, and pedestrian mobility. To provide information on environmental and soil conditions, the MVP, city of Milwaukee, Wisconsin Department of Natural Resources, U.S. EPA, and the U.S. Geologic Survey conducted scientific investigations of the valley's soil and groundwater. Of particular concern were initial indications that groundwater flow might be moving between parcels, which meant that contamination could be spreading and that the cleanup of one property might not improve groundwater conditions adequately.

The city of Milwaukee used funds from the EPA Brownfields Redevelopment Pilot Grant to conduct an additional environmental site assessment. A group made up of scientists, lawyers, environmentalists, real estate professionals, and state agency representatives assisted with the direction of the study.[10] Their first recommendation was that an "area-wide" approach be taken rather than a site-specific one. They also recommended that the study be divided into two parts: a physical characterization of the groundwater (location, flow, and so on) and a chemical sampling to determine the nature of area-wide contamination. Modeling for the physical characterization revealed that the two major receptors for shallow groundwater were Milwaukee's Deep Tunnel System and Lake Michigan. Fortunately, however, the travel time to these receptors was very slow and would allow for the natural attenuation of many dissolved contaminants.

To complete the physical characterization and begin chemical sampling, the city of Milwaukee received an additional $150,000 from the EPA. Sampling revealed that groundwater impacts greater than background or DNR regulatory standards were not present on a valley-wide basis, and that groundwater quality at any point in the valley was reflective of its relative location. Thus, sites with no soil contamination were unlikely to find groundwater contamination. Furthermore, subsurface conditions were found to be conducive to biodegradation, making natural attenuation a viable remedial option for groundwater contamination related to specific properties. Overall, the study concluded that there was minimal risk from existing groundwater contamination, which alleviated many area-wide concerns. While individual properties may have site-specific concerns, their respective landowners and purchasers could manage them individually without fear of their sites would be recontaminated by adjacent parcels.

While minor efforts were taken in the 1970s to improve roads in the valley, major projects were initiated in the early 1990s with the planning of the Hank Aaron State Trail, Miller Park, the Sixth Street Viaduct, and the eventual development of Canal Street. While the individual projects are important, more important was the fact that they brought the attention and resources of various stakeholders and government agencies to the valley. In 1991, the Wisconsin State Legislature directed the Department of Natural Resources (DNR) to study the feasibility of establishing a Henry Aaron State Park on the Menomonee River adjacent to Milwaukee County Stadium.[11] More comprehensive planning for a greenway trail to connect the valley from west to east was initiated in 1992 with the DNR taking the lead in planning, constructing, and managing the trail. Other partners included the city of Milwaukee (involved primarily in raising funds, releasing land, and maintaining the trail), various federal agencies (financial support for accessories), local community groups and neighborhood associations (e.g., Friends of the Hank Aaron State Trail have helped to raise awareness and funds), and private landowners (e.g., Miller Park Stadium Corporation and the Sigma Group donated easements for the trail and to help finance develop-ment and renaturalization activities). The state trail, Wisconsin's first in an ur-ban area, officially opened in 2000 on the valley's west side and was connected to Sixth Street in the valley's east end by 2007.

Construction of Miller Park for the Milwaukee Brewer's also commenced in late 1996 and was completed in 2001. As part of the project, 260 acres immedi-ately surrounding the park were improved through the spending of $72 million in government funds, with $36 million from the state of Wisconsin, $18 million from Milwaukee County, and $18 million from the city of Milwaukee.[12] Much of this went to improve accessibility to the stadium and the west end of valley through freeway relocation, new entrances and exits, and new roads and walk-ways. Numerous amenities and landscaping features were also added around the stadium that complemented the Hank Aaron trail and provided many Milwau-keeans with a glimpse of what a revitalized valley could look like.

On the opposite end of the valley, long-term discussions about replacing the almost 100-year-old Sixth Street Viaduct were beginning to bear fruit. In 1991, the city and state signed an agreement affirming the city of Milwaukee as the lead agency responsible for the design and construction of the viaduct. Con-struction costs of $50 million were to be shared between the state (75 percent), county (12.5 percent), and city (12.5 percent).[13] Despite several delays, con-struction commenced in 2000 and what could have been a standalone bridge project was now touted as a "Gateway to the Menomonee Valley." The sleek, sail-like, cable-stayed bridge took fifteen months to construct and slopes down 900 feet (274 meters) from the north end of the valley to bring vehicles and peo-ple down to the valley floor at Canal Street and then slopes back up to meet the south end.

With major new access points on the west and east end of the valley, the next major infrastructure project was the reconstruction of Canal Street to con-nect the two points. The city and state began to reconstruct Canal Street from the Sixth Street Viaduct west to 25th Street east beginning in 2004. That proj-ect included pavement reconstruction, new traffic signals, a railroad spur, a multi-use trail, and a roundabout at 25th Street. In the summer of 2004, the governor of Wisconsin and Milwaukee's mayor jointly announced a package under which $5 million in federal transportation funds and $3 million in city money would be used to extend Canal Street from 25th Street west to Miller Park. The project was completed in 2006 and was estimated to have cost more than $40 million in total, with approximately $2.5 million for demolition and site remediation.

Designing a Sustainable Vision

A signal event in the valley's transformation took place in 1999 when the EPA awarded a $250,000 grant to the Sixteenth Street Community Health Center through its Sustainable Development Challenge Grant Program to look into ways of incorporating sustainability into the valley's redevelopment. Sixteenth Street organized a two-day charrette in which design professionals, nonprofits, government agencies, students, and community members were charged with the task of "raising the bar on redevelopment and restoration activities for Milwaukee's Menomonee River Valley." The goal was to forge a strategy that could attract high-quality investors and family-supporting jobs to the valley, restore property value to the tax rolls, reestablish a sense of pride in the community among Milwaukeeans while reducing environmental impacts.

Seven so-called Keys for Sustainability were put forward to guide the charrette and link it to the city's Land Use Plan and to the infrastructure activities being planned for the valley. These keys included: (i) transportation and circulation, access, and linkage, responsive to infrastructure plans; (ii) mixed use and density; (iii) bundling utilities in a single corridor; (iv) cost-effective environmental remediation and engineered solutions based on site conditions and uses; (v) green building; (vi) open space and habitat restoration; and (vii) using the river as an amenity. The charrette resulted in the production of a comprehensive report entitled *Vision for Smart Growth*. It outlined ideas for the eastern, central, and western portions of the valley.[14] The exciting plans and designs addressed each of the Keys for Sustainability and provided an inspiring description of "what could be," which brought further attention to the valley's assets and potential. The report also confirmed that a broader, sustainability oriented approach was both viable and attractive.

In 2002, Sixteen Street, MVP, and the city initiated consultation to develop more concrete guidelines for both green building and family-sustaining wages. The *Menomonee Valley Sustainable Design Guidelines* provides guidance and lessons learned from other projects to help simplify sustainable design, enhance building performance, improve aesthetic quality, and expedite the municipal and state permitting and approvals process.[15] The first iteration of the guidelines were completed in 2004 in line with the U.S. Green Building Council's LEED rating system and touch on the following issues:

- Site Design
  Site Analysis and Planning
  Storm Water Management
  Natural Landscape
  Parking and Transportation
  Exterior Site Lighting
- Building Design and Energy Use
  Building Design
  Energy Efficiency
  Daylighting and Internal Lighting
  Alternative Energy
  Building Commissioning
- Materials and Resources
  Exterior and Interior Materials
  Water Conservation
- Construction and Demolition
  Waste and Recycling
  Erosion and Dust Control
  Pre-Occupancy Controls for Indoor Air Quality
- Indoor Environmental Quality
  Indoor Air Quality
  Acoustic Quality
- Operations and Maintenance
  Operations Manual and Monitoring
  Facility Maintenance
  Maintenance and Stewardship of Site and Landscape Elements[16]

In 2002, MVP also convened a workgroup of business and community representatives to establish a family-sustaining living wage target for the valley. In 2003, MVP recommended that employers moving into the valley pay a wage of $12 per hour. In 2005 this recommendation was formally adopted as policy for land sales by the city. This wage was more than double the minimum wage in Wisconsin, which had been raised to $5.70 per hour in 2005 from the previous rate of $5.15 per hour. Employers are also encouraged to provide health insurance to those in their employ. Employers not offering the Family Sustaining Wage for all employees are asked to prepare a sustainable wage plan summarizing the steps they will take to meet the family-sustaining wage in the medium term of one to three years. MVP also recommended that employers recruit a workforce reflective of Milwaukee's population and recruit workers via several local nonprofit organizations. Given that the Menomonee Valley is in a federal renewal community, employers can also qualify for significant tax credits ($1,500 per person) if they hire workers who live in the community.

From Vision to Plan to Development

Redevelopment of the 140-acre Milwaukee Railroad Shops property in the western end of the valley into an industrial center provided the most exciting opportunity for stakeholders to convert sustainable visions, designs, and guidelines, into a reality. In 2002, the Sixteenth Street Community Health Center, together with the city of Milwaukee and other sponsors, organized a national design competition referred to as Natural Landscapes for Living Communities to plan the redevelopment and greening of the shops property, even before it had been acquired by the city. Once home to a cluster of railroad-related manufacturing plants that started operation in 1879, the property had been abandoned in 1985 when the Milwaukee Road went bankrupt. The blighted site later became the subject of Milwaukee's largest eminent domain action and the Redevelopment Authority of the city of Milwaukee eventually acquired the land from Chicago-based CMC Heartland Partners for $3.55 million in August of 2003.

The land use, infrastructure, and sustainability visions that had evolved during the planning and design charrette exercises were now entrenched as the following criteria presented to the four finalist design teams[17]:

- Design an industrial park accommodating at least 1.2 million square feet of development;
- extend Canal Street;
- expand the Hank Aaron State Trail;
- interconnect the railroad property to Mitchell Park and neighborhoods to the north and south of the valley;
- devise site-specific storm- and floodwater management techniques;
- resolve site-specific environmental and geo-technical issues;

FIGURE 3.1. Rendering of the Menomonee Valley Industrial Center and Community Park (courtesy of Wenk Associates Inc.)

- landscape the area; and
- establish community connections to the site by means of open space planning, educational opportunities, and signage.

The winning design was selected in the summer of 2002 (see figure 3.1). It was put forward by the team of Wenk Associates, Applied Ecological Services, and the architecture, planning, and engineering firm HNTB. It incorporated the full range of criteria listed above and involved the integration of natural process and development in a manner that recognizes the valley as an industrial and transportation hub and seeks to regenerate the landscape while reconnecting the community.[18] The design provided for 70 acres of light industrial development, a 1-mile segment of the Hank Aaron State Trail, and 70 acres of streets, parks, and natural areas along the banks of the Menomonee River. From this design, the city generated the Menomonee Valley Industrial Center and Community Park Land Use Plan in 2006 to guide redevelopment.

To make the site "shovel ready" for redevelopment, the city established a $16 million dollar Tax Increment Financing District in 2004 to pay the cost of site remediation, demolition, filling and grading, storm water utilities, local roadways, and infrastructure. The site required massive cleanup, demolition, removal, and management of 6 miles of brick sewers, asbestos, and more than 1 million square feet of old building foundations as well as the trucking of 700,000 cubic yards of fill from a nearby interchange project to create an environmental cap that would protect human health and the environment and raise the site out of the flood-plain. The city of Milwaukee has aggressively raised funds for remediation and redevelopment activities, winning more than twenty local, state, and federal grants and dozens of private donations totaling $24 million.[19] The goal of the city was to achieve flexible closure for the site such that future property owners were not required to manage environmental closure of their individual properties. In addition to soil contamination, many new buildings constructed in the valley also need passive methane/soil gas collection systems that are funded in part by public tax credits and incentives.[20] The Menomonee Valley Community Park portion of the shops site provides an amenity for businesses located in the valley and green space for local residents. Some of the park space was not economically feasible to develop due to its odd shape, and some portions contain demolition debris converted into vegetated bluffs that are encumbered with environmental use restrictions consistent with the Wisconsin Department of Natural Resources approved Remedial Action Plan for the area.[21] The storm water portion of the park also provides essential infrastructure by conveying, storing, and treating storm water for the adjacent parcels in the industrial site, as well as for Canal Street and other internal roads. The shared storm water facility makes it unnecessary for developers to set aside land and build their own private detention ponds, saving money and also allowing the city to maximize the build-out of the industrial site. Annual management costs are shared through fees among individual business owners in the industrial center and the city of Milwaukee.

Since preparing the site in 2006, six buildings have been constructed and two parcels recently purchased (see figure 3.2). The city is ahead of schedule in terms of land sales, despite the economic downturn, and properties have sold for

FIGURE 3.2. Menomonee Valley Industrial Center 2010 (Christopher DeSousa)

slightly more than initially expected. The industrial projects that have been developed thus far include:[22]

- Palermo Villa constructed a 135,000 square feet frozen pizza production facility on 9 acres of land in September 2006. Palermo now employs 420 people and recently purchased an additional 3.1 acres for a 55,000-square-foot expansion.
- Badger Railing fabricates ornamental iron and steel for railing, stairs, and other products, completed their facility in the summer of 2007 and currently employs 41 people.
- Caleffi Hydronic Solutions, which makes solar water heating and other products, opened their building in the Valley in 2007 and currently employs 28 people. Their facility houses its main offices, warehousing, and assembly operations and features radiant heat to warm the floors, natural and energy-saving lighting, as well as solar hydronic heat that supplements the high-efficiency boilers.
- Taylor Dynamometer manufactures engine dynamometers that test engines for power and torque. They opened in May 2008 and currently have 39 employees.
- Derse, a manufacturer of high-tech trade show exhibitions, completed construction of its 160,000-square-foot building in 2009 and was the first industrial building in the city of Milwaukee to receive LEED Silver certification from the U.S. Green Building Council.

• Charter Wire manufactures steel products and constructed its 160,000-square-foot facility in 2009. It employs 115.
• Ingeteam, a supplier to the wind and solar energy industries, is building an 114,000-square-foot factory that is expected to generate 275 jobs by 2011.

While most of these firms have relocated from other parts of the Milwaukee region, some foreign firms such as Ingeteam and Caleffi have also moved into the valley. Several new businesses in the center have also used new market tax credit loans through the Milwaukee Economic Development Corporation for their projects. MVP notes that by 2011 there should be 1,100 jobs in the center and only 12 acres left for sale (on three separate parcels), which is on target for their goal of 1,200 jobs.[23] The Tax Increment District is also on target to meet its $45 million goal by 2012.

Sustainable Development Moves East

Following the success of the west end's conceptual design, Wenk and Associates worked with MVP and the city to develop a vision for the central and eastern valley. Much of the plan deals with creating a "spine" for the valley—connecting it via Canal Street and the Hank Aaron State Trail discussed above. Several other notable developments that occurred in the central valley include the Sigma Group headquarters in 2003, the former Stockyards property, for which the living-wage guidelines were initially created, and the iconic Harley Davison Museum.

The development of a new headquarters building for the Sigma Group, an environmental engineering and services company with extensive involvement in valley affairs, set a high bar for buildings in the valley. Sigma addressed a variety of soil, groundwater, methane, and geotechnical challenges in the planning, design, orientation, and construction of their facility. Their site also accommodates public access to the Menomonee River with a walkway that borders the river's edge and links up with the Hank Aaron Trail. Both the building and site incorporate numerous green building features, including natural day lighting, stormwater management, beneficial reuse of materials, and a high-efficiency HVAC system. The building materials also complement the neighboring drawbridge and blend in with the industrial look of the valley. Indeed, Sigma was honored with the 2003 Mayor's Design Award for the project.

Upon completing its headquarters in December 2003, the Sigma Group worked with the Sixteenth Street Community Health Center to evaluate the impact of their project on the Menomonee Valley and in relation to their previous office space.[24] The intent of the study was to provide measurable impacts on several dozen short- and long-term sustainability-oriented benchmarks. Variables examined related to environmental impacts (e.g., soil risk, air emissions, stormwater discharge, tree canopy, resource utilization, increase in public river access), economic/business impacts (e.g., real estate value, annual tax revenue, employment, security, aesthetic), and employment and social benefits (e.g., employee commute, employee morale, employee participation in the community). This study provided an example of how developers should consider the broader sustainability implications of their buildings on the valley.

Another notable project across the street from Sigma is the Canal Street Commerce Center, a light industrial and office building on the former Milwaukee Stockyards property that now houses Proven Direct Inc., a commercial printing and direct mail firm. Also housed at the center is Prolitec Inc., which provides scents for use in office buildings and other commercial properties. At the eastern gateway to the valley, Harley Davidson constructed a museum that, while initially criticized for its low job density, was praised for incorporating the Menomonee Valley Sustainable Design Guidelines, storm water treatment areas, and public river access.

With the Menomonee Valley Industrial Center filling up on the valley's west end, the city's focus continues to shift east. The Department of City Development has started creating a detailed development plan for several parcels in the eastern and central valley. For example, the city of Milwaukee recently proposed a $6.4 million Tax Increment District for the 17-acre Reed Street Yards property that would be used for public improvements including new roads, water, sewer, riverwalk, an extension of the Hank Aaron State Trail, and dock wall repairs. The new district would help fund construction of building foundations and environmental remediation as well. Many of the smaller, privately owned parcels are also being primed for redevelopment.

Tracking Valley-Wide Sustainability

In order to track progress toward sustainability, the Sixteenth Street Community Health Center collaborated with the University of Wisconsin–Milwaukee on the

Menomonee Valley Benchmarking Initiative. The core objectives of the MVBI as defined by the partners at the outset of the project were several-fold: to raise awareness in the community regarding the current state of the Menomonee Valley and the progress made toward its revitalization; to create an information clearinghouse on data related to environmental, economic, and social indicators; and to promote the principles of sustainability in an urban context by exploring issues and assembling data in a more holistic manner that considers economic, environmental, and social concerns. Other objectives were to generate a practical synthesis of the raw data for the benefit of a wide variety of users and to stimulate research interest in the valley as a complex laboratory for studying urban environments.

In 2001, Indicator Work Group meetings focused upon the triple bottom line of social, environmental, and economic performance were held with stakeholders to determine key "issues of concern" for the valley, and to select specific "indicators" for investigating those issues.[25] The coordinators of the study and the stakeholders agreed that the MVBI should not focus on historical trends and legacies, but evaluate the valley's future progress based on its conditions at the start of the new millennium. A voting scheme was used to narrow the list of indicators to about fifty, with the economic work group identifying four key issues and twenty-one benchmarks, the social/community work group identifying four key issues and eighteen benchmarks, and the environmental work group identifying four key issues and twelve benchmarks.[26]

Preparing the first MVBI report involved identifying stakeholders willing to supply existing data or gather new data, and then to report the results. While some of the data could be gathered from existing U.S. Census Bureau data and municipal records sources, a significant amount had to be collected from scratch. For this reason, it was felt that establishing a protocol and making arrangements for future data collection was an important component of the MVBI process. Measuring and tracking the state of economic activity in the valley was a central focus of the MVBI. Given that much of the information on business activity and employment for the area was not available, a survey designed by stakeholders from the economic work group was administered to valley businesses by mail and then followed up with telephone calls. As for environmental benchmarks, the partners worked with a number of key scientists from the university to establish a water-quality monitoring network to analyze biotic integrity and physical water quality in the Menomonee River. They also worked with the Wisconsin Department of Natural Resources (DNR) to analyze data from local air-monitoring stations, while information on land coverage and bird activity was gathered by graduate students and an array of volunteers from local organizations and nonprofits. For the community indicators, data on recreation and art were gathered by university students as part of independent study and fieldwork classes. Housing and crime data were obtained from relevant city departments, while health and pollution data pertaining to fertility rates, lead poisoning rates, Ozone Action Days, and other indicators were gathered via local and state health agencies.

The results of the first State of the Valley study in 2003 were disseminated through a short summary pamphlet and a project website, while a more formal hard-copy and web report were produced for the 2005 study.[27] The report commences with an overall introduction to the valley and the MVBI, and includes maps of the study areas. Indicator analyses are then sorted into three sections— economy, environment, and community—and each section commences with an introductory page that highlights the most important results from the section and presents an index of the issues and indicators examined. The analysis of each indicator addresses three fundamental questions: (1) what has been measured? (i.e., benchmark, sources of data, and methodological approach); (2) why is it important? (i.e., explains the indicator's role in achieving sustainability); and (3) how are we doing? (i.e., describes the performance of each indicator). The analysis of each indicator is summarized on a single page, while tables, figures, and maps are employed to help clarify the results by providing a snapshot view of performance. Following the indicator analyses, a section entitled Vital Signs presents raw data by census tract, intended for use by local community groups for their planning and programming activities.

Overall, MVBI has been attempting to educate the public, inform policy-making efforts, and monitor the performance of renewal activities by gathering analytical information reflective of overall redevelopment in the area. It has generated a useful synthesis of data, helped promote principles of sustainability in an urban brownfields context, and brings together stakeholders in a collaborative effort. Recently, funding has been awarded by the U.S. EPA to conduct a 2011 MVBI study.

Lessons Learned

While efforts to bring employment back to brownfield sites have faced continued challenges from deindustrialization, Milwaukee continues to press forward in an attempt to reap the substantial benefits of employment-oriented redevelopment. In addition, the city has raised the bar in terms of creating and implanting a vision for sustainability that not only remediates and reuses brownfield property, but also incorporates family-supporting wages, sound design, ecological restoration, and connections to the community. The challenges associated with reindustrialization, however, require a more vigorous management approach that incorporates a variety of policy and funding mechanisms in order to make them attractive to potential investors and developers. Sharing the costs and risks related to site preparation and development make projects more viable and attractive when carried out along with schemes to improve basic infrastructure and the physical environment.

Several key lessons that emerge from the Menomonee Valley redevelopment experience that can be applied by other cities interested in sustainable urban economic development include:

- Make early efforts to consult and understand the needs of the community and affected stakeholders in order to better incorporate their ideas into visions and plans.
- Involve respected stakeholders and community representatives who were active in the community before the project, will be there throughout the project, and will remain in the community long after it is completed.
- Undertake market research and scientific studies to assess the scope of problems, needs, possible solution strategies, and even post-development impacts, as sound science helps demystify barriers and point to practical solutions.
- Facilitate and support public private partnerships that allow for balanced participation of multiple stakeholders, help enhance buy-in and faith in the process, and make stakeholders more willing to compromise, be patient, and contribute to that process.
- Offer early seed funding, such as the EPA grants used in the valley, to explore sustainability and to help incorporate it throughout the planning and development process.
- Ensure that local government, in particular, is willing to play—and capable of playing—a central role in visioning, planning, site acquisition, site preparation, project funding, redevelopment, and post-closure activities.
- Work tirelessly to pull together funding from all levels of government and

other sources in order to address complex brownfield projects, infrastructure, industrial redevelopment, and sustainability.

As reported in MVP's 2009 annual report, Milwaukee's success in revitalizing the Menomonee Valley's includes the following:[28]

- 300 acres of brownfields redeveloped
- 20 new companies
- 7 company expansions
- 4,200 jobs created
- 45 acres of native plants
- 7 miles of trails
- $3.60 in private investment for every $1 in public investment
- 10 million visitors annually to entertainment destinations in the valley
- $66 million increase in taxable property values from 2002 to 2009
- 900,000 square feet of energy-efficient buildings designed and constructed
- 475 individuals have volunteered their time on boards, committees, and working teams
- 260 organizations have offered pro bono assistance

There is no standard step-by-step guide for undertaking a sustainable urban economic development project, especially one oriented toward industry. The approach taken by any individual community must reflect both structural conditions like geography and how past land uses have shaped an area and resulting environmental impacts as well as situational factors like prevailing economic conditions and funding availability. The Menomonee Valley Redevelopment project, however, provides a useful approach that can point many communities in the right direction. As Milwaukee's experience with the Menomonee Valley shows, there are many economic, social, and environmental reasons to justify taking a triple bottom line approach to urban revitalization.

Acknowledgments

The author would like to thank Laura Bray, Corey Zetts, David Misky, and Ben Gramling for supplying information for this study. Portions of this work were performed under a subcontract with the University of Illinois at Chicago and made possible by grant number TR-83418401 from the U.S. Environmental Protection

Agency, and its contents are solely the responsibility of the author and do not necessarily represent the official views of the University of Illinois.

Notes

1. Christopher A. De Sousa, *Brownfields Redevelopment and the Quest for Sustainability* (London: Elsevier Science/Emerald Group Publishing, 2008), 215.

2. John Gurda, *The Menomonee Valley: A Historical Overview* (Milwaukee: Menomonee Valley Partners, 2003), 1.

3. John Gurda, *The Making of Milwaukee* (Milwaukee: Milwaukee County Historical Society, 1999), 126.

4. Gurda, *Making of Milwaukee*, 128.

5. Sam White et al., *The Changing Milwaukee Industrial Structure, 1979–1988* (Milwaukee: The Urban Research Center, University of Wisconsin–Milwaukee, 1988). See also, City of Milwaukee, *Menomonee Valley 1975 Business Needs and Attitudes Survey* (Milwaukee: Report prepared for the City of Milwaukee Department of City Planning by Dun and Bradstreet Inc., 1975).

6. Gurda, *The Menomonee Valley*, 14.

7. Gurda, *The Menomonee Valley*, 15.

8. City of Milwaukee, *Market Study, Engineering, and Land Use Plan for the Menomonee Valley* (Milwaukee: Report prepared for the Department of City Development, City of Milwaukee, by Lockwood Greene Consulting, Fluor Daniel Consulting, Trkla, Pettigrew, Allen, and Payne, Inc., and Edwards and Associates, 1998).

9. City of Milwaukee, *Land Use Plan*, 6-3–6-11.

10. City of Milwaukee, *Menomonee River Valley Brownfields Pilot Project, Interim Report, Redeveloping Milwaukee's Menomonee Valley: Developing an Aqua-shed Framework for Groundwater Regulatory and Remediation Alternatives* (Milwaukee: Report funded by the U.S. Environmental Protection Agency, the City of Milwaukee, the Milwaukee Economic Development Corporation, and the U.S. Geological Survey, 2002). See also, C. P. Dunning et al., *Simulation of Ground-Water Flow, Surface-Water Flow, and a Deep Sewer Tunnel System in the Menomonee Valley, Milwaukee, Wisconsin* (Denver: U.S. Department of the Interior and the U.S. Geological Survey Scientific Investigations Report 2004–5031 conducted in cooperation with the U.S. Environmental Protection Agency, Region 5, and City of Milwaukee, 2004).

11. Wisconsin Department of Natural Resources, *Henry Aaron State Trail, Feasibility Study Master Plan and Environmental Assessment* (Madison: Menomonee Valley Greenway Advisory Committee, National Park Service, and Wisconsin Department of Natural Resources, 1996).

12. Munsey and Suppes, "Milwaukee Brewers Miller Park," 2007, www.ballparks.com/baseball/national/miller.htm (3 May, 2010).

13. Lori Lovely, "Milwaukee's Old Sixth Street Viaduct Yields to Modern Cable-Stayed Spans," *Construction Equipment Guide*, www.constructionequipmentguide.com

/Milwaukees-Old-Sixth-Street-Viaduct-Yields-to-Modern-Cable-Stayed-Spans/1384/ (3 May, 2010).

14. Sixteenth Street Community Health Center, *A Vision for Smart Growth: Sustainable Development Design Charrette Milwaukee's Menomonee River Valley 1999–2000* (Milwaukee: Sixteenth Street Community Health Center, Department of Environmental Health, 2000), 21.

15. Menomonee Valley Partners, *Sustainable Design Guidelines for the Menomonee River Valley* (Milwaukee: Menomonee Valley Partners, City of Milwaukee, and the Sixteenth Street Community Health Center, 2006).

16. Menomonee Valley Partners, *Guidelines*, 5.

17. Sixteenth Street Community Health Center. *Menomonee River Valley National Design Competition, Executive Summary* (Milwaukee: Competition sponsored by the Sixteenth Street Community Health Center, Menomonee Valley Partners Inc., the City of Milwaukee, the Milwaukee Metropolitan Sewerage District, Wisconsin Department of Natural Resources and Milwaukee County, 2002), 1.

18. Sixteenth Street Community Health Center, *Menomonee River Valley National Design Competition* (Milwaukee: Sixteenth Street Community Health Center, Department of Environmental Health, 2002), 20–24.

19. Dave Misky and Cynthia Nemke, "From Blighted to Beautiful." *Government Engineering* May–June (2010): 14–16.

20. City of Milwaukee, *Menomonee Valley Industrial Center and Community Park Master Land Use Plan* (Milwaukee: City of Milwaukee, Redevelopment Authority of the City of Milwaukee, 2006), 9.

21. City of Milwaukee, Menomonee *Valley Industrial Center*, 13.

22. See www.renewthevalley.org/.

23. Personal e-mail correspondence with Corey Zetts, Menomonee Valley Partners, on May 17, 2010.

24. The Sigma Group, *Locating in Milwaukee's Menomonee River Valley: An Impact Report* (Milwaukee: The Sigma Group and the Sixteenth Street Community Health Center, 2004).

25. As Matthew Slavin notes in chapter 1, key to the 3BL approach is measuring the environmental, social, and economic efficacy of sustainability initiatives via a more comprehensive framework that considers the interests of a wide array of stakeholders.

26. For more information about the MVBI process see De Sousa et al., 2009.

27. Menomonee Valley Benchmarking Initiative, *2005 State of the Valley: Evaluating Change in Milwaukee's Menomonee Valley*, (Milwaukee: Sixteenth Street Community Health Center, Department of Environmental Health and the University of Wisconsin–Milwaukee, Center for Urban Initiatives and Research, 2005), www.mvbi.org.

28. Menomonee Valley Partners (MVP), *A Decade of Transformation, Momentum for the Future, 2009 Annual Report* (Milwaukee: Menomonee Valley Partners Inc., 2010), 8–9.

Chapter 4

Phoenix, the Role of the University, and the Politics of Green-Tech

JONATHAN FINK, ARIZONA STATE UNIVERSITY

> States across the nation are increasingly seeking to leverage the science and technology assets found at their research universities as a source of competitive advantage.
>
> — Battelle Memorial Institute

The global economic crisis that began in 2008 had a particularly harsh impact on cities of the Southwestern United States. Over the previous few decades Phoenix had experienced the fastest growth of any major American city. This demographic dynamic was linked to an unprecedented housing and construction boom that made many individuals and companies wealthy. Like the gold rushes of the nineteenth century, this get-rich-quick success dampened potential interest in alternative models that would require longer-term investment, like the creation of strong public institutions and more knowledge-based jobs.

At the same time that Sunbelt cities like Phoenix were embracing automobile-based hyper-growth, cities in other parts of the United States, especially the Northwest, were acknowledging and adapting to a world of more limited resources. In the process, they were finding new economic opportunities and improving quality of life for their residents. In the minds of environmental activists and urban planners, a dichotomy was drawn between the slower-growth, denser, less car-centric urban forms typified by Portland and Vancouver, B.C., and the no-holds-barred growth and sprawl of Phoenix and Las Vegas. By the mid-2000s, Phoenix became a poster child for how not to achieve the increasingly popular civic goals of "urban sustainability" and "livability."

And yet, as is often the case, the reality of a place is more complex than its stereotypes. The metro Phoenix region took several steps as early as the 1980s that facilitated the launching of an ambitious yet pragmatic green agenda nearly twenty years later. The governance aspects of this unusual economic development story have been described by others.[1] This chapter focuses on a series of knowledge-based initiatives—several led by universities—which brought together academic, business, and government interests in innovative ways tried in few other parts of the country. While the ongoing economic crisis and political changes have slowed some of those programs, new ones continue to emerge. Indeed the region's little-heralded and still-incipient sustainable technologies emphasis is one of the few factors contributing to its resilience, somewhat blunting the impact of the current downturn.[2]

It is too early to know how the "Green Phoenix" story will play out. Phoenix faces a number of sustainability issues including water scarcity, air pollution, the urban heat island effect, and influxes of immigrants fleeing economic, political, and environmental distress. In this, as well as its libertarian politics, Phoenix may be more representative of conditions faced by most of the world's cities as they deal with the challenges of a changing climate, resource depletion, and population growth than those of wetter, cooler, wealthier, more homogeneous, and more progressive cities of the Northwestern United States and southwest Canada. However, in order for society to successfully address these growing global threats, all major cities will need to determine how to balance their environmental, economic, and social priorities.

A Recent History of Phoenix

The growth of metro Phoenix took off in the 1950s, as World War II veterans that had been trained in the area returned, and as air conditioning made summers more tolerable. Industrialization of production home-building expanded in the 1950s and 1960s, making home ownership more affordable—especially in and around Phoenix, which had an abundance of relatively cheap, undeveloped land. That, coupled with the mild winter climate, laid the groundwork for future rapid population growth. The economy transitioned from an agricultural to a service orientation during this period, with suburbs spreading into previous farmland to the south, east, and west and into pristine desert to the north. Indian reservations partly blocked the sprawl to the east and south, and large municipal parks enclosed most of the mountain ranges that punctuated the urban landscape.[3]

The postwar economy of Phoenix featured many electronics firms. Motorola had started a research laboratory in the city in the 1940s and opened electronic manufacturing facilities in the 1950s. By the 1980s, Motorola, Intel, and some of their suppliers formed the core of a semiconductor manufacturing cluster. Allied Signal, Raytheon, and Goodyear were among the many early defense contractors in central Arizona. These firms were later joined by others including Boeing, which made Apache helicopters in Mesa; General Dynamics, which purchased some of Motorola's defense-oriented divisions in Scottsdale; and Gilbert-based Spectrum Astro, which built and launched satellites. Most of the major automobile makers had hot-weather test tracks in and around metro Phoenix, although they maintained little other presence. Several healthcare providers including Banner Health and Catholic Healthcare West became major employers in the region. A few other corporations and banks were based in Phoenix, including Dial, Greyhound, U-Haul, Pinnacle West, and Arizona Bank. However, by the end of the twentieth century, only a few large companies and no large banks were still headquartered in Phoenix. These were replaced by local entrants Avnet, America West Airlines, PetSmart, and Insight Enterprises—but none of these were directly involved in technological innovation. The most dramatic and disconcerting loss was that of Motorola, long the region's dominant high-tech company, due in large part to the off-shoring of manufacturing jobs to Asia, and because of increased product design competition from Asia and Scandinavia.

One explanation for the corporate flight from Arizona is that the lack of critical mass of locally based companies made other sites appear more attractive from a synergistic standpoint. Another is that the low level of government investment in social services, especially schools, made it difficult to recruit mid-level executives with young families. Whatever the cause, the result was that the corporate philanthropy and civic leadership that had previously existed and that was common in older, comparably sized cities was mostly absent by the end of the 1990s.

The growth of the metro area was originally polycentric, with Phoenix, Mesa, Scottsdale, Tempe, Glendale, Chandler, and others merging geographically but remaining independent in their pursuit of resources, jobs, and prestige. Because the state legislature had essentially forced the cities to rely on local sales tax for their public revenue, competition for shopping malls, big-box stores, automobile dealerships, and supermarkets became intense.[4] This led to economic inefficiencies and a monotonous aspect to the built environment. It also overshadowed the pursuit of high-tech companies that offered higher-paying jobs with benefits.

The politics of Arizona, and Phoenix in particular, followed national trends, becoming increasingly polarized during the two Bush and Clinton presidencies. Most significantly, from an economic development perspective, a cooperative culture of pragmatic leaders (of both parties), which had prioritized the metro Phoenix region's well-being in the 1970s, gave way to a more rigid politics. Antigovernment ideologues came to dominate the Arizona legislature, blocking measures and investments intended to promote the growth of newer high-tech industries. A series of scandals in the 1980s and 1990s brought down many members of the legislature and two Republican governors, and served to further lower the public's opinion of its political leaders and tarnish Arizona's national reputation.

An exception to this trend was Arizona's intentional and successful establishment of economic clusters, beginning in the 1980s with the creation of the Arizona Strategic Partnership for Economic Development (ASPED), later reconstituted as the Governor's Strategic Partnership for Economic Development (GSPED). These nonpartisan advisory committees, consisting of industry, government, and academic representatives, worked to facilitate economic development around specific industrial groupings as well as strengthen the state's fundamentals for economic growth such as public education, capital formation, and transportation infrastructure. Two governors in particular actively promoted this approach, Jane Hull (1997–2003) and Janet Napolitano (2003–2009). Hull, formerly a long-time Republican legislator, created the Arizona Partnership for the New Economy (APNE) in 1999. APNE went beyond ASPED and GSPED to consider not only the emergence of new high-tech industries, but also how those technologies could infiltrate and transform the ways society works. Napolitano, a Democrat and former Arizona attorney general, created the Governor's Council on Innovation and Technology (GCIT), in which she played a very active lead-

ership role. Hull and Napolitano both supported legislation that would help enact the recommendations of these task forces, the goals of which included a
better-educated workforce, the ready availability of venture capital, better coordination of state-based research and development, the strengthening of industry
alliances, adoption of technological advances by government, and a greater emphasis on an improved quality of life.[5]

One of the outgrowths of the APNE process was the commissioning of Battelle Memorial Institute to prepare a series of three technology-oriented, long-
range economic development roadmaps for Arizona.[6] The plans were funded by
the Arizona Department of Commerce, the Arizona Board of Regents, and the
private, biomedically focused Flinn Foundation. All of these plans analyzed the
competitive strengths of the three state universities and identified priority areas
for cultivation and investment.[7] In the non-biotechnology arenas, the top areas
with the greatest potential based on numbers of faculty, grants, and publications
were (1) advanced communications and information technology, and (2) the
broad domain of "sustainable technologies." Battelle laid out a detailed timeline
for forming a "new economy" in Arizona. In broad terms, they proposed that
with sufficient public and private sector investment, three synergistic technology
platforms could come online sequentially over the following fifteen years: advanced communications and information technology within five years, biomed-
icine and biotechnology in five to ten years, and sustainable technologies in ten
to fifteen years.

A common theme of Battelle's recommendations—both in their Arizona
analysis and in studies they did in other parts of the country—was that the expertise distributed across the state or region should be pooled for competitive advantage. Thus, for instance, they identified nearly 500 faculty members at University of Arizona (UA), Arizona State University (ASU), and Northern Arizona
University (NAU) working in the broad area of sustainability and proposed a series of strategies and administrative structures that would take advantage of those
collective intellectual assets. As will be described below, this idealized approach
was commonly thwarted by interinstitutional and intrastate rivalries.

The Role of Universities in Arizona's Clean Tech Development

In historical terms, universities have often paved the path in identification of a
city or region with new technology platforms. Silicon Valley and Route 128 in

Boston are two of the best known examples. In those cases, much of the inspiration came from private universities (Stanford; MIT and Harvard; respectively). Administrators and faculty at public universities have added motivation to try to impact their economies because of the possibility of better justifying their research functions and budgets to legislators and business leaders.

Although today's focus on green technology in Arizona is centered in Phoenix, much of the state's knowledge-based industrial experience began 100 miles to the south in Tucson, home of the University of Arizona. UA is the state's land-grant university, with the only public medical and agricultural schools. For more than half a century, as the state's two other public universities—ASU in metro Phoenix and NAU in Flagstaff—focused largely on teaching, UA was where companies and government looked for technologically relevant ideas and talent. In the 1960s, UA became recognized as an international research leader in two key sectors that would eventually relate to sustainability: optics and hydrology.

Now the College of Optical Sciences, UA's optics program emerged from the presence of world-class telescopes taking advantage of the clear skies on the mountains surrounding Tucson. It gave rise to many start-up companies and the growth of a southern Arizona-based cluster, under the moniker of "Optics Valley." These skills contributed significantly to the development of telecommunications, computing, and aerospace expertise in the state. They also helped UA space scientists win large grants and contracts from NASA for planetary exploration and astronomical research. Today, UA's lens-making talents are also being applied to concentrating solar energy cells.

UA's hydrologic sciences proficiency is another outgrowth of place-based priorities. With a school of agriculture in a desert environment, there was strong pressure to find ways to locate and conserve water resources. Expertise in hydrology combined with climate science to create the ability to forecast future water availability based on tree-ring data, remote sensing of snowpack, and computer models. UA's hydrologists partnered with colleagues in other arid parts of the world, including the Middle East and Australia. UA also collaborated with the U.S. Geological Survey, which co-located an office on the UA campus, and the Arizona Department of Water Resources. A few of the water-related topics that received less attention at UA—including urban hydrology, water quality, and clean-up technologies—eventually became central to Arizona State University's urban-oriented sustainability portfolio.

ASU and NAU had different areas of expertise related to sustainable technologies. As far back as the 1960s, ASU had engineers and architects working on solar energy technology from both theoretical and applied standpoints. In the early 1990s, ASU opened the first photovoltaic testing laboratory (PTL) in North America. One of only three in the world at the time of its opening, the PTL was a place where companies could send their solar panels and cells to certify that they met performance standards. By running this facility, ASU built relationships with many of the world's top photovoltaic (PV) companies. ASU architects became leaders in the design of energy-efficient buildings with innovations such as the incorporation of PV into their structure, appliances running on direct current, and high-performance insulation. As discussed later in this chapter, these twin legacies of engineering and architectural expertise would, years later, form the basis for the growth of a solar cluster in partnership with local companies, utilities and government leaders.

In the 1970s, an Australian expert in microcharacterization moved to ASU's chemistry department, where he helped create the leading center for electron microscopy in the United States. Funded by the National Science Foundation, the Center for High Resolution Electron Microscopy was made available to local industry, which used it to help improve various manufacturing processes. Combining characterization with complementary expertise in electrical engineering and supply chain management, ASU became known as a place where companies could turn to learn how to improve their high-technology manufacturing.

A third area of expertise, remote sensing of urban environments, grew out of strong connections to NASA's planetary exploration program. This linkage began with the purchase by ASU's Chemistry Department of a large collection of meteorites in 1960. Subsequent recruitment of faculty for the resulting Center for Meteorite Studies brought in planetary geologists that also had interest in examining earth from space. The ability to use remote sensing to look at cities helped ASU win, in 1997, the National Science Foundation's competition for an urban Long Term Ecological Research (LTER) program. ASU's urban LTER (one of only two in the country) focused on the impact that the city of Phoenix had on its underlying desert ecosystem and vice versa, and formed the foundation for what eventually became, seven years later, the Global Institute of Sustainability (GIOS). ASU's sustainability programs established close partnerships with state agencies for monitoring and modeling urban air quality, water availability, and public health.

Meanwhile, Northern Arizona University was cultivating an environmentally oriented curriculum and research portfolio. In particular, it emphasized forestry, restoration ecology, climate studies, and renewable energy. Although limited by size, small state budget allocation, and a mission that was primarily oriented toward teaching, NAU harnessed the enthusiasm of its faculty members and created a robust, regionally oriented sustainability initiative that supported local industry in forest services, tourism, biotechnology, and distance education.

From an economic development perspective, it made great sense for Arizona's three state universities to collaborate in order to better compete with other states and regions in the United States. In practice, this was frequently complicated by inherent rivalries and real or perceived competition to get resources from the Arizona Board of Regents (ABOR) and legislature. ABOR consisted of a governor-appointed group of lawyers, ex-politicians, and business leaders, each of whom tended to have allegiance to one or another of the three state universities. The lack of cooperation was also a function of history. UA had long been the state's flagship university. In the 1990s, as ASU and NAU began to establish themselves as leaders in particular niche areas of research, some members of the UA faculty and administration, and their supporters in ABOR and the legislature, tried to protect their longstanding advantages by slowing this emergence. The failure of the universities to work together frustrated politicians and ABOR members alike as they tried to create statewide strategies. However, during the first decade of the twenty-first century, economic development initiatives emerged on which all three schools agreed to cooperate. In particular, they collaborated effectively through the APNE and GCIT processes and in administering the Technology and Research Initiative Fund, described in greater detail in the next section.

Proposition 301 and the Technology and Research Initiative Fund (TRIF)

Following the lead of their neighbors in California and other western states, Arizona voters in the late 1990s became enamored of the initiative process, partly because it allowed them to enact laws and regulations that could not be easily modified by the legislature or governor. In 2000, Arizonans passed Proposition 301, which enacted a twenty-year, 6/10-of-a-cent sales tax increase dedicated to the improvement of schools and K-12 teachers' pay, especially in rural parts of the state.[8] Lobbyists for economic development interests and for the state universities arranged for the bill to also allocate up to 12 percent of the generated revenue to the creation of the Technology and Research Initiative Fund (TRIF), which could be used for research at the three state universities in support of economic development goals identified by APNE. Administration and allocation of TRIF, estimated to potentially total up to $1.5 billion over twenty years, fell to ABOR, which required that UA, ASU, and NAU derive detailed plans for how these resources would be used to achieve the goal of technology-oriented economic development.

The regents decided that each of the universities could have up to three specific and complementary research focus areas. These would be selected on the basis of existing strengths and their potential for innovation, the goal being to diversify the state's economy and improve its competitiveness. The chosen topics included optics, water, and biotechnology for UA; manufacturing, materials, and biotechnology for ASU; and environmental research, distance education, and biotechnology for NAU. Each school was also expected to use some of the funding to enhance workforce development and technology transfer. The universities were to put together coordinated planning documents showing how their funds would provide citizens of the state with a return on their investment. This represented an unprecedented degree of cooperation across the state university system, and was also the first official acknowledgment that university-based research was a potential instrument for statewide economic development.

Over the next eight years, TRIF was used to support the launch of major initiatives based at all three state universities and their host cities. In particular, the Biodesign Institute at ASU, the BIO5 Institute at UA, and the Center for Microbial Genetics and Genomics at NAU leveraged Proposition 301 funds and brought in large amounts of federal and private-sector revenue. The scale of interdisciplinary and interinstitutional planning that Proposition 301 engendered carried over to other major science-based programs including the Translational Genomics Research Institute in Phoenix and Flagstaff, and Science Foundation Arizona, launched in 2006.

The Arrival of Michael Crow as President of Arizona State University

The flight of corporate headquarters from Phoenix in the 1990s coupled with the growing unpopularity of elected officials resulted in something of a leadership vacuum in the region. In 2002, Michael Crow became the sixteenth president of ASU, coming from Columbia University where he had been executive vice provost, a position similar to but more powerful than the vice president for research at most other universities. Crow had had great success in promoting entrepreneurial activities at Columbia and was nationally recognized for his studies of technology transfer, university-based innovation, and public-private research and development partnerships. He made it clear that the primary attraction of the ASU presidency was the unique combination of a young, large, and fast-growing university within a young, large, and fast-growing city. Also significant was the fact that ASU was the only major university in what was soon to become the fifth largest city and fourteenth largest metropolitan statistical area in the country. Crow quickly set about to intimately link the future of the university with that of the region—perhaps more than had been done in any other urbanized area.

Eschewing the traditional antipathy between Arizona's legislature and higher education, President Crow began to cultivate conservative members of the state's House and Senate, presenting them with a series of investment propositions. Crow's basic case statement was that if government would commit the upfront resources to provide additional infrastructure, the resulting research and associated economic development activity by and around the universities would generate sufficient revenue to more than refill the public coffers. Variations of this argument were made repeatedly over the next eight years to different audiences of potential "investors": state legislators, cities, corporations, foundations, and individual donors. The only standard academic revenue source he did not pursue was direct appropriations, or earmarks, from Congress. By all measures, his was a remarkably successful strategy.

Another of Crow's distinctive positions was that a public university had obligations to society that extended beyond the core missions of providing students with a first-class education and conducting research. For instance, Arizona's public universities had freshman-to-sophomore year retention rates that were considerably lower than many of their peers from other states. Rather than simply blaming these statistics on inadequate teaching and oversized classes in Arizona's high schools, Crow admonished ASU's College of Education to produce many more high-quality secondary school teachers. He also endorsed a proposal to have ASU establish K–12 charter schools on each of its four campuses, where teaching innovations could be tested and perfected before being transferred to the public school system as a whole. A separate, university-based program, funded by private philanthropy, addressed the connections between homelessness and family harmony. This commitment of the university community to broader societal goals, described under the heading of "social embeddedness," gained Crow and ASU regional as well as national attention. It also suggested that any sustainable technology focus in Phoenix that involved ASU would place value on social as well as environmental and economic outcomes.

Research Infrastructure Legislation

The passage of Proposition 301 in 2000 provided operating funds for new research projects and programs at the three state universities related to economic development. But it soon became clear that the success of that initiative was jeopardized by a lack of laboratory facilities in which the research could be conducted. At the same time, an economic downturn in 2002 seriously impacted the state's dominant construction and real estate industries. In response, ASU President Crow and UA President Peter Likins worked with the Arizona business community, pro-education legislators, and newly elected Governor Janet Napolitano to create legislation that would authorize bonding for $440M of new construction at UA, ASU, and NAU. Following a lobbying campaign led by the construction industry that emphasized the potential for associated job creation, the bill passed, leading to the building of major new facilities at all three universities. This significant expansion of the state's research capacity was especially important because Arizona is one of the few states that do not include capital funds in their funding formulae for public universities.

ASU's Downtown Phoenix Campus

Another example of Crow's ability to leverage ASU's value to obtain outside investment was the public financing of the university's Downtown Phoenix Campus (DPC). The first of the eight tenets of Crow's New American University agenda is "leveraging place."[9] Probably no other collaboration between the university and its surrounding region better exemplifies this aspiration than the DPC.

At the time of his arrival at ASU in 2002, the city of Phoenix was seeing an accelerating exodus of residents from its downtown area, which had been losing population to the suburbs over the previous few decades. At the time, ASU had a small presence in a partially abandoned shopping center in the downtown area. In a series of discussions with Mayor Phil Gordon and members of the city council, Crow proposed that a significant portion of a citywide ballot initiative be dedicated to the creation of a new ASU campus in downtown Phoenix capable of serving more than 15,000 students. ASU was interested in expanding the overall enrollment on its various campuses (DPC would be its fourth), while also attempting to generate a critical mass of faculty researchers and teachers involved in urban issues and public outreach that could benefit from the downtown setting. For its part, Phoenix wanted to establish a core of twenty-four-hour residents that could spur the establishment of a more vibrant downtown culture and economy.

In March 2006, the initiative passed with a 66 percent plurality, authorizing the sale of bonds that provided ASU with $223 million.[10] This was in addition to $100 million worth of buildings that the city had already purchased and donated to the university. According to city and university officials, this was the first time in U.S. history that a municipal government funded the expansion of a state university campus. ASU moved several programs to the DPC that could take advantage of being located in the business and government hub of the state, which also offered proximity to several major hospitals. Within two years, the DPC housed the schools of nursing, journalism, and public programs. The latter offers degrees in social work, public affairs, and community resources and development.

Another key economic development and transportation consideration was the design of the new campus around a stop for the planned light rail system, which opened two years after the launch of the DPC. The planners for the project surveyed a variety of options for the location of the campus but quickly converged on the idea of making sure that all new facilities would be within a five-minute walk of the central intermodal transportation hub. There was considerable doubt about the viability of public transportation in an auto-centric region. However, thanks to the strategic location in the downtown area and incentives to encourage them to leave their cars behind, the students helped to model new behaviors for the general public. Valley Metro, the Phoenix light rail system, now takes twenty-two minutes to link the DPC with ASU's primary campus in Tempe (45,000 students), and ASU-affiliated passengers are one of the largest components of its ridership. This is another case where the university has helped catalyze the "greening" of the region.

President Crow's Involvement with Green Tech in Arizona

The emergence of green tech as a state economic development priority was also consistent with Crow's agenda and philosophical leanings. At Columbia, one of his proudest accomplishments was merging the university's many environmental programs under a single umbrella called the Earth Institute. This large group of experts became best recognized for their research and teaching about the evidence for and impacts of global climate change.

Crow had also arranged for Columbia to take over the Biosphere 2 facility in Oracle, Arizona, just north of Tucson. Biosphere 2 had been created by oil tycoon Ed Bass to see whether a group of individuals could live together in a totally enclosed environment for a period of months to years, as preparation for a possible future escape from an environmentally compromised Earth. Columbia wanted to transform this counter-culture icon into a giant laboratory facility and spent tens of millions of dollars of Ed Bass's money upgrading the infrastructure while also building an onsite campus for research and teaching about environmental sciences and policy. Crow's vision for Biosphere 2 was that it would eventually become a national laboratory for climate research and related technology, modeled after the Department of Energy's research laboratories in California, New Mexico, and Tennessee.[11]

Upon arriving at ASU, Crow proposed that the university redefine itself by embracing the emerging concepts of sustainability in its research, teaching and business operations. He brought in international sustainability leaders as advisers and authorized the recruitment of senior faculty members to strengthen these capabilities. A long-term goal of this strategy was to create "green" economic development opportunities for the metro Phoenix region, consistent with the earlier Battelle recommendations. In 2004, Crow enticed a wealthy donor to pledge $25 million to create the Global Institute of Sustainability (GIOS) and encouraged the faculty to establish the world's first degree-granting School of Sustainability (SOS). In 2007, he gave the GIOS director a second title of University Sustainability Officer, with authority to oversee and influence all of ASU's business operations to make sure that they conformed to the environmental and social principles espoused in the institute's research and teaching. This centralization of functions related to sustainability was unprecedented in any academic institution. Among the initiatives that it engendered were the installation of more than ten megawatts of PV on the roofs of ASU's buildings and parking structures, a comprehensive recycling program, and the launching by Aramark, the country's largest academic food service provider, of its first on-campus organic restaurant.[12] Crow also arranged for GIOS to have an influential board of trustees, which included some of the country's leading faculty members and industrialists interested in sustainability and economic development.[13]

Flexible Display Center

Just as UA research had spawned a burgeoning and unique optics industrial cluster in Tucson, ASU sought to bring novel high-tech economic development to metro Phoenix. An important opportunity arrived in 2002 when the Army announced a competition for a $44 million, university-based Flexible Display Center (FDC). The ultimate goal was to develop wearable, low-cost, low-power wireless communication devices that soldiers in the field could use to receive information about battlefield situations. Combining a number of different emergent technologies, the proposed FDC would need to bring its new innovations to the premanufacturing stage and would require the involvement of many different companies, both established and start-up. One of the most challenging aspects would be setting up licensing arrangements that would allow the companies to retain some of their proprietary intellectual property while sharing other components. The intention was for the consortium to simultaneously develop primary military applications while coincidentally spurring the growth of a variety of low-power, wireless, flexible electronic consumer products, so that commercial competition would accelerate evolution of the technology.

Leveraging TRIF resources and its new Biodesign Institute, ASU mounted its most comprehensive proposal preparation effort ever, bringing together an interdisciplinary team of its most experienced scientists and engineers as well as outside consultants including Washington-based "rent-a-generals" to provide advice about army-based site visits. Technology transfer experts from President Crow's former office at Columbia University were also involved. Despite spending more than $700,000 in proposal preparation, ASU was considered a long shot as it lacked specific display expertise, did not have much prior experience in working with the army, and had not competed for this magnitude of funding before.

The team found a unique competitive edge in a recently abandoned, flat-panel display research and manufacturing facility that Motorola had built a few years earlier in ASU's Research Park. After a series of complex negotiations, Motorola gave the university an option to purchase the building for less than a third of its original $100 million cost, contingent upon the army awarding ASU the grant. This option, and a creative approach to technology transfer, became the decisive factors, as ASU beat Cornell, Princeton, and the University of Texas at Dallas (which had close connections to Texas Instruments) to win the award. The university then purchased the 275,000 square foot facility, which contained more than 50,000 square feet of clean room space. During the first five years of the program, ASU and its partners in the army, other universities, and more than two dozen companies produced prototypes that represented the United States' primary entry into the embryonic yet highly competitive global flexible electronics industry. In 2008, the army agreed to provide ASU with $50 million of Phase 2 funding.[14]

While flexible displays can form the basis for lighter-weight, lower-power consumer electronic devices, the other green spinoff application of the FDC is in solar technology. Displays use electricity to generate and emit light, while photovoltaic systems do the opposite: absorb light energy and convert it into electricity. With its capacity to handle not only the development of new devices, but also the early stages of their manufacture, the FDC offers solar technology companies unique partnering opportunities. ASU is currently taking advantage of these through the co-location of their new Solar Power Laboratory.[15] Several of the different strategies for designing flexible displays—including organic LEDs, amorphous silicon, and electrophoretic systems—are being explored for their potential solar applications.

The Creation of Science Foundation Arizona

In 1996, Columbia University appointed William Harris as the first president of Biosphere 2, reporting to Michael Crow. Harris had previously served as assistant director for mathematical and physical sciences at the National Science Foundation. In 2001 he became the founding director general of Science Foundation Ireland (SFI), a nonprofit organization that allocates substantial levels of Irish research funding to universities and industry in order to boost science- and technology-based economic development. SFI's three priority technological investment areas paralleled those identified by Battelle for Arizona: information/communications, biotechnology, and sustainability.

In 2005, ASU's President Crow began making the case that Arizona should view its economic development as being like that of a small country, citing Ireland as an appropriate analog in terms of population and other metrics. He proposed to Governor Napolitano and industry leaders that a Science Foundation Arizona (SFAz), modeled after SFI, could catalyze critical R&D, through matching grants and other targeted outlays, positioning Arizona to compete more effectively against better established states like California, New York, and Massachusetts. The idea appealed to Napolitano, who made it one of her signature initiatives. Crow worked with elected officials and business leaders to keep the proposal nonpartisan, repeating the political strategy and return-on-investment logic that had helped persuade the Arizona Legislature to pass the research infrastructure bill in 2003.

In June 2006, the legislature and governor appropriated $35 million for SFAz with the goal of "developing the necessary resources for Arizona to become globally competitive in science and engineering."[16] A year later the legislature approved an additional $100 million, spread over four years, which required matching funds from the private sector. Harris was recruited to be the first president of SFAz. Upon his return to Arizona in 2006, he met with industry and academic leaders to formulate an investment strategy that emphasized topics that would be complementary to existing local R&D funding sources, such as the Flinn Foundation's support of the state's biomedical research agenda.

Over the next several years, SFAz became an invaluable source of matching funds for grants, fellowships for students and post-docs, and a strong driver of large-scale partnerships across the state university system.[17] However, despite its early success, SFAz became a target for politically motivated budget cuts when the economy soured and Napolitano stepped down as governor to become President Obama's secretary of homeland security. As will be discussed in the final section of this chapter, the future prospects for SFAz are cloudy.

Recruiting Solar Manufacturers to Phoenix

Arizona is an obvious place to develop and deploy solar technologies. Even before it became a university in 1958, ASU had one of the nation's first solar research programs, based in its engineering and architecture departments. This expertise persisted and grew through the interests of ASU faculty over the ensuing decades. By 2005, ASU had assembled a diverse set of solar-related programs and skills spread across more than a dozen departments, including architecture, construction, physics, electrical engineering, mechanical engineering, chemistry, biology, business, and materials science. Yet, despite this homegrown knowledge base, when it came to installation of photovoltaic systems for generating electricity Arizona persistently lagged behind other states and countries. Solar was seen as one of the most prominent missing components of any green economic development strategy for Phoenix.

As cited earlier, ASU possessed one solar-related asset that no other academic institution in the world had: the Photovoltaic Testing Lab (PTL). Besides helping to provide access to the companies whose solar panels they tested, the PTL also trained influential technicians that were distributed throughout the industry. The rest of ASU's interdisciplinary solar expertise also made it an attractive partner for companies competing for federal renewable energy research grants. Yet strangely, the economic development leadership in Phoenix as late as early 2007 had still not capitalized on the local solar potential, despite Governor Napolitano's commissioning of an Arizona Solar Electric Roadmap Study by a task force overseen by the Arizona Department of Commerce.[18]

Here again, ASU asserted itself on behalf of the community. Two senior research administrators from the university and the director of the PTL traveled to Germany and China in 2007 to meet with representatives of eight leading solar companies.[19] These included SolarWorld, Solon, Schott, Q Cells, and Suntech, as well as with the member of the German Bundestag (parliament) responsible for Germany's groundbreaking feed-in tariff.[20] Their message was that Arizona represented an ideal site in which to set up a U.S. manufacturing presence because of the proximity to the California market, affordability of housing and labor, availability of academic research partners and the PTL, and favorable energy policies. Their visits contributed to an enhanced awareness of Arizona among the global solar industry, later capitalized on by the Greater Phoenix Economic Council (GPEC), the region's principal economic development organization.

Based on the Germany and China visits, the ASU administrators identified Suntech as the most promising target, both because of its size (it is now the world's largest manufacturer of solar panels) and its potential interest in research collaboration. They visited Suntech's CEO and senior leadership several times in China and California and, along with senior administrators of Arizona Public Service and SFAz, cohosted a visit they made to Phoenix in July 2008, including arranging meetings with Governor Napolitano, leaders of the Department of commerce, and several local companies. Recognizing that Suntech had strong research ties with University of New South Wales in Sydney, Australia, where their CEO, Zhengrong Shi, had received his PhD, ASU lured two faculty members from University of Delaware that had been fellow graduate students with Shi. After subsequent negotiations led by GPEC, Suntech in 2009 agreed to open a manufacturing site in metro Phoenix, its first in the United States Discussions are currently underway between GPEC and other Chinese manufacturers to expand metro Phoenix's growing solar cluster. The entrance of Suntech onto the local scene illustrated the influence that a prominent green tech corporation can have on regional economic development policies and politics. In late 2009, Arizona legislators—opposed to what they perceived to be overly generous government subsidies of the solar, biofuels, and wind power industries—proposed that nuclear power be counted toward the percentage of the state's energy mix that was mandated to come from renewable sources. This radical reinterpretation would have eliminated subsidies for the solar industry and essentially driven all of Arizona's renewable energy projects to other states. Suntech publicly announced that if the legislation passed, they would not come to Arizona. That threat motivated Governor Jan Brewer to convince her fellow Republicans in the legislature to withdraw their bill, preserving one of the strongest incentives for development of a green tech economy in the state. Keeping the PTL as a unique asset with which ASU could help the region create a robust solar power industry was another strategic economic development goal of the university. By 2007, as global solar manufacturing expanded, especially in Asia, PTL could no longer keep up with demand. Turnaround time on panel evaluations increased dramatically, causing client companies to complain. In response, Underwriters Laboratories (UL) announced plans to open a competing facility to PTL in San Jose, supported by the emerging renewable energy interests in Silicon Valley, and taking advantage of California's aggressive state inventive programs for using solar power.[21] ASU countered this threat by opening negotiations with PTL's largest international rival, TUV-Rheinland. These discussions, led by ASU's Office of the Vice President for Research and Economic Affairs, resulted in the creation of a commercial joint venture, TUV-PTL, in renovated and greatly expanded facilities near ASU's Tempe campus.[22] Not only did this move retain PTL's important ties with the solar industry, it expanded its customer base, created new jobs, and did so in what became the world's premier commercial solar testing lab. Furthermore, it gave Arizona access to one of the world's largest technology testing companies, with associated long-term benefits.

The "Energize Phoenix" Project

President Crow's expansive mandate for the university, combined with his personal interest in environmental issues and his relentless pursuit of institutional resources and recognition all came together in one of ASU's most lucrative sustainability initiatives. Prepared collaboratively by ASU faculty members and administrators, leaders of the state's largest utility (Arizona Public Service), and the city of Phoenix, the Energize Phoenix proposal sought federal stimulus (ARRA) funds to create jobs, reduce environmental impacts, and strengthen neighborhoods. The project obtained $25 million from the U.S. Department of Energy in May 2010 to install various technologies that reduce energy use and improve the overall energy efficiency of buildings along a ten-mile stretch of the new light rail line in downtown Phoenix, while concurrently working to change the behavior of the residents in the surrounding communities so they would also use less energy.

ASU's ongoing role in the project is to monitor and analyze the impact and financial savings associated with the new infrastructure and to try to learn about the personal investment decisions and behaviors that lead to energy efficiency. The project is intended to be scalable through creative financing mechanisms so that the lessons learned can be directly applied across the entire city of Phoenix and into the surrounding metro region by reinvesting the savings that come from energy conservation. The infusion of new federal dollars came at a particularly opportune time because city budgets were painfully stressed by a reduction of state funds. This is an example of a sustainability opportunity that ASU identified and led in order to benefit the broader community, but from which faculty members and students will also gain valuable research experience and support.

Lessons Learned and Relevance to Other Cities

This chapter highlights some of the unique events and characters responsible for helping to bring metro Phoenix, and Arizona more broadly, into the "green economy." Critical factors included early success in coordinating high-tech development across the state through the establishment of economic clusters; an emphasis on leveraging Arizona-specific assets, like semiconductor expertise and the potential for academic partnerships, to promote solar manufacturing; and the ability of academic leadership to persuade a spectrum of legislators to view public research universities as entrepreneurial enterprises worthy of temporary but large investments rather than as government agencies entitled to steadily increasing, recurrent budgets.

Yet, the most recent episode of the metro Phoenix story reveals that green economic development gains remain vulnerable. The same fiscally conservative Republican leaders that were receptive to nonpartisan, return-on-investment pitches for research infrastructure made an about-face and eliminated public funds for Science Foundation Arizona when the state budget came under pressure and the Democratic governor stepped down to join the Obama Administration. Legislative enthusiasm for using Arizona-based renewable energy to help the United States gain independence from unstable foreign governments has recently been offset by the suspicion that all sustainability initiatives are somehow connected to "socialistic" climate change conspiracies. Support for locally based solar thermal projects that were among the most ambitious in the world have run up against the recognition that such systems require large amounts of water, which in Arizona is already over-allocated. Interuniversity cooperation on green technology development, encouraged by the business community and the promise of joint funding from Science Foundation Arizona, has waned as faculty members retreat to their historical interests in parochial intrastate competition. Incipient collaboration on advanced technology development across Tucson and Phoenix is being shelved as the two metro areas resume jockeying for statewide technological dominance, which ironically is becoming irrelevant as they merge demographically into one "Sun Corridor Megapolitan" region.[23] Even Proposition 301, the flagship initiative that started Arizona on its recent path to a more diversified technological future is under threat as desperate legislators look for any resources they might reappropriate to fill yawning budgetary holes, and as cutbacks in consumer spending reduce the sales tax revenues on which TRIF depends.

The fragility of Phoenix's recent progress toward a green future may reflect a lack of depth to the support for those more progressive outcomes. Seattle, Portland, San Francisco, Chicago, New York, and Austin have all put in place policies and initiatives that parallel those seen in Phoenix during the last decade. What's different is the political context in which those other cities have made their moves toward sustainability. While in each such setting, a mayor, CEO, or other civic leader may have put forward one or more specific ideas, they have taken root, become nourished, and thrived in a diverse culture of popular interest. The cities were already poised to accept these new concepts as logical extensions of widely held values and historical assets.

In metro Phoenix, many of the green advances ultimately arose from the influence of a single charismatic leader, Arizona State University's president, Michael Crow. But other than the brief period when Governor Napolitano used her position to push for similar goals, Crow's technocratic view of a future shaped in sizable measure by a university's actions was not reciprocated or complemented by any other players or constituencies that shared his vision, energy, and institutional clout. Even within ASU, there is a sense that Crow's long-term impact may be fleeting, because his well-formulated ideas were grafted onto an academic setting that had not yet matured sufficiently to fully appreciate and incorporate them.

The underlying question for Phoenix, as for any city that is plotting its way to a greener future, is how quickly and long-lastingly can transformation occur through technological and political means, if the culture is not yet sufficiently receptive?

Notes

1. Rob Melnick and John S. Hall, "Regional Roles and Relationships: A Fifty-Year Evolution of Governance in Metropolitan Phoenix, 1960–2008," in *Governing Metropolitan Regions in the 21st Century*, ed. Don Phares (Armonk: M.E. Sharpe, Inc., 2009), 154–74.

2. The author was engaged in several of the activities described in this chapter, through his administrative service to Arizona State University (ASU), as vice provost for research (1997–2002), vice president for research and economic affairs (2002–2007), director of the Global Institute of Sustainability (2007–2009), and university sustainability officer (2007–2008). As a consequence, this account may emphasize the importance of ASU disproportionately relative to other institutions.

3. Patricia Gober, *Metropolitan Phoenix: Place Making and Community Building in the Desert* (Philadelphia: University of Pennsylvania Press, 2005), 248.

4. Grady Gammage, Jr., *Phoenix in Perspective* (Tempe: Herberger Center for Design Excellence, Arizona State University, 1999), 192.

5. Morrison Institute for Public Policy, *The New Economy: Policy Choices for Arizona* (Tempe: Morrison Institute for Public Policy, 2000), 16.

6. Battelle Memorial Institute, Technology Partnership Practice, *Positioning Arizona for the Next Big Technology Wave: Development and Investment Prospectus to Create a Sustainable Systems Industry in Arizona* (Cleveland: Battelle Memorial Institute, 2004), 43.

7. Battelle Memorial Institute, Technology Partnership Practice, *Positioning Arizona and Its Research Universities: Science and Technology Core Competencies Assessment* (Cleveland: Battelle Memorial Institute, 2003), 140.

8. Arizona Proposition 301(2000), 2010, www.ballotpedia.org/wiki/index.php/Arizona _Proposition_301_%282000%29 (1 July 2010).

9. Arizona State University, *New American University*, n.d., http://newamericanuniversity .asu.edu/ (1 July 2010).

10. Leah Hardesty, "Phoenix voters approve funding for ASU downtown campus," *Arizona State University News Service*, 2006, www.asu.edu/news/stories/200603/20060315 _phoenixcampus.htm (1 July 2010).

11. When then executive vice provost Michael Crow and the president and provost of Columbia University all left their positions in 2002, the incoming administration severed ties with Biosphere 2, which now is run by the University of Arizona.

12. Karen Leland, "ASU to deploy largest university solar installation," *Arizona State University News Service*, 2008, http://asunews.asu.edu/20080617_solar (1 July 2010). Judith Smith, "ASU recycling program expands—and compacts," *Arizona State University News Service*, 2008, http://asunews.asu.edu/20080814_recycling (1 July 2010). Kerry Lepain, "What's on your plate, ASU?," *Arizona State University State Press Magazine*, 2010, http:// statepressmagazine.com/2010/01/18/whats-on-your-plate-asu/ (1 July 2010).

13. ASU Global Institute of Sustainability, "Board of Trustees," n.d., http://sustainability .asu.edu/about/our-people/our-board-of-trustees.php (1 July 2010).

14. Nick Colaneri, "Army continues Flexible Display Center support," *Arizona State University News Service*, 2009, http://asunews.asu.edu/20090129_flexdisplay (1 July 2010).

15. Joe Kullman and Karen Leland, "New lab aims to advance solar energy industry," *Arizona State University News Service*, 2008, http://asunews.asu.edu/20080711_solarlab (1 July 2010).

16. Science Foundation Arizona, "History," n.d., www.sfaz.org/about-sfaz/our-history .aspx (1 July 2010).

17. Battelle Technology Partnership Practice, *Measuring Up: 2010 Annual Report Card on How Arizona's Technology Sector Is Performing and the Contributions of Science Foundation Arizona*. (Cleveland: Battelle Memorial Institute, 2010), 9.

18. Navigant Consulting, Inc., *Arizona Solar Electric Roadmap Study* (Burlington: Navigant Consulting, Inc.,2007), 189.

19. Vice President for Research and Economic Affairs Jonathan Fink; Associate Vice President for Economic Affairs Rob Melnick; and PTL Director Govindasamy Tamizhmani.

20. Hermann Scheer, *Energy Autonomy* (London: Earthscan Publications Ltd., 2007), 320.

21. Underwriters Laboratory, "UL creates largest solar testing lab in North America," *Quality Digest*, 2009, www.qualitydigest.com/inside/quality-insider-news/ul-creates-largest -solar-testing-lab-north-america.html (1 July 2010).

22. TUV Rheinland PTL, www.tuvptl.com/.

23. Grady Gammage, Jr., John S. Hall, Robert E. Lang, Rob Melnick, and Nancy Welch, *Sun Corridor Megapolitan* (Tempe: Morrison Institute for Public Policy, 2008), 52.

Chapter 5

LEED in the Nation's Capitol: A Policy and Planning Perspective on Green Building in Washington, D.C.

GERRIT KNAAP, AMY GARDNER, RALPH BENNETT,
MADLEN SIMON, AND CARI VARNER

Buildings represent a nexus of impacts and opportunities for people and the environment.

Chris Pyke, U.S. Green Building Council[1]

Washington, D.C., and its metropolitan region are national leaders in the development and implementation of the United States Green Building Council (USGBC) Leadership in Energy and Environmental Design (LEED) rating system. According to SustainLane.com, Washington, D.C., ranks second among the nation's fifty largest cities in the number of LEED-certified buildings per capita. This chapter provides a policy and planning perspective on how LEED standards have been implemented in Washington, D.C. and in selected counties in the Washington metropolitan region, and what other cities and counties can learn from their experiences. A case is made for continuation of LEED development as a key to the future of sustainable development.

The USGBC was established in 1993 as a nonprofit organization bringing together architects, construction companies, product manufacturers, engineers, consultants, and others interested in creating more sustainable buildings. The

USGBC takes a multidisciplinary approach, with no one profession owning the green building process. Headquartered in Washington, D.C., the USGBC pioneered the concept of standards for green buildings in 1993. LEED is coming into use internationally, with Canada, India, and Italy as early adopters of LEED rating systems overseas and certification of developments in other international locations available through the USGBC.

Although competing standards exist, LEED has garnered wide support throughout the United States. In Washington, D.C. and its surrounding metropolitan area, there are more than 1,730 LEED-certified buildings and developments (see figure 5.1). The District of Columbia alone is home to more than 750 LEED certified buildings and developments ranging from commercial office space to larger mixed-use developments. Additionally, there are twenty-two

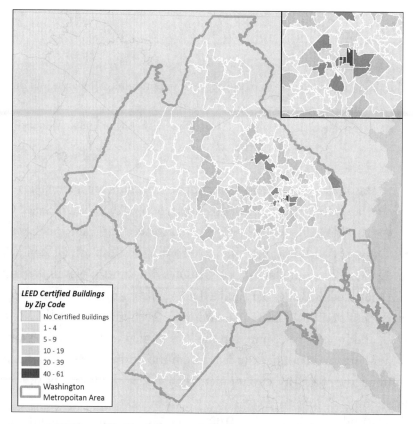

FIGURE 5.1. LEED certified buildings and developments in the DC metropolitan area with inset focusing on DC (Credit: Graham Petto)

LEED-ND developments in the metro area, including ten in D.C. and three in Arlington, Virginia.[2]

Vigorous LEED activity in the D.C. metropolitan region is the result of a synergy of factors including the location of nongovernmental organizations in the nation's capitol, the role of the federal government in construction, early adoption of green building standards into legislation, and the location of a key private sector player in the real estate market in D.C.

What Is LEED?

The U.S. Office of the Federal Environmental Executive (OFEE) defines the design of green buildings as (1) "the practice of increasing the efficiency with which buildings and their sites use energy, water, and materials," and (2) "reducing building impacts on human health and the environment through better siting, design, construction, operation, maintenance, and removal throughout the complete life cycle."[3] The notion of energy-efficient buildings is hardly new. The ancient Egyptians, for example, positioned their buildings to capture the heating energy of the sun and the cooling energy of the wind. In more modern times, several early-twentieth-century skyscrapers, including the Flatiron and the New York Times buildings in New York City, featured deep-set windows while the Carson Pirie Scott department store in Chicago had retractable awnings. These features were designed to control interior temperature while lessening the impact on the environment. During this period there were, however, no uniformly accepted design standards for low-impact buildings. The only incentive to design for energy efficiency was the cost savings that accrued to the building owners or occupants. Whether a building was designed with low-impact features and what assortment these features might incorporate was solely and exclusively a matter to be decided by a building's developer and owners.

Interest in energy-efficient building designs began to grow rapidly during the 1970s. This period saw the "glass box" begin to dominate the American skyline. As Matt Slavin mentions in chapter 1, the oil crises of the 1970s sparked a new wave of environmentalism, and a progressive set of architects, environmentalists, and ecologists began to promote building efficiency as an approach to environmental conservation, giving impetus to what we know today as the green building movement. At the state level, Governor Jerry Brown gained approval in

California for an energy-efficiency building code, called Title 24, in 1978. In the late 1970s, President Jimmy Carter and Congress enacted federal incentives for renewable energy. Carter also installed solar panels on the White House, which were unceremoniously ripped down as soon as Ronald Reagan took office. In 1992, the green building community once again focused on the White House as model of green building design. Launched during the Clinton administration, the greening of the White House program was designed to improve energy efficiency and environmental performance by identifying opportunities to reduce waste, lower energy use, and make appropriate use of renewable resources. In March 1996 it was reported that the White House greening project resulted in a savings of more than $150,000 per year in energy and water costs, landscaping expenses, and expenditures on solid waste.[4] The success of this initiative led to the makeover of other iconic federal facilities, including the Pentagon, located in Arlington County across the Potomac River from Washington; the Presidio in San Francisco; and the downtown Washington, D.C. headquarters of the U.S. Department of Energy.

The idea of setting industry-wide uniform standards for green buildings grew out of an initiative by the USGBC. Of the various programs and activities undertaken by the USGBC, LEED is by far the most significant. The proposal to create a USGBC green building rating system emerged as the subject of a paper presented by David Gottfried, a founder of the USGBC and the organization's first staff president, to the organization's first convention, hosted by the American Institute of Architects in 1993. Gottfried's idea for a U.S. green building rating system drew upon the BREEAM rating system previously established in the UK and the BEBAC system established in British Columbia, Canada. In the spring of 1995, Rob Watson of the Natural Resources Defense Council chaired a ratings systems committee that led to the development of LEED. The committee generated several drafts of what a green building ratings system might look like, resulting in development of the LEED 1.0 rating protocol. However, LEED 1.0 was never released commercially. Instead, during the summer of 1999, a group of technical experts convened for a weekend at the Rockefeller estate in Pocantico, New York, to initiate a series of refinements to previous work. The culmination of these efforts appeared in the form of LEED 2.0. Based on version 2.0, the USBGC certified its first twelve buildings in March 2000.

The original green building certification program developed by the USGBC is now known as LEED-NC or new construction (including major renovations).

Since the release of the initial LEED-NC rating and certification system, nine additional LEED certifications have been established by the USGBC. Included are certifications for existing buildings, operations and maintenance, commercial interiors, core and shell, schools, retail, healthcare, homes, and—more recently—neighborhood development. The neighborhood-development rating system, LEED-ND, takes a district-wide approach to fostering sustainable development rather than focusing on a single building.

LEED for Core and Shell and LEED for Commercial Interiors are particularly important, as these standards regulate the design of the building type that makes up the bulk of the building stock of downtown business districts of cities, as well as suburban office park developments. These are the large and ubiquitous buildings that define our urban environments. The success of LEED for Core and Shell and LEED for Commercial Interiors, the standards for commercial office buildings, have been given special momentum by CoStar, the commercial real estate data service founded in Washington, D.C., which was early to include energy and sustainability data in its listings. This private initiative, combined with legislation in D.C., has made sustainability an important focus for owners of office space. The Green Building Act of 2006 mandated LEED certification for commercial buildings. The District of Columbia's 2008 Clean and Affordable Energy Act requires commercial property owners to provide energy performance data to the city for public access, reinforcing the ability of the market to enable selection of energy efficient and sustainable buildings.

LEED for Schools is a significant standard for several reasons. First, it provides an opportunity to influence a major public building type that is a mainstay of building programs of municipalities across the country. Second, the design of schools has the potential to influence future generations. It has been argued that LEED-certified buildings provide better learning environments through improvements to day-lighting, indoor air quality, environmental systems, and acoustics. And, students in sustainably designed schools grow up with examples that will, hopefully, influence decisions to adopt more sustainable practices in their own lives.

LEED for Neighborhood Development (LEED-ND) received important impetus in the D.C. metropolitan region. The region was an early leader in community development, including the early-twentieth-century towns of Greenbelt and Columbia in Maryland and Reston in Virginia. More recently, one of the first New Urbanist residential projects, the Kentlands, was built in the

Washington suburb of Gaithersburg, Maryland, starting in 1988. After the development of Seaside, Florida, the Kentlands was the first nonrecreational illustration of New Urbanist town planning principles. An impetus to LEED-ND arose when the Chesapeake Bay Foundation building outside Annapolis was completed and certified LEED Platinum in 2001. Questions were raised about LEED's relationship to settlement patterns since the foundation had located on a remote site, which virtually required automobile access—but achieved LEED highest rating. Those questions resulted in the Congress for the New Urbanism's joining with USGBC to formulate a standard that would describe denser, pedestrian-friendly settlement patterns, which, under the rubric of smart growth, were seen to be a far more sustainable alternative to traditional postwar development, which came to be described as sprawl. The LEED-ND standard was released in 2009, providing a powerful tool for considering sustainable design at the community level, with respect to patterns of use, density, and transportation. While the regulation of individual buildings is undeniably important, LEED-ND could have a far greater influence than any of the other standards, which relate only to the design of individual buildings.

The number of buildings LEED certified under the various standards has increased rapidly, and certification in many jurisdictions has evolved from a voluntary program to a regulatory requirement. Washington, D.C. was the first major U.S. city to require LEED compliance for development projects built by private investors. In 2006, the District of Columbia adopted its Green Building Act, which requires compliance with LEED standards at the certified level for all privately developed building projects including new construction or major renovations of 50,000 square feet or larger. The act also requires all city-owned commercial development projects to attain LEED certification. Under the act, all district-funded housing projects were required to follow similar standards and the mayor of Washington was required to adopt environmental building standards for schools. In fact, at the time the act was adopted, both LEED for Homes and LEED for Schools were still in their development phases and had yet to be commercially released by the USGBC. With the Green Building Act, Washington, D.C. was getting out ahead of the USGBC, adopting in advance standards that were yet to be written. The act included measures for compliance and verification along with incentives for early adoption and for reaching higher levels of LEED certification.[5]

From Voluntary to Regulatory

The USGBC describes LEED as a "voluntary, consensus-based tool that serves as a guideline and assessment mechanism for the design, construction, and operation of high-performance, green buildings and neighborhoods."[6] The objectives of LEED include:

- Defining "green" by providing a standard for measurement
- Preventing "greenwashing" (false or exaggerated claims)
- Promoting whole building, integrated design processes
- Recognizing leaders
- Establishing market value with recognizable national "brand"
- Raising consumer awareness

Such characterizations and objectives are common among programs that certify other items, such as automobiles, schools, consumer products, and professionals. The value of certification lies in the additional revenues that such certification provides. Certification makes economic sense if the value of certification exceeds the cost of meeting the standards. The central argument for incurring any potential additional up-front cost of building to LEED standards is that LEED certification generates a premium payback to the developer or owner of a building or development project. Payback from LEED can be derived from several sources. One source is a reduction in building operating costs: the measures credited should produce operational savings for the certified project in terms of reduced expenses for energy and water, for example. Payback can also be measured in terms of increased rents and above market capital appreciation of a property or development. A 2008 study by CoStar concluded that there is indeed a "strong economic case for developing green buildings." According to CoStar President and Chief Executive Officer Andrew Florance, "Green buildings are clearly achieving higher rents and higher occupancy, they have lower operating costs, and they're achieving higher sale prices."[7] The rapid adoption of LEED by the development industry suggests that many developers perceive that LEED-certified development does generate payback.

Over the years many state and local governments and school districts have adopted various types of LEED initiatives, incentives, and regulations. In some cases these incentives and regulations apply only to government buildings, but in others they apply to some or all developments in the community. Thus, over time, LEED has evolved from a largely voluntary, market driven rating system to one that is increasingly adopted as a regulatory requirement.

Technical Components

The LEED system is organized by categories that describe the building construction process from site selection to performance after completion. For LEED for Building Design and Construction, which has become the basic standard, rating categories include sustainable sites, water efficiency, energy and atmosphere, materials and resources, and indoor environmental quality. Also included is a category for innovation in design, intended to promote innovation in green buildings by awarding additional points for innovative techniques not covered by the other categories. Each category has prerequisite requirements that provide a threshold for performance; no points are awarded for meeting the prerequisites. Credits in each category are assigned points according to their importance, from 1 for small measures to 19 points (the latter the maximum in a range of from 1 to 19) to "Optimize Energy Performance."

The total number of possible points achievable is 100; the familiar "precious metal" ratings are assigned according to total score: 80 and above qualifies as platinum; 60 to 79 points qualifies as gold; 50 to 59 points qualifies as silver; and 40 to 49 points qualifies as certified. The weighting of the credits was adjusted for the 2009 version to reflect changing priorities, for example, for energy over materials.

The LEED system relies heavily on standards derived from other organizations like the American Society of Heating, Air Conditioning, and Refrigeration Engineers (ASHRAE), sometimes offering choices among methods and standards, or simply awarding points according to compliance with appropriate industry standards. Scoring is conducted online by a LEED-accredited professional involved in the project, who manages the submission of data supporting the project's compliance with various credits. USGBC contracts with individuals to manage the scoring, awarding points or not, based on the submitted data. This third party verification is a strongly advocated attribute of the LEED system that distinguishes it from most other rating systems.

The award of a LEED certification to a building or development project has been understood to be permanent: once a building acquires its certification, it retains the certification. However, the permanency of LEED certification has led to some controversy over the degree to which, once constructed, LEED buildings are actually operated to the high performance standards to which they have been designed. It was noted above that recent changes to the LEED rating system have been incorporated to stress the importance of energy use. This reflects one particular controversy. As National Public Radio has reported, "LEED certification has never depended on actual energy use. . . . You can use as much energy as you want and report it and keep your (LEED certification) plaque."[8] The U.S. Green Building Council has responded to these concerns by issuing revised standards in 2009 that require owners of LEED-certified buildings to report their energy usage for a five-year period following receipt of certification. The goal is to assure long-term performance consistent with the building's represented design. In addition, this requirement will make it possible to systematically gather data on LEED-certified buildings. It remains to be seen what will happen should a building's out year performance fail to meet the rated standard. At the present time, no procedures exist for revoking LEED certification or ensuring compliance beyond the initial certification.

LEED Provides Impetus to Alternative Green Building Standards

The increasing importance of sustainability has been accompanied by a proliferation of other green standards and codes. This is especially true in the home-building market where the complexity of LEED for Homes, together with the added cost of an approved "provider," has prompted a number of self-rating standards. These include the National Green Building Standard, sponsored by the National Association of Home Builders, Energy Star for Homes from the United States Environmental Protection Agency and the Department of Energy, Green Globes, and the Living Building Challenge. Other green building standards and codes, some developed before and some after LEED, include:

- Green Communities: Green Communities is a standard developed by the Enterprise Foundation for affordable housing developments. The District of Columbia requires compliance with this standard for all housing development assisted by public funding.
- Local Green Building Codes: LEED rating systems were not intended to be used as the basis for local government building codes, but components of LEED have been adopted as such in many jurisdictions. In Montgomery County, Maryland, for example, according to a law enacted in 2006, new buildings and additions larger than 10,000 square feet with at

least 30 percent public funding must meet the LEED Silver standard. Compliance with the standard may be demonstrated either by certification by the USGBC or by the county's director of permitting services, who assumedly becomes the third-party verifier.

- CalGreen State Building Code: The state of California has adopted its own Green Code called CalGreen. It was adopted in early 2010 and will come into effect on January 1, 2011. Promotional material for the code emphasizes cost savings, claiming that the cost of certification under the code will be included in the building permit fee. CalGreen is patterned on LEED in its organization and its provision of mandatory and voluntary provisions—a novel feature for a building code.
- International Codes: The International Code Council has developed an International Green Construction Code whose first draft was opened for comment in the summer of 2010. It, too, is patterned on the LEED standards with its topical organization and its requirements and electives. This organization provides the foundation for building codes in many jurisdictions in the United States including Virginia, Maryland, and the District of Columbia; its Green Construction Code has been endorsed by the U.S. Conference of Mayors and wide adoption of the code can be expected.

The U.S. General Services Administration (GSA) undertook a study of thirty green building rating systems in 2006. Based on the analysis, the LEED rating system received the highest rank, further cementing LEED's dominance not only for private developers but for use by the federal government in its building activities as well.[9]

LEED in D.C.

As noted earlier, Washington, D.C. ranked second in the nation for having 18.1 LEED registered and certified buildings per hundred residents.[10] D.C. is one of the green-building leaders nationwide, although competition from cities like Portland, Oregon, Chicago, and Seattle is fierce. A number of nongovernmental organizations based in D.C., including USGBC, and their leaders have worked together and independently to position the nation's capital as a center for innovation and dedication to the green building movement. The Washington, D.C. metropolitan area and region have followed suit, and some of the communities that surround Washington, D.C. have the most progressive green building policies and regulations in the United States.

The story of the D.C. metropolitan area's leadership in LEED begins in 2005, when the Kyoto Protocol went into effect for 141 nations that ratified it. Since the United States was not one of the nations that ratified the treaty, mayors of hundreds of cities took matters into their own hands at the U.S. Conference of Mayors and signed onto the Mayors Climate Protection Agreement, which bound them to the same stipulations as the Kyoto Protocol. They pledged to reduce carbon emissions by 7 percent below 1990 levels by 2012 and committed to promoting sustainable building practices using the U.S. Green Building Council's LEED program.[11] As of 2010, more than 1,000 mayors had signed on to the agreement.

Following that signing of the agreement by mayors in the D.C. region, they turned to the Metropolitan Washington Council of Governments (COG), which is an association of twenty-one local governments including Washington, D.C. and its surrounding local jurisdictions in Virginia and Maryland. The communities pledged to work together as a region to pursue ways to achieve the goals outlined in the Climate Protection Agreement, which includes the implementation of green building initiatives.[12] In 2007, COG released the first result of the collaboration—the report "Greening the Washington Metropolitan Region's Built Environment," which detailed current efforts in the region to support green building and established policy goals for future development.[13]

Leading the way regionally in turning those recommendations into regulation, Washington, D.C. enacted the Green Building Act in 2006, phasing in compliance with LEED standards for both public and private development within the city's municipal limits. The act positioned Washington as the first major U.S. city to require LEED compliance for private projects. The new green building standards will be mandatory in the district by 2012 for private construction projects with 50,000 square feet or more. Public projects currently have to comply with the standards.[14]

The act also includes an incentive program, designed to encourage early adoption of the new standards by developers. The incentive program is to include a "Green Building Expedited Construction Documents Review Program" by which construction documents that comply with code requirements and other laws must be approved within thirty days of submission.[15] A grant program will make funding available for buildings that seek LEED certification, providing further incentive for compliance.

Action was not limited to the district alone. Other jurisdictions within the metropolitan area also have enacted legislation and provided incentives for buildings that reach LEED standards, starting as early as 2000.[16]

Arlington County, Virginia

Arlington County in northern Virginia stands out as a national model for green building and development. Originally adopted in October 1999, Arlington County's green building incentive program was revised and enhanced in December 2003 and again in March 2009. The program allows commercial projects and private developments earning LEED Silver certification to develop sites at a higher density than conventional projects.[17] The county also offers expedited development review and other incentives to program participants. Analysis of the program has shown it to be effective not only in creating additional density, but also in increasing the number of LEED-certified buildings in the county, especially commercial office space.[18] Arlington's green building regulations have in turn served as a model for other jurisdictions across the United States, which have basically copied their density bonus incentives verbatim into their building codes.[19]

Fairfax County, Virginia

Fairfax County, Virginia, is located in northern Virginia and is home to the affluent community of McLean. In February 2008, the county adopted a policy that all county projects greater than 10,000 square feet must achieve LEED Silver certification. The policy applies to the construction of new county buildings and renovations or additions to existing buildings. However, the policy does not apply to county-constructed single-family homes, town houses, or low-rise multifamily buildings. Instead, the Energy Star rating system will be used for these types of buildings. The county estimated that this new policy will impose an additional 2 to 4 percent in construction costs, but will be offset by annual energy savings.[20]

Montgomery County, Maryland

Montgomery County enacted its Green Buildings Law in 2006. New buildings and additions larger than 10,000 square feet with at least 30 percent public funding must meet the LEED Silver standard. Compliance with the standard may be accomplished by USGBC or by the director of permitting services, who assumedly becomes the third-party verifier. A real estate tax credit scheme was enacted in 2006 as well, granting property tax reductions to buildings that meet various LEED certifications. All new county schools must achieve a LEED Silver certification. Silver Spring, Maryland, is home to Blair Towns, the nation's first LEED-NC certified multifamily project in the country.[21]

Prince Georges County, Maryland

In September 2007, Prince George County established its Green Building Program, which was created by executive order. The program is run by an executive steering committee consisting of representatives from various county departments and has the following mission:

> Promote energy-efficiency and healthy buildings, create a sustainable environment and protect the health, safety and welfare of those who live and work within Prince George's County.

Pursuant to that mission, the Prince Georges County Goes Green program (as it is called) has made various goals for the county explicit, including Goal 2, which states "Design, construct and incorporate Green Building principles into all future county facilities/buildings, inclusive of office buildings, public schools, libraries, recreational facilities, etc." In their 2009 annual report, it was reported that two facilities, Vansville Elementary School and Vansville Community Center (which adjoins the elementary school), were built to LEED Silver Certification. Five buildings were scheduled to meet LEED Gold Certification, four were scheduled to meet LEED Silver Certification, and two were scheduled to incorporate Green Building principles.[22] The Barack Obama Elementary School, which was completed in 2010, achieved LEED Gold Certification.

The county also aims to "establish incentives for existing and new privately owned commercial buildings and developments to achieve LEED Silver Certification and/or an equivalent utilizing Green Building principles." Steering committee members are working with the development community at-large to consider a real estate tax incentive program for LEED-certified office buildings as well as a personal property tax credit or deferral program for tenants of LEED-certified buildings. Also considered is an expedited permitting process for the

FIGURE 5.2. Photo of CoStar Group's headquarters office at 1331 L Street, NW, in Washington, D.C. (Photo Credit: CoStar Group Inc.)

development and construction or tenant permitting of LEED-certified buildings in the county. However, at this time, no additional effort has been made to formalize these incentives.[23]

The Role of the Market

It should be noted that it was not regulation and incentives alone that positioned the D.C. metro area as a nationwide leader. A confluence of public and private forces, including legislation and CoStar's initiative, caused developers to realize that they were going to have to pursue sustainable development to comply with local regulations and to stay competitive locally as well as nationally, especially in the office market. As competition between developers increased, pursuing LEED certification became a hallmark of trophy office developments that could attract the best tenants. In the D.C. market, tenants were not necessarily seeking out LEED developments at first, but upon seeing those buildings and their benefits as well as comparable ones that did not have certification at the same price point, they consistently chose LEED developments.[24] CoStar's D.C. headquarters, a LEED Gold-certified building, exemplifies the trend towards sustainable commercial development in Washington (figure 5.2).

Part of the strength with which developers embraced the LEED development in Washington, D.C. stemmed from the involvement of the Building Industry Association in the development of the Green Building Act. The stipulations of the act were worked out in collaboration between government and businesses; the result was workable and successful for both. This kind of collaboration between the public and private sectors has been critical for the success of green building regulations.

Private developers have embraced LEED because it is perceived as creating underlying wealth in the terms of the asset value of the properties they develop.

The Federal Government

The federal government has played a significant role in the proliferation of LEED buildings and development in the D.C. metro area. In 1997, the Department of Energy provided $200,000 to the USGBC for the development of the LEED rating system, resulting in the creation of the LEED system.[25] The efforts of the USGBC in marketing and branding the system have proved successful, as has their probusiness approach, which urges municipalities to provide incentives for certification, not just mandates.[26] Perhaps more so than any other form of sustainable development initiative in the United States, LEED points to the successful confluence of public and private interests in the effort to create a more sustainable urban environment. Governments have embraced LEED to reduce energy and water consumption and mitigate other environmental externalities.

All new construction projects administered by the federal government's General Services Administration (GSA) must achieve a level of LEED Silver; the impact this has had on the D.C. market is substantial.[27] The GSA is one of the largest property owners in D.C. and manages the design and construction of all federal buildings. This dedication to LEED standards by the U.S. government provided a huge push to the strength of LEED development in the D.C. region and beyond. Besides funding the construction of thousands of square feet of LEED-certified office and support buildings in the region, the GSA reevaluates the green building rating systems every five years, and thus provides an impetus to keep the USGBC and LEED at the forefront of sustainable thinking while providing a strong business incentive to D.C. architects and developers to hire LEED-educated professionals and create LEED-certified buildings and communities.[28]

Case Studies

Twinbrook Station, Maryland

Twinbrook Station in Rockville, Maryland, is transforming 26 acres of existing commuter parking lots adjacent to the red line of the Washington, D.C. Metro subway system into a 2.2-million-square-foot, mixed-use community. At full build-out, the project will include 1,595 multifamily residential units, 220,000 square feet of ground-floor retail, 325,000 square feet of Class-A office space, and a new Village Green. Twinbrook Station is a joint effort of the JBG Companies and the Washington Metropolitan Area Transit Authority (WMATA). It was the first project in the Washington, D.C. area to be awarded Stage 2 LEED for Neighborhood Development (LEED-ND) Gold-level certification for its plan.

Twinbrook Station was well into the planning phases when LEED-ND was released, but it already had many of its planning principles in place and the developer realized that pursuing LEED-ND would serve not only to bring the project recognition, but would push them to incorporate additional sustainable development best practices into Twinbrook's planning and construction. From JBG's perspective, pursuing LEED certification was a benefit for the project. First, it demonstrated to the end-users, residents, commercial tenants, and visitors/shoppers the commitment of both the developer and the municipality to sustainable development. Second, it communicated this dedication to smart growth design principles and stringent review to the community and approving jurisdiction. Last, in the eyes of JBG, building to LEED standards could help attract funding, as private investors and lenders are more actively pursuing sustainable development investment opportunities.

From the beginning, JBG forged a close working relationship with the Rockville community and city officials. Initial plans for the development would not have been permissible by Rockville's zoning requirements, resulting in the entire site being approved as a Planned Unit Development. However, since Twinbrook Station's approval, Rockville has responded by revisiting its zoning code and has changed its requirements to facilitate this type of smart growth development. In the end, the municipality encouraged JBG to incorporate additional green development practices, such as lower building-parking ratios, into their plan. Twinbrook Station has become an exemplar for the application of form-based codes in the region.

In pursuing LEED-ND, changes were made, including the addition of compact fluorescent lighting fixtures, programmable thermostats, retail tenant water submetering to encourage responsible water use, low-flow fixtures, the use of paints and adhesives with low volatile organic compound (VOC) levels, a green roof, and a nonsmoking policy. Throughout the construction process, LEED-ND certification also helped to motivate the contractor and the property management teams to focus on sustainability issues and adhere to the highest standards, such as documenting onsite recycling.

Twinbrook Station has been designated a Smart Growth project by the Washington Smart Growth Alliance, received the International Charter Award for Excellence from the Congress for the New Urbanism, and was selected as the site for a USGBC national launch event announcing the LEED-ND standard. The project has resulted in the adoption of smart growth development principles in the area, and serves as a nationwide model for LEED-ND.

Stoddert Elementary School, Washington D.C.

In August 2010, a ribbon-cutting ceremony was held for the newly renovated and expanded Stoddert Elementary School in Washington, D.C. The original building, built in 1932, with an addition in 1993, only had capacity for 220 students, but was operating with 285 pre-kindergarten to fifth grade students. The new addition, designed by D.C.-based architecture firm Ehrenkrantz, Eckstus & Kuhn (EEK), added 47,300 square feet and cost $34.3 million to complete. It included fourteen new classrooms, a new gym, media center, cafeteria, community, and administrative spaces. Onsite, the addition also included new athletic fields and a playground, a forty-two-car parking lot, and a drop-off area. The addition increased capacity to 300 students, alleviating the overcrowding the school was experiencing, and achieved a LEED Gold certification under the LEED for Schools program.

Stoddert is the first school in the District of Columbia to be fully served by a geothermal system, which provides heating and cooling for the building from the ground. The project architects estimate that the geothermal wells will allow for 30 percent savings in energy costs per year, paying for the system in six to eight years. Noise levels in the building were also a major consideration for the designers; acoustic blankets and full-height partitions were added wherever possible.

Another innovative feature of the design is an interactive kiosk that allows students to monitor the building's energy consumption and other resources, helping to ensure that the building performs as promised by the LEED standards, and educating students about energy consumption and sustainability. The connection that the building makes between its green features and education was critical. Daylighting, outdoor learning spaces, and improved ventilation to maintain a high level of air quality are all features that achieved LEED Gold Certification, while improving the experience for users of the building.

Conclusions

While the LEED rating systems, certification processes, and measured outcomes have their flaws and their critics, LEED has been a success if measured in sheer quantity of projects certified and its impact on jurisdictions. It has withstood comparison with and provided impetus for the generation of competing systems. LEED's success can also be understood in the degree to which it has served as a framework for both public and private entities to create enforceable sustainable guidelines for the creation of buildings and cities. In fact, LEED's ultimate success may be its ultimate irrelevancy, if the International Code Council's Green Construction Code, patterned on the LEED standards, becomes widely adopted.

Washington, D.C. is a center of LEED-related activity and influence. The governance and institutional structure of the District of Columbia and its metropolitan region has provided a fertile environment for LEED application. The district, literally and figuratively, consists of two entities—the city of D.C. as the seat of the federal government, and the federal government that inhabits it—and both entities are committed to green building. The GSA's commitment to LEED Silver is significant as it is one of the largest property owners in the city. The city's Green Building Act provides a lessons-learned example for other cities around the country in the importance of public/private collaboration toward the development of regulatory measures.

LEED's success in D.C., as measured in the degree and methods by which it has been disseminated, can serve as an effective model for other cities. However, lessons from D.C. extend beyond the means by which the system has been adopted. Single-building certification has become commonplace, yet it may be the LEED-ND system that comes to exert a sizeable impact on cities and their planning and regional growth. In cities such as D.C., with expanding metropolitan areas, the aggregation approach to growth areas may offer tangible and measureable improvements with widespread environmental benefits.

The LEED-ND system was conceived in 2004 to expand the LEED concept to aggregations, rather than the one-off building. The goal was to "foster neighborhoods that have a gentler impact on the environment, that reduce carbon emissions and that meet broader social and quality-of-life goals, such as housing affordability and locating jobs near homes."[29] While aimed at new developments more than redevelopment, the LEED-ND standard could nevertheless be applicable to redevelopments, attracting financing to otherwise difficult-to-develop land, such as a brownfield development.[30]

Thus, we learn from D.C. that in the one-off single-building strategy, implemented through voluntary measures at the building scale, LEED offers a limited approach to sustainability. The most fertile ground for sustainable regulation, whether the LEED system, jurisdictional or code mandate and adoption, may be in standards such as LEED-ND, which aim to optimize results over more than one building, extending to the patterns of use, density, transportation, and ultimately transforming the places in which we live.

Notes

1. Chris Pyke, "Acknowledgements: From the Director of Research at USGBC," *The Journal of Sustainable Real Estate* 1, no. 1 (2009), www.costar.com/josre/JournalPdfs/00-Preface-Contents-Board.pdf.

2. Analysis by Graham Petto from the National Center for Smart Growth Research and Education using Green Building Certification Institute (accessed through the USGBC website) data on LEED buildings and development found here: www.gbci.org/main-nav/building-certification/leed-project-directory.aspx.

3. Building Design and Construction, "White Paper on Sustainability," Novermber, 2006, www.docstoc.com/docs/2200447/Green-Building-History-of-Green-Building.

4. Office of the President. "The Greening of the White House." Washington, D.C.: Office of the President of the United States, n.d., http://clinton3.nara.gov/Initiatives/Climate/greeningsummary.html.

5. Sarah Karush, "D.C. Council Passes Green Building Rules," Associated Press, December 6, 2006, www.washingtonpost.com/wp-dyn/content/article/2006/12/06/AR2006120600165.html; Howrey, LLP, "Washington, D.C. Enacts Green Building Requirements for Private Projects, *Construction WebLinks*, April 16, 2007, www.constructionweblinks.com

/Resources/Industry_Reports__Newsletters/Apr_16_2007/wash.html (accessed September 2, 2010); and the District of Columbia, *The Green Building Act of 2006*, http://green.dc.gov /green/lib/green/pdfs/GreenBuilding_act06.pdf (accessed September 30, 2010).

6. U.S. Green Building Council, "Foundations of LEED," July 17, 2009, www.usgbc.org /ShowFile.aspx?DocumentID=6103 (accessed September 30, 2010).

7. Andrew C. Burr, "CoStar Study Finds Energy Star, LEED Bldgs. Outperform Peers," CoStar Group, March 26, 2008, www.costar.com/News/Article.aspx?id= D968F1E0DCF73712B03A099E0E99C679.

8. Franklyn Cater, "Critics Say LEED Program Doesn't Fulfill Promises," *NPR*, September 8, 2010, www.npr.org/templates/story/story.php?storyId=129727547.

9. Kevin Kampschroer, *Federal Green Buildings*, statement before the Subcommittee on Government Management, Organization, and Procurement of the House Committee on Oversight and Government Reform, July 21, 2010, U.S. General Services Administration, www.gsa.gov/portal/content/159125 (accessed September 12, 2010).

10. Greater Washington Initiative, *Greater Washington Energy Efficiency and Sustainability Industry Report*, 2010.

11. The United States Conference of Mayors, *U.S. Conference of Mayors Climate Protection Agreement*, www.usmayors.org/climateprotection/agreement.htm (accessed September 12, 2010).

12. Metropolitan Washington Council of Governments, www.mwcog.org/ (accessed September 12, 2010).

13. Metropolitan Washington Council of Governments, "Environment: Green Building," www.mwcog.org/environment/greenbuilding/ (accessed September 12, 2010).

14. Howrey, LLP, "Washington, D.C. Enacts Green Building Requirements for Private Projects."

15. Howrey, LLP, "Washington, D.C. Enacts Green Building Requirements for Private Projects."

16. COG Intergovernmental Green Building Group, *Greening the Metropolitan Washington Region's Built Environment: A Report to the Metropolitan Washington Council of Governments Board of Directors*, December 12, 2007.

17. U.S. Green Building Council, "Public Policy Search," www.usgbc.org/PublicPolicy /SearchPublicPolicies.aspx?PageID=1776 (accessed September 12, 2010).

18. *Green Building Density Incentive Policy for Site Plan Projects*, February 27, 2009, report presented to County Board of Arlington County, Virginia, March 14, 2009, www .arlingtonva.us/departments/EnvironmentalServices/epo/PDFfiles/file69951.pdf (accessed September 2, 2010).

19. Shannon Sentman (LEED AP, Chair of the National Capital Region Chapter of the USGBC), personal communication, September 2, 2010.

20. *Fairfax County Sustainable Development Policy for Capital Projects*, www .fairfaxcounty.gov/dpwes/construction/sdpolicy.pdf (accessed September 5, 2010).

21. COG Intergovernmental Green Building Group, *Greening the Metropolitan Washington Region's Built Environment*.

22. Prince George's County Goes Green, *Goes Green Steering Committee's Annual Report to County Executive Jack B. Johnson*, Spring 2009, www.princegeorgescountymd.gov

/Government/AgencyIndex/GoingGreen/pdf/2009-annual-green-report.pdf (accessed August 23, 2010).

23. George Nicol (Acting Associate Director, Permits and Review Group, Department of Environmental Resources), personal communication, August 23, 2010.

24. Sentman, personal communication, September 2, 2010.

25. *Environmental Building News*, "DOE Funds USGBC's Development of LEED," October 1, 1997, www.buildinggreen.com/auth/article.cfm/1997/10/1/DOE-Funds-USGBC-s -Development-of-LEED/ (accessed September 12, 2010).

26. Sophie Lambert (Director, LEED ND), personal communication, August 31, 2010.

27. U.S. General Services Administration, *Sustainable Design Program*, www.gsa.gov /portal/category/21083 (accessed September 12, 2010).

28. Sentman, personal communication, September 2, 2010.

29. Steve Law, "Next Big Thing: Green Neighborhoods," *Sustainable Life*, March 11, 2010 (accessed from U.S. Green Building Council, *USGBC in the News*, www.usgbc.org /News/USGBCInTheNewsDetails.aspx?ID=4336, September 21, 2010).

30. Law, "Next Big Thing: Green Neighborhoods."

Chapter 6

The Greening of Mobility in San Francisco

AARON GOLUB AND JASON HENDERSON

In a democracy there is simply no reason to adopt major changes in policy as a result of scholarly studies or technical findings. There is every reason, however, to adopt policies that respond to vocal and persistent interest groups that demonstrate they have staying power in the political arena. Whether or not cycling catches on in America will depend upon the success or failure of grassroots movements like the one that is now thriving and growing in the San Francisco Bay Area.

Martin Wachs, University of California at Berkeley, 1998[1]

San Francisco has witnessed a flurry of interest in alternative transportation during the last fifteen years. Much of this interest has been inspired by grassroots movements to envision a new kind of city and act on that vision to foster a "politics of possibility." This chapter explores the launching of two successful green mobility initiatives: the expansion of the city's bicycle transportation program and the launching of a citywide car-sharing service. The impacts of these initiatives have been profound, affecting not only travel, parking, and automobile ownership, but also the planning code of the city of San Francisco. These developments point to the important role mobilization by grassroots activists and social entrepreneurship played as prime movers behind the city of San Francisco's green transportation initiatives.

Why San Francisco?

The City by the Bay occupies 47 square miles on the northern end of the San Francisco Peninsula bounded by the Pacific Ocean to the west, San Francisco Bay to the north and east, and the peninsula cities and San Jose to the south. Its beautiful, hilly topography and stunning views and beaches are a blessing and a challenge: they've created a highly desirable place attracting diverse populations for more than 150 years, while forming natural development constraints resulting in relatively dense settlements. Because of these dense settlement patterns and relatively good public transit options, San Franciscans rely heavily on alternatives to automobile: about 45 percent of internal trips are by walking, cycling, or public transit, compared to the U.S. average of only about 13 percent for those modes.[2] Today, almost 30 percent of households in the city are car-free, and for many this is by choice, not necessity. The city has one of the lowest rates of daily vehicle miles traveled (VMT) per person, at under 10 miles a day, compared to the national statistic of more than 30 miles. It also has one of the lowest per-capita automobile ownership rates in the United States, at 510 automobiles per 1,000 persons, compared to the national statistic of 784 automobiles per 1,000 persons.[3]

Compared to most U.S. cities, it appears San Francisco is already pretty "green." However recent trends of rising population, density, wealth, and car-ownership are challenging those characteristics. San Francisco is increasingly a bedroom community to other job centers, and much of this commuting is by automobile, causing increasing congestion on freeways and local streets in San Francisco.[4] Further still, concerns about energy consumption, local air quality, safety, greenhouse gas emissions, and affordability are growing louder every year. While already in a good position, the city will have to make new efforts to improve transportation to meet these existing and new challenges.

Many of the approaches to greening transportation place emphasis on alternative modes such as public transit, walking, and cycling. Yet, there are various constraints to doing so in San Francisco—most notably, the already crowded roadways of the city will need to be reconsidered for other uses as alternatives take more priority. San Francisco has the highest density of automobile registra-tions in the entire United States, at more than 8,000 motor vehicles (conven-tional automobiles, sport utility vehicles, and commercial trucks) per square mile—five to ten times that of a typical suburb.[5] The contradiction of low car ownership but high automobile density makes San Francisco an interesting petri dish for anyone advocating "livable communities," smart growth, new urbanism, or transit-oriented development. San Francisco has a decent palimpsest to re-duce car use, but the sheer density of automobiles makes it extremely con-tentious because already scarce road space must be reallocated from automo-biles. There is no room for adding bike lanes to roadside shoulders as in many American cities where bicycling is taking hold, and there is no excess road ca-pacity for creating exclusive bus lanes. In short, promoting even more sustain-able transportation in San Francisco requires substantial political will. This chapter will provide a brief examination of how that political will was created by grassroots movements to rethink the city in fundamental ways.

The actions documented below were not initiated by elected officials or trained planners or transportation engineers. They were initiated by groups of citizens envisioning a more sustainable city and inspired by the politics of possibility—creating a social movement by demonstrating through action that some vision is possible and that preconceptions formerly held could be challenged.

Ultimately, the two movements we describe—to create a system of public car-sharing and to increase cyclists' access to public road space—create the po-litical will to change the way San Franciscans get around by calling citizens to act on these visions and organize around them. Car-sharing was begun by a small group of people thinking about the way sharing could become an integral part of a sustainable society. Cycling was promoted by a group of people who felt that the use of public road space was something to be fought for instead of being left to the technical domain of planners and engineers. These two move-ments are having profound impacts not only on travel in San Francisco, but more fundamentally on how city planning and private development take place in the city. We begin by looking at the birth of car-sharing and its impacts on travel in San Francisco. Then, we trace the explosion of interest in cycling in the city from the contentious Critical Mass movement to the family friendly Sunday Streets program.

Car-Sharing

At first glance, trading the convenience of one's personal, private car for the occasional use of a shared car, owned and maintained by others and located somewhere out in the public realm, seems supremely countercultural in the United States. It appears there are places all over the nation however, where this idea makes sense and has increased in popularity. Though no programs existed before 1994, in mid-2009, there were roughly 280,000 car-share members sharing about 5,800 vehicles in the United States with these numbers growing roughly 20 percent per year.[6] While several cities in the Northwest, including Vancouver and Portland, saw formal car-sharing start before San Francisco, its home-grown, not-for-profit operator City Carshare opened in March of 2001 and has since become one of the largest in the United States. As of June 2010, it had 13,000 members sharing 330 vehicles at 180 pods in San Francisco, Oakland, and Berkeley. What's more is now in the same city, another for-profit operator has moved in to offer car-sharing service in competition with City Carshare, and they both appear to be thriving.

In this section, we chronicle the rise of this increasingly important component of the transportation system in San Francisco. First, we briefly explain how the system itself works, and then explore how it came to be. Then, we review the results of several studies of the impacts of car-sharing on travel, parking demand, and car ownership in San Francisco.

What Is Car-Sharing?

Car-sharing dates back to the 1940s in Northern Europe and most notably with the electric car-sharing system in central Amsterdam in the 1970s and 1980s.[7] San Francisco saw an early experiment in car-sharing in its Short-Term Auto Rental program, though it only lasted from 1983 to 1985. Eventually, with improvements in communication technologies, modern car-sharing took off with systems introduced in Europe and Canada in the early 1990s. Portland, Oregon, was the site of the first car-sharing system in the United States, with its CarSharing-Portland opening in 1998.[8] Phone-based reservation systems eventually gave way to Internet-based ones, and new car-sharing systems opened in cities across the United States. By 2002, there were 24 operators in North America with about 17,000 members sharing 766 vehicles.[9]

Though there are always variations from operator to operator in terms of the payment structure, membership fees, and vehicles types, a common model did emerge from these early systems with the following basic principles:

1. To use vehicles, one must be a member.
2. The operator screens new members for insurance purposes.
3. Some operators charge a small membership fee (typically monthly or yearly).
4. Members have a device (e.g., card-key) for gaining twenty-four-hour access to vehicles.
5. Vehicles are picked up and returned to the same place (called a Point of Departure—POD—typically a parking space with easy public access).
6. The member makes a reservation for a vehicle before using it.
7. The operator owns, insures, fuels, cleans, and maintains the vehicles being shared.
8. The operator provides a credit card for gasoline purchase when the car is in use.
9. Users are asked to fuel the vehicle when the tank gets below some specified level (generally 25 or 50 percent of a tank).
10. The operator arranges for PODs for vehicles.
11. The parking spaces used for PODs are off-limits for general public use, even when empty.
12. The user pays for the use of the vehicle by the hour or mile (or a combination of both).
13. Members are fined if vehicles are returned late, dirty, with too little fuel, and so on.

For a member, car-sharing takes place by making a reservation online or by phone through a voice-operated menu sometime before they need it (though it can be made instantly, so long as the car is available). The system shows them, based on their location, where vehicles are available for the reservation period they request. The user can specify the kind of vehicle from the POD they want or do searches anywhere in the system—even in other cities if they are members of a multicity network like Zipcar. Once the reservation is placed, the car is available to the user and their cardkey activates the car. Figure 6.1 shows a POD in San Francisco with a selection of cars from both City Carshare and Zipcar. Reservations can be extended on-the-go as long as the car is still available.

FIGURE 6.1. Head to head competition: City Carshare vehicles sit parked in their POD along Market Street in San Francisco, while on the far side of the lot sit six Zipcar vehicles. Photo: Jason Henderson.

The Rise of Car-Sharing in San Francisco

Currently in San Francisco there are two car-sharing operators: the nonprofit City Carshare (CCS) and the for-profit Zipcar. CCS opened for public membership in March of 2001, while Zipcar started operating in San Francisco in 2005. Gabriel Metcalf, one of the founders of CCS, recounted how the system was begun.[10] Interestingly, the idea for car-sharing began not out of a specific interest in improving the transportation system in San Francisco but in broader interests in social change and creating new institutions and social practices. Interests in cooperative ownership, bartering, and alternative economies led Gabriel and two friends to begin dreaming about starting car sharing in San Francisco in 1995 after reading a feature in *Rain* magazine on the Stattauto system in Germany.[11] The three formed a larger group of interested friends and colleagues in order to gather information about parking access, insurance policies, vehicle lease and purchase options, and system management technologies. In 1998, Gabriel made a trip to experience Seattle's car-sharing system and to meet with Tracey Axelsson, the founder and executive director of the Cooperative Auto

Network (CAN) in Vancouver, British Columbia (the oldest car-sharing co-op in North America). By then, the group in San Francisco began smaller experiments in sharing vehicles while assembling the financing, technical and operational expertise, and parking spaces for the large system they envisioned. Regular meetings with friends turned into larger events and fundraisers.

By 2000, they were sharing several cars and had created an Internet-based reservation system. While they had hoped to make an "open source" platform for their reservation system, which other car-sharing systems could use, they had to settle for a custom system to meet their immediate needs. They secured parking spaces from the city of San Francisco in city-owned lots, avoiding at first on-street parking spaces because of street cleaning concerns. Parking spaces were also secured from other institutions including schools, hospitals, and commercial property owners. The city public transit agency, MUNI, is funded in part from parking revenues, and MUNI expressed concern about lost revenues from space donation to car-share vehicles. However, the size of the operation seemed innocent enough to avoid a major protest. Being seemingly small and "under the radar" helped overcome other potential resistances during the initial experiments.

Starting with a fleet of about fifteen chartreuse-green Volkswagen Beetles, City Carshare opened to the general public in March of 2001. By the end of 2001 it had about 1,000 members sharing 31 vehicles parked in 12 PODs.[12] Growth nationally produced major investments in car-sharing and national scale, multi-city, for-profit operators soon emerged. Not surprisingly, the healthy car-sharing market in San Francisco attracted two prominent national firms, Flexcar and Zipcar, in late 2005. They merged under the Zipcar banner in October 2007. Because of such fast growth, it is hard to get exact current measures of car-sharing activities in San Francisco. As of June of 2010, City Carshare had roughly 13,000 members sharing 330 vehicles at 180 PODS in San Francisco, Oakland, and Berkeley. Zipcar also had about 800 vehicles in the City of San Francisco, though membership numbers were not available.

By 2006, the popularity of car-sharing led to calls for codifying requirements for car-sharing parking in new developments. A section was added to the San Francisco City Planning Code that set requirements for car-sharing in all new developments of one space for developments of 50 to 200 units, two for 200 units with one space added per 200 additional units.[13] Similar requirements were placed on nonresidential developments as well, and were recently expanded to cover the entire city.[14] This occurred alongside a broader movement to drastically restrict parking in most inner neighborhoods, eventually leading to the adoption of parking maximums and no parking minimums in many neighborhoods. In these areas with restricted parking allowances, however, car-sharing spaces do not count toward the maximum.

Impacts of Car-Sharing in San Francisco

Numerous studies have been made of the transportation impacts of car-sharing, and several have focused on the San Francisco area.[15] Car-sharing can have impacts on several aspects of transportation systems, such as household car-ownership and parking demand; car use; and demand for "alterative" transportation such as public transportation, cycling, and walking. Research across North America shows extremely significant impacts: households, after joining car-sharing groups went from owning an average of .47 vehicles (already somewhat lower than typical North American households) to .24 vehicles.[16] In the group of about 6,000 surveyed households that joined car-sharing, almost 1,400 vehicles were "shed"—equal to almost half of the vehicles owned by the group, and about 7 vehicles per vehicle shared. Even more vehicles were reduced because car-sharing households avoided the planned purchase of vehicles.

Research specifically focused on the San Francisco Bay Area showed similar impacts. In a long-term comparison of car-sharing households and a control group of households, membership was found to significantly influence car ownership.[17] Tracking households' car reductions and acquisitions between 2001 (before car-sharing) and 2005, it was found that car-sharing households shed about 7 vehicles per 100 households, while control households gained about 3 vehicles per 100 over the period.[18] Looking at overall travel patterns, car-sharing made up 4.8 percent of members' total daily trips, and 5.4 percent of total vehicle miles traveled (VMT) by members. The overall most popular form of conveyance by members—representing 47.6 percent of all trips—was "non-motorized" (i.e., walking or cycling). Non-car-share members were twice as likely to use a private car, and significantly less likely to take transit, compared to members. Members generally took "green modes" to work or school: nearly 90 percent of their journeys to work or school were by public transit, foot, or bicycle—a far higher share than for nonmembers.[19]

Based on these various studies, it appears that when households use car-sharing, they behave differently than when they own their own vehicle. The bulk of the costs of owning a car is in the depreciation and insurance, and it ends up being relatively cheap to operate it day to day. Plus, once you've paid for a vehicle, it behooves you to use it. Car-sharers pay the costs of depreciation and insuring the vehicle per use, so they experience much higher costs per use and therefore use it more judiciously. When they don't drive much, even those higher costs per use end up being cheaper than owning a vehicle. This is why, for urban dwellers who may already take public transit or bike to work, car-sharing makes sense and has grown in popularity rapidly. (For those who commute by car, however, car-sharing doesn't make a lot of sense.) Furthermore, in places like San Francisco, parking can be difficult, so car-sharing alleviates the worry of storing the vehicle when not in use.

VMT and car-ownership reductions can become significant as the number of car-sharers grows in the city. Assuming the roughly 25,000 car-sharing members in the Bay Area are distributed in 15,000 households with two-thirds in San Francisco, roughly 3 percent of the 320,000 households in the city contain car-sharers. The effects of this small membership can become significant. Parking pressures in core neighborhoods can be alleviated by the reduction in vehicle ownership, while congestion can be reduced because of the tendency for car-sharing households to drive less in general. Reduced parking pressures produce secondary impacts, because less cruising for parking can reduce local congestion and impacts on other road users. Further down the chain, reduced car ownership reduces the use of nonrenewable resources, energy and local and global emissions from vehicle production. It is estimated that, nationally, car-sharing has reduced the total demand for automobiles by between 90,000 to 130,000 vehicles.[20]

The Explosion of Bicycling in San Francisco

As previously suggested, car-sharing can provide a practical complement for people who otherwise chose walking, bicycling, or public transportation as their primary mode of daily transport. With only 1 percent of all trips, bicycling makes up a very small share of daily travel in the United States.[21] But with increased gasoline prices and congestion, more public awareness of the relationship between global warming and driving, and interests in physical activity, bicycling has experienced a miniboom in many U.S. cities. Chicago, New York, Portland, Seattle, and many smaller university cities have experienced significant increases in utilitarian bicycling.[22] In this section, we look closely at the substantial growth in cycling in San Francisco and the movement that helped to spur it. In San Francisco it is estimated that 5 percent of adults use bicycles as their main mode of transportation (up from 2 percent in 2001) and 16 percent ride a bike at least twice a week.[23]

Bicycling is poised to be a substitute for many short-range automobile trips, and has enormous potential to contribute to reductions in vehicle miles traveled. Nationally, roughly 72 percent of all trips less than 3 miles in length are by car, a spatial range that an average cyclist can cover easily.[24] Data for San Francisco are probably similar. Unlike walking or transit, the bicycle can be practical for running many errands, even in conventional lower-density suburbs. Bicycles do not require expensive, long-term capital investment or operating costs like that of transit and so can be deployed quickly. And in many respects bicycling is among the most equitable forms of urban transportation because it is affordable and accessible to almost everyone.[25]

Yet "bicycle space"—an interconnected, coordinated, multifaceted set of bicycle lanes, paths, parking racks, and accompanying laws and regulations to protect and promote cycling—has been extremely difficult to implement in the United States. Lack of political will to develop bicycle space has been a major barrier. There is no strong national bicycle policy with dedicated funding programs as there are for automobiles. Advocacy for bicycling has been a largely local, fragmented, and isolated effort. Therefore, the few cities that have established a political will to promote bicycling—and that have seen significant increases in bicycling—are worth considering.

In San Francisco, an 11,000-member bicycle organization has lobbied hard for the production of bicycle space, and the city has experienced a rather rapid upsurge in bicycling. Between 2005 and 2009, bicycling increased 53 percent, accounting for 6 percent of all trips in 2009, and amounting to 128,000 daily trips.[26] In some inner neighborhoods of San Francisco the mode share of bicycling is above 10 percent for all trips. This is despite the fact that much of the terrain over which bicyclist travel in the city is quite hilly. What makes San Francisco interesting is that during much of the last decade very little bicycle infrastructure has actually been built. For reasons described below, litigation has tied up the city's bicycle plan for almost five years. While it will likely be resolved in the fall of 2010, and bike lanes will likely proliferate thereafter, what has been remarkable in San Francisco is the increase in bicycling regardless of the provision of new bike lanes. This says something about the city's political culture and could inform those in other places that are seeking to develop bicycle space. Bike lanes are not enough—politics matters.

Critical Mass and the Bicycle Movement

Through the early and mid-1990s, despite a growing and vocal San Francisco Bicycle Coalition (SFBC), the city of San Francisco was reluctant to aggressively pursue bicycling systematically, and instead pursued a "low-hanging fruit" policy of striping bike lanes only if they did not impact car traffic. Bike lanes were placed on streets with very low vehicular volumes and very wide rights-of-way. When a bike lane approached a busy intersection or street segment with moderate or high car traffic, bike lanes were "dropped." The lane would simply end and bicyclists would be left to fend for themselves in the traffic. Moreover, when bike lanes were striped they were placed within the dangerous "door zone" of parked cars, because of reluctance to make them wider since that would also require removing car space. The city's unspoken priority was to ensure that bike lanes did not impact car space and so few real improvements for cycling were made, and few people were seen cycling in the city. It was a lonely and sometimes daunting existence for San Francisco cyclists in those days.

In San Francisco the frustration over the lack of political will to create bicycle space led to bicyclists creating their own spaces. These were the spaces of "critical mass" bicycle rides, which, beginning in 1992, occurred on the last Friday of every month in downtown San Francisco (critical masses eventually spread to New York City, Chicago, and globally to cities like Rome and Vancouver). Figure 6.2 shows the typical Friday evening CM procession. The name Critical Mass (CM) is as implied: a critical mass of cyclists that once reached, can recapture urban space from the automobile, enabling the mass to progress through city streets unimpeded, and to block intersections in a way that makes most motorists resigned to simply wait for its passage. The name was inspired by *Return of the Scorcher*, an independent documentary film that included a narrative observing hundreds of cyclists bunching at an intersection in China and pushing their way into traffic. Bicyclists would wait until they had critical mass to push

FIGURE 6.2. Safety in numbers: Several thousand critical mass riders proceed south-west on Howard street in the South of Market district of San Francisco in June, 1996. Photo: Chris Carlsson.

into the stream of cross-traffic, and the phrase was borrowed by local activists or-ganizing the monthly ride.

The small group of early CM participants were experienced, utilitarian cy-clists, but the rides helped them realize the possibilities of safe, car-free bicycle space. CM helped reframe the questions about urban sustainability and pushed the debate about street space. For many participants, CM reclaimed connectiv-ity to community and showed the possibilities of a humane city.[27] They felt that the bicycle was ideal for the eco-city of the future, as a swift, graceful, quiet, low-energy form of transport that takes up very little space. Through CM, participants found that bicycling could make streets a safe place, and it empowered a new sense of possibilities for urban living. According to one early participant "when you realize it can be different, you feel empowered and you see where we can go."[28] Furthermore, the ride reflected a movement without a central organizer, set of demands, or rigid plans. It was only there to demonstrate the possible. In the words of CM cofounder Joel Pomerantz:

> I'm sure policy-makers think about the looming monster of Critical Mass when they think of bikes, and the scary part is probably that they can't fit it into their category system. It's not a holiday, nor a parade, nor a demonstration, nor a sport. What is it? It's not an organization or particular group of any kind.[29]

Through the early and mid-1990s the monthly rides, although growing, were largely innocuous and drew little media criticism or police response, although incidents between motorists and cyclists did occur from time to time and police did occasionally try to tame the rides. In 1996 the *San Francisco Chronicle* used an image of CM in a promotional advertisement of the city, celebrating San Francisco's authentic dissident character. Participation expanded into the thousands on warmer spring and summer evenings, and the annual Halloween CM became a masquerading spectacle. Then in June of 1997, a sedan carrying the mayor of San Francisco, Willie Brown, was delayed by a passing CM. Known to be intemperate at times, the mayor directed the police to crack down on CM. Over the next month an exceptional amount of media attention focused on CM and the broader conditions of bicycling in the city. Upward of 5,000 cyclists appeared at the next month's CM, and a showdown with police ended in a melee of more than 200 arrests and images of police violently subduing cyclists. Every arrest was dismissed in court but, more important, bicycling was now front and center in a local politics increasingly concerned about congestion and the state of the public transit system in the city in mid-1997.

After the melee Mayor Brown asked the SFBC: "what do you want?" That was a first for bicycling in the city.[30] The SFBC, now in the limelight and growing in numbers because of CM, asked for eight specific bike lane projects, most of which would require removing car space to make bicycle space. The mayor directed his traffic department to hold hearings around the city in 1997 and 1998 while bicycle advocacy flourished in the city. Hundreds of cyclists attended these meetings, and the SFBC took a more aggressive position that the city needed to move beyond its low-hanging fruit approach.

Although the SFBC made pains to differentiate itself from CM, the fallout from CM strengthened the SFBC, which had 1,700 members by 1998 and was gaining allies with some local elected officials on the city's board of supervisors. Some key streets were made more welcoming to cyclists. For example, the city approved a "road diet" and bicycle lanes for Valencia Street, a level route through the city's Mission District and a core SFBC membership stronghold. Advocates had lobbied for this for almost a decade to no avail, mainly because of merchant and motorist opposition. Now the city felt it had to do something due to the political upwelling after the CM melee.

When bicycle lanes were added to Valencia Street in 1999, bicycling increased by 144 percent. The success of the Valencia Street project further emboldened bicycle activists, and proved that with adequate infrastructure more people would choose to bicycle. It came to be supported by shop owners, after the fact, and today Valencia is a thriving retail and entertainment corridor. By 2004, 16 percent of all trips on the street were by bicycle. A long-awaited resurfacing and widening of bike lanes to address the door zone safety hazard was nearing completion in 2010.

Success, however, exposed the raw truth of limited road space in San Francisco; some of the space for automobiles would need to be removed if bicycling were to get a fair shake. This threatened motorist convenience, and through concerns of car drivers' "levels of service," the city's transportation agency stalled on more radical bicycle lane proposals because of the fear that it would inconvenience too many motorists. While CM continued with rides of several hundred participants in winter months and several thousand participants in summer months, the SFBC responded to the unwillingness of city planners and engineers to reconfigure streets with open and aggressive political campaigning during city elections. Moreover, the city political establishment backed off of cracking down on CM.

By the mid-2000s, and with almost 5,000 members and growing every day, the SFBC had almost every local elected official concerned about the "bicycle vote," and very few elected officials spoke against the notion of bicycling, although ambiguity about how to implement bicycle space was widespread among many politicians. In 2005, with a clear probicycle majority on the city's legislative body, the SFBC pushed through a bicycle plan that, while modest, would have transformed traffic conditions on a handful of city streets. The plan was approved without an environmental analysis that is usually required for transportation projects, because the city decided to waive the analysis thinking that bicycling was good for the environment. It seemed very logical at the time, and for a brief moment the bicycle movement was euphoric and anticipating dramatic improvements while also beginning to plan for an even bolder bicycling expansion for the next decade.

With political success comes backlash. The city of San Francisco was sued for its bicycle plan by a lone blogger unsympathetic to the demands of CM. In question was how San Francisco's politicians and planners, eager to placate the politically potent SFBC, circumvented typical environmental review for the new bicycle plan for the city, reasoning that bicycles were environmentally benign and met urban sustainability goals such as reducing carbon emissions and providing more mobility choices. The lone litigant challenged the waiver of environmental review, claiming that bike lanes would cause congestion and this needed to be studied and documented. In November 2006, a judge ruled that San Francisco had to conduct the study, thus delaying implementation of bicycle space. The legal ruling was not against bicycle space per say, but against implementation without detailed traffic impacts analysis.

The litigation was a major setback for bicycling in the city, and it fostered a sense of confusion and cautious inaction among the city's political leaders. It tempered the momentum for change — exactly what the litigant wanted. Beyond bicycling, it made local politicians less enthusiastic about removing car space to provide exclusive bus lanes or other methods of improving transit. Yet it also inspired advocates to propose changes to the California Environmental Quality Act traffic impact analysis, which could deprioritize drivers' level of service and prioritize impacts on cycling and walking. Though yet to be adopted, the San Francisco County Transportation Authority eventually produced a formal proposal.[31] The judge recently lifted the injunction on ten of the projects in the bicycle plan that he stated were needed for safety reasons, and finally, on August 26, 2010, the city was found to be in full compliance with court-required environmental reviews of traffic and parking issues.[32] Now, the city can move forward immediately on 35 bike projects, adding 34 new bike lanes to the existing 45 miles.

Sunday Streets and New Momentum

While under injunction the city embraced the "Cyclovia" concept first introduced in Bogotá, Columbia, and now found in several other Latin American cities and New York City as "Sunday Streets." The Sunday Streets program in San Francisco temporarily opens long segments of streets only to bicyclists, walkers, and other nonmotorized users while banning automobiles. The idea of doing a Cyclovia event in San Francisco came from the SFBC in 2008. After visiting a similar event in Portland, Oregon, the SFBC worked closely with the city and with physical fitness, health, and urbanist organizations to hold a Sunday Streets event in September 2008. Unlike CM, the advocates took a more mainstream and less confrontational approach, but promoted the same ends—to provide a car-free space for safe bicycling (and in this case, walking, jogging, or skating).

Advocates framed Sunday Streets to appeal to a broader segment of the political establishment beyond simply sustainable transportation activists. For example, the concept was framed as providing much-needed open space in neighborhoods lacking adequate parks and recreation—such as Chinatown, the Mission District, and the low-income Bayview neighborhood in the Southeastern sector of the city. The target audience of the initial Sunday Streets was a hypothetical young mother with two children who had difficulty juggling her children's recreation needs. She could not let her kids play in front of the house because of automobiles, but then she had to lug her children across town to Golden Gate Park to find safe recreational opportunities. The idea to bring the parks to underserved neighborhoods had a very strong social justice angle. Families with children have indeed packed Sunday Streets events. In June 2010, 25,000 people were estimated to have enjoyed the Sunday Street event in the Mission District. Large numbers of free-roaming children could be found throughout the length of the open roadways. These are children rarely seen on bicycles or walking in the city on a normal day, because their parents are afraid and chauffeur their children in cars or on public transit. A huge latent demand for bicycling has been discovered via Sunday Streets.

While the first Sunday Streets did not explicitly engage the sustainable transportation vision, immediately after the first event organizers got numerous e-mails and phone calls suggesting that many people became more excited about bicycling because of the event. Attendees pointed out that they had forgotten how easy it was to ride a bicycle, and that riding a bicycle for distances of 3 to 5 miles was easier than they thought. Children were also nagging their parents to bicycle more. As one key organizer put it, Sunday Streets showed that "people aren't afraid of bicycling or walking for transportation, rather, they are afraid of car traffic."[33] Sunday Streets is expanding people's "politics of possibilities," and more people are realizing that car traffic is a profound mental barrier to bicycling in a city that is otherwise generally easy to bicycle in.

Like CM a decade before, Sunday Streets builds political support for removal of car space in order to have safe cycling and walking spaces in the city. Rather than an adversarial message, the emphasis now is on safety for children and parents and on providing more equitable access to open space.

Sunday Streets continues today, and the success of Sunday Streets led to a cautious optimism about rethinking San Francisco's streets. For example it reignited a decades-long debate about banning cars on San Francisco's signature thoroughfare, Market Street. Not to be outdone by Mayor Gavin Newsome, who claimed to have come up with the idea for Sunday Streets, his political rivals on the San Francisco Board of Supervisors called for a study to reduce car traffic on Market Street.[34] Instead of a total ban, the city has taken an innovative approach to experiment with forcing diversions for private automobiles at key points along the thoroughfare. The pilot project, initiated in early 2010 and modified incrementally, also includes using soft-hit posts to create a barrier between a generously wide and now green-painted bike lane and motorized lanes.

In May 2010 the city released preliminary results that suggested 200 fewer private cars were using Market Street during rush hour periods.[35] The interim study also showed that transit travel times decreased by almost one minute, and that bicyclists and taxi drivers liked the forced right turn of private cars. The results have been positive and more data are being collected to get environmental clearance and to make the diversion permanent. Taking an incremental approach rather than a comprehensive approach is more cautious, but it is also changing the order of implementation. Instead of making a design proposal and then spending years studying it, the approach is to make modest changes and study the impacts as they unfold in real time. As a trade-off, the SFBC and other advocates have backed off their bolder vision of a completely car-free Market Street from a decade earlier.

Conclusion

In the early 1990s there were few bike lanes, fewer cyclists, and no formal car-sharing in San Francisco. In 2010 bike lanes have slowly proliferated throughout the city, and the only thing that holds them back from gushing forth is an injunction that will likely end in 2010. On many mornings more cyclists are found on Market Street than automobiles, and bicycling is rapidly increasing, with its mode share projected to reach 10 percent of all trips citywide in the next few years. Inspired by the success on Market Street, the city is experimenting with innovative temporary street closures, diversions, and the creation of "parklets" in some curbside parking spaces. The SFBC is beginning a new campaign to push for a set of strategic east-west and north-south bicycle trunk routes crossing the city. Several new land use plans that eliminate automobile parking requirements for much of the eastern part of the city have been adopted with the expectation that more local trips will be on bicycles.

Car-sharing can now be seen all over the city, with Zipcars and City Carshare cars making up significant portion of the local automobile travel and PODs on nearly every block in the densest neighborhoods. From a simple idea to a very mainstream tool for planners and developers, the small group starting City Carshare has had a big impact. For many in San Francisco, car-sharing makes access to a car possible while saving money, reducing the total numbers of cars parked in a neighborhood and, in turn, reducing the number of cars searching for that rare open spot, therein reducing emissions, noise, and impacts on cyclists and pedestrians. The city is now considering dedicating some on-street parking for car-sharing PODS and new transit-oriented, land use development codes also require that new development include car-sharing. The impact has even made it to the statehouse in Sacramento where a bill was introduced (when) to allow anyone in the state to put their vehicles into car-sharing systems for public use.[36]

These results are largely due to the persistent advocacy by well-informed, passionate, and at times savvy advocates. They all began with visions and by organizing around that vision, fostered a politics of the possibilities for urban space that is not dominated by automobiles. Sharing cars and cycling were seen as distinctly un-American and distinctly outside of the dominant trends in the 1990s of rising congestion and car ownership in the city. The grassroots efforts pushed the envelope for residents and for the city. Incrementally, and not without pushback, many of the ingredients of a vision for urban sustainable transport are becoming institutionalized in San Francisco, and the city is at the leading edge of a national transformation promoting bicycling and car-sharing. In an era of paltry national leadership on global warming and energy security, San Francisco has taken as global civic duty to be out front and provide inspiration for sustainable transportation advocates elsewhere.

Notes

1. Martin Wachs, "Creating Political Pressure for Cycling." *Transportation Quarterly* 52, no 1. (1998): 6–8.

2. SFCTA (San Francisco County Transportation Authority) *Countywide Transportation Plan* (San Francisco: County of San Francisco, 2004), 39.

3. SFMTA (San Francisco Municipal Transportation Agency). *2008 San Francisco State of Cycling Report* (San Francisco: San Francisco Bicycle Program, Department of Parking and Traffic, Municipal Transportation Agency, 2009), 22.

4. SFCTA, *Countywide Transportation Plan*, 41.

5. SFMTA, *San Francisco State of Cycling Report*, 22.

6. Susan Shaheen, Adam Cohen, and Melissa Chung. "Carsharing in North America: A Ten-Year Retrospective." *Transportation Research Record: Journal of the Transportation Research Board* 2110 (2009): 35–44. Also see Elliott Martin, Susan Shaheen, and Jeffrey Lidicker. "Carsharing's Impact on Household Vehicle Holdings: Results from a North American Shared-Use Vehicle Survey." Forthcoming in *Transportation Research Record: Journal of the Transportation Research Board*, 2010.

7. Shaheen, et al. *Carsharing in North America: A Ten-Year Retrospective*, 35–44; David Brook, CarsharingUS Blog, entry posted January 8, 2010, CarsharingUS Blog, http://carsharingus.blogspot.com/ (12 June 2010).

8. David Brook, "Carsharing—Start Up Issues and New Operational Models." Paper presented at Transportation Research Board 83rd Annual Meeting, Washington, DC, January 11–15, 2004; Shaheen et al., *Carsharing in North America*.

9. Shaheen et al., *Carsharing in North America*.

10. Gabriel Metcalf, personal interview with Gabriel Metcalf, cofounder of City Carshare. San Francisco. 20 June 2010.

11. Michael LaFond, "Cooperative Transport: Berlin's Stattauto (Instead of Cars)." *Rain Magazine*, 1995, http://afo.sandelman.ca/afz/issue9-II.html (20 June 2010)

12. Robert Cervero, "City CarShare: First-Year Travel Demand Impacts." *Transportation Research Record: Journal of the Transportation Research Board* 1839 (2003): 159–66.

13. Section 166 was added to the Off-Street Parking and Loading Article (Article 1.5) See: City of San Francisco. City of San Francisco Planning Code, Article 1.5: Off-Street Parking and Loading. City of San Francisco. http://search.municode.com/html/14139/level1/A1.5.html (24 June 2010).

14. John Wildermuth. "City Working to Make Car-Sharing More Popular." *San Francisco Chronicle*, 6 August 2010.

15. Cervero, City CarShare: First-Year Travel Demand Impacts; Robert Cervero and Yu-Hsin Tsai. "City Carshare in San Francisco, California: Second-Year Travel Demand and Car Ownership Impacts." *Transportation Research Record: Journal of the Transportation Research Board* 1887 (2004): 117–27; Robert Cervero, Aaron Golub, and Brendan Nee. "City Carshare: Longer-Term Travel Demand and Car Ownership Impacts." *Transportation Research Record: Journal of the Transportation Research Board* 1992 (2007): 70–80; Martin, et al., *Carsharing's Impact on Household Vehicle Holdings: Results from a North American Shared-Use Vehicle Survey*.

16. Martin, et al., *Carsharing's Impact on Household Vehicle Holdings: Results from a North American Shared-Use Vehicle Survey*.

17. Cervero, et al., *City Carshare: Longer-Term Travel Demand and Car Ownership Impacts*.

18. Cervero, et al., *City Carshare: Longer-Term Travel Demand and Car Ownership Impacts*.

19. Cervero, et al., *City Carshare: Longer-Term Travel Demand and Car Ownership Impacts*.

20. Martin, et al., *Carsharing's Impact on Household Vehicle Holdings: Results from a North American Shared-Use Vehicle Survey*.

21. USDOT (United States Department of Transportation). *The National Bicycling and Walking Study: 15-year Status Report* (Washington, DC: USDOT, 2010), 22.

22. John Pucher and Ralph Buehler. "Making Cycling Irresistible: Lessons from the Netherlands, Denmark, and Germany." *Transport Reviews* 28, no. 4 (2008): 1–57; Harry J. Wray, *Pedal Power: The Quiet Rise of the Bicycle in American Public Life* (Boulder: Paradigm Publishers, 2008.); Jeff Mapes, *Pedaling Revolution: How Cyclists Are Changing American Cities.* (Corvallis, Oregon: Oregon State University Press, 2009)

23. SFMTA, *2008 San Francisco State of Cycling Report*, 22.

24. USDOT, *The National Bicycling and Walking Study*, 22.

25. Wray, *Pedal Power*.

26. SFMTA, *2008 San Francisco State of Cycling Report*, p 22; SFMTA, *2009 San Francisco State of Cycling Report*, p 22.

27. Joshua Switzky, "Riding to See." In *Critical Mass: Bicycling's Defiant Celebration*, edited by Chris Carlsson, 186–92 Oakland, CA, AK Press, 2002.

28. Cheryl Brinkman, personal interview with Cheryl Brinkman, President of Livable City, and Organizer of Sunday Streets. San Francisco. 24 June 2010.

29. Hugh D'Andrade, SFCriticalMass.org Blog, posted May 25, 2010; SFCriticalMass.org Blog. www.sfcriticalmass.org/ (accessed June 23, 2010).

30. David Snyder. 2008. Interview with David Snyder, former executive director of SFBC. San Francisco, June, 2008.

31. SFCTA (San Francisco County Transportation Authority). *Automobile Trips Generated: CEQA Impact Measure and Mitigation Program*. San Francisco: County of San Francisco, 2008.

32. Rachel Gordon and Jill Tucker, "Ruling Paves Way for San Francisco Bike Lanes." *San Francisco Chronicle*, 6 August 2010.

33. Brinkman, personal interview.

34. Rachel Gordon, "New S.F. Study: Phase-In Market St. Car Ban." *San Francisco Chronicle*. 10 May 2009, A-1.

35. SFMTA (San Francisco Municipal Transportation Agency). *Pilot Study of Required Right Turns on Eastbound Market Street*. San Francisco: San Francisco Municipal Transportation Agency, 2010b, p 2.

36. Michael Cabanatuan, "State Bill Offers Twists to Expand Car-Sharing." *San Francisco Chronicle*, 29 April 2010.

Chapter 7

Wind, Waves, and Watts: Creating a Clean Energy Future for Honolulu

MATTHEW I. SLAVIN, DOUGLAS A. CODIGA, AND JASON J. ZELLER

The future of Hawaii requires that we move more decisively and irreversibly away from imported fossil fuel for electricity and transportation and towards indigenously produced renewable energy and an ethic of energy efficiency. . . . The very future of our land, our economy, and our quality of life is at risk if we do not make this move and we do so for the future of Hawaii and of the generations to come.

Energy Agreement to the Hawaii Clean Energy Initiative (October 2008)

Hawaii currently uses imported oil to generate the vast majority of the electricity it uses; its dependence on oil-fired generation is more than thirty times the national average. This chapter examines plans to transform Honolulu, the state's largest municipality, into one powered primarily by renewable energy. We begin with an overview of how Honolulu came to be heavily dependent upon oil for electricity generation and how the Hawaii Clean Energy Initiative emerged during the first decade of the twenty-first century as a response to this overdependence. The initiative amounts to nothing less than a paradigm shift that would enable Honolulu to drastically reduce its dependence on imported oil and rely primarily on renewable energy sources such as wind, solar, and other clean energy resources. The initiative will also require Honolulu to use energy more efficiently, green its building stock including development of the world's largest deep sea water air conditioning system, expand use of electric vehicles, and construct an undersea electric transmission cable to allow renewable energy generated on Oahu's neighboring Hawaiian islands to be transmitted to Honolulu. If various obstacles can be overcome, the Hawaii Clean Energy Initiative affords an opportunity to transform Honolulu into perhaps the most energy independent municipality in the nation.

Honolulu's Oil Conundrum

With a population of 910,000 Honolulu is the eleventh most populous municipality in the United States. Located on the island of Oahu, Honolulu does not function as an independent city government. Since 1907, the city of Honolulu and Oahu County have been consolidated into a single municipal government, the City and County of Honolulu. The combined municipality occupies all of the island of Oahu. In a state with an estimated 2010 residential population of almost 1.2 million, 75 percent of all Hawaiians live on Oahu within the municipal limits of Honolulu.[1] Honolulu's population may add as many as 100,000 more people on a seasonal basis due to an influx of part-time residents and visitors. Honolulu is Hawaii's predominant economic center. Seventy percent of all those employed in the state work in Honolulu.[2] Historically Honolulu's main industries have been tourism, the military, property development, and agriculture, although the significance of agriculture has declined in recent years.

Energy professionals use the phrase "fuel mix" to describing how electricity is generated for consumption by homes, businesses, and industry. In Honolulu, it's not much of a mix. Approximately 87 percent of the electricity currently consumed in Honolulu is generated by oil that is used to fuel the power plants that produce Honolulu's electricity. Electricity production accounts for 26 percent of all petroleum fuel consumed in Hawaii with most of this being consumed on Oahu. For the United States as a whole only 3 percent of electricity consumed is generated from oil. Coal-fired electricity accounts for an additional 13 percent of Honolulu's electricity with the remainder being generated by renewable energy resources.[3] Honolulu's overwhelming dependence upon oil to generate electricity has made it highly vulnerable to the supply disruptions and price spikes that have characterized global oil markets since the first Arab oil embargo in 1973.

To fully appreciate the nature of the energy challenge facing Honolulu, it is useful to understand how the island city came to be so dependent upon petroleum-fueled generation. Honolulu is the only large U.S. municipality surrounded entirely by water. The Hawaiian Islands do not have any indigenous oil, natural gas, or coal deposits. Moreover, the islands lack major rivers and offer little in the way of hydropower potential. Commercial nuclear generation of electricity has never been considered a viable option in Hawaii in part because there are few if any sites appropriate for a nuclear plant on the relatively small, sloping volcanic islands, but moreso because of strong public opposition. Hawaii is one of a handful of states whose constitutions effectively ban commercial nuclear generation. On November 7, 1978, Hawaii's constitution was amended to ban construction of commercial nuclear energy plants on the Hawaiian Islands unless two-thirds of the members of both houses of the Hawaii legislature vote to approve construction of such a plant.[4] Few observers believe that overcoming this threshold is possible.

How Honolulu Became So Oil Dependent

The roots of Honolulu's modern development can be traced to 1893. In what effectively amounted to a coup d'état, American and European sugar and pineapple plantation owners overthrew Hawaii's native system of monarchical governance. U.S. Marines were sent to Hawaii and the islands were annexed in 1898. In 1900 Hawaii became a federal territory. Rapid population growth followed, driven in part by a failure of the Puerto Rican sugar crop in 1889. Island-based plantation owners increased sugar cane production to fill this gap and recruited farm workers from Japan, the Philippines, and Puerto Rico and, to manage the plantations, from Portugal. Between 1900 and 1910, Honolulu's population increased from 58,000 to 80,000. The settlement of Kalaupapa (the precursor to today's Honolulu) had functioned as the center of royal governance and commerce on Oahu since the early years of the 1800s. In 1907, the territorial government merged Kalaupapa and Oahu County to create the City and County of Honolulu.[5]

In the aftermath of Japan's victory over a Russian fleet in the Russo-Japanese War of 1904–1905, U.S. naval planners began to look for a harbor to base a fleet in the Pacific to counter a possible Japanese threat. In 1912, the navy began construction of the naval base at Pearl Harbor, one of the world's great natural harbors. At the time, the U.S. fleet was converting from coal to oil to fuel its battle fleet. The navy constructed oil tanks and other oil-related infrastructure to refuel the ships that would be based there. Being a liquid, bulk oil was easier and less expensive to transport by sea than coal and also has a higher energy density than coal. Oil was given a further impetus as the fuel of choice by the island's location. Oahu is 2,500 nautical miles from Los Angeles where in 1892 oil was discovered on a site nearby what is now Dodgers Stadium. Other discoveries followed and by 1923 the region was producing a quarter of the world's oil supply. To the west from Oahu, it is 4,000 miles to the island of Sumatra where oil had been discovered in 1885. By 1911, Royal Dutch Shell was shipping 4 percent of the world's oil from the Indonesian archipelago.[6] Unlike the major industrial centers of the Eastern and Midwestern United States, which came to depend upon coal from nearby coalfields to fuel electricity generation, Honolulu's fuel of choice was oil, which could easily be shipped by sea from the two oil-producing regions. The amount of oil imported into Hawaii from the U.S. mainland has declined over the years. Today, 88 percent of Hawaii's oil imports originate in foreign lands, with the leading suppliers being Indonesia, Vietnam, Saudi Arabia, Thailand, and Brunei. The comparative figure for the nation as a whole is 66 percent.[7] Hawaii is not only much more reliant on oil for electricity generation than the United States as a whole, but the state is also more reliant on foreign suppliers as well.

The growth that Honolulu experienced during and following the Second World War gave further impetus to an oil-based energy sector. Particularly instrumental was travel by jet aircraft, which led to significant growth in Honolulu's population. Between 1950 and 1960, the population of Oahu expanded by 41 percent, from 353,000 to 500,000. Additional growth pushed the island's population to more than 630,000 in 1970. As population grew, so did the number of cars on Honolulu's roads. Local oil refinery capacity expanded to produce fuel for planes and cars, further deepening Honolulu's reliance upon oil.

As with every American city, Honolulu experienced disruptions as a result of the oil crises of the 1970s. However, given its overdependence upon oil for electricity generation, the impact upon Honolulu and Hawaii was much more profound. Between 1972, the last full year before the Arab oil embargo began in October 1973, and 1982 when oil shortages resulting from the Iranian Revolution began to subside, global oil prices increased from about $2 a barrel to almost $40, equivalent to a rise from about $20 to $100 a barrel if measured in real 2008 dollars. Retail electricity prices in Hawaii during this period increased by almost 500 percent, from $0.025 per kilowatt-hour (kWh) to over $0.11 per kWh. The price rise resulting from the 1973 Arab oil embargo caused airlines to cancel flights between Honolulu and the mainland United States and Japan. A decline in tourism increased unemployment, which peaked during this period at 9.9 percent in January 1976, two percentage points higher than the nation as a whole.[8]

These events prompted Hawaii's first significant foray into renewable energy. In June 1974, the Hawaii Natural Energy Institute was created at the University of Hawaii. The institute's purpose was to "coordinate and undertake the development of non-polluting natural energy resources."[9] An energy planning and conservation program was also created within the state's Department of Business, Economic Development and Tourism. Perhaps the most prominent outcome of efforts launched during the 1970s was development of the Puna Geothermal Venture, which commenced operation on the Big Island of Hawaii in 1981, producing three megawatts of electricity. The initial Puna plant was intended as an experimental project and closed in 1989. A newer, larger geothermal generating facility commenced operation nearby in 1993. The second plant currently has a generating capacity of 30 megawatts of electricity, equivalent to 20 percent of the Big Island's power needs, and plans exist for its expansion.[10] The Puna project will, however, do little to meet the needs of Hawaii's economic and population center of Honolulu, because the Big Island is separated from Oahu by more than 200 nautical miles of water. At the present time no electrical transmission links exist between any of the Hawaiian Islands. As will be seen, establishing a grid that will allow electricity supplied by Oahu's neighboring islands to be transmitted to Honolulu is a key objective of the Hawaii Clean Energy Initiative.

The Hawaii Clean Energy Initiative

The global price of oil began to decline during the mid-1980s, offering relief to consumers in Hawaii and across the nation. This continued despite a price upswing associated with the first Gulf War in 1990. Following a price cut by Saudi Arabia, a barrel of crude oil could be purchased for an average price of $14.44 in 1986. Generally low prices continued, despite a brief price upswing associated with the first Gulf War in 1990. Disregarding the brief price spike during and following the 1990 invasion of Iraq, prices rose again gradually before dropping below $15 in 1998 due to the Asian currency crisis. Prices began a gradual climb again in the period preceding and surrounding the September 11 attacks. Afterward the world price of crude oil began to climb steadily, driven in large part by a growing U.S. domestic and global economy and by rising demand from China and East Asia. In August 2005, the price reached $60 per barrel before continuing on a rapid price escalation that brought the average global price of crude oil peaking at an "eye-watering" $140 per barrel in July 2008.[11]

Electricity rates in Hawaii paralleled the rise in oil prices. In July 1992 the average cost of a kilowatt-hour of electricity across all end use customers in Hawaii stood at $0.09, ninth highest in the United States. By July 2001, the U.S. Energy Information Administration reported that Hawaii was home to the highest retail electricity rates in the county, at $0.142 per kWh. According to figures presented at a workshop in 2005 titled *Energy and Hawaii: The Need for Options, Strategic Integrated Policies, and Change*, between 1990 and 2003, the average cost of electricity on Oahu increased by 37 percent. Across Hawaii as a whole, the increase was 62 percent. Nationwide, the figure was only 13 percent.[12] By July 2005, the average in Hawaii stood at $0.187 per kWh; it rose to more than $0.20 in October of the same year. With global oil prices rising to over $140 per barrel in July 2008, electricity rates reached $0.49 during peak periods of energy use, four times the national average. The *Wall Street Journal* reported electricity prices in Honolulu as having "gone through the roof."[13] Yet the most expensive electricity rates of any large municipality in the country did not ensure that Honolulu's businesses and residents could be secure in the knowledge that when they reached to turn on the lights, the lights would indeed go on. While little additional capacity had been added to Oahu's power grid in recent years, electricity consumption had increased significantly. The increase was driven in large part by increased use of home air conditioning, which rose by a third between 1996 and 2005. As a result, Hawaiian Electric Company (HECO), the electric utility serving all of Oahu, which normally seeks to maintain a 30 percent margin of electricity generating supply over the peak amount consumed at any given time, found its reserve margins approaching only 20 percent. Honolulu was facing not only the most expensive electricity in the country, but uncertainty over the sufficiency of the island's capacity to generate electricity as well.

In the aftermath of the March 2003 invasion of Iraq, President George W. Bush began to focus upon increasing the nation's energy security by encouraging substitution of domestic sources for imported fuels. CNN summarized a speech the president made in laying out his approach. Arguing that U.S. dependence on overseas oil imports amounts to a "foreign tax on the American people," CNN reported, "President Bush on Wednesday proposed a series of energy initiatives, including more oil refineries and nuclear plants, to combat the problem."[14] With the highest electricity rates in the country, greater reliance upon oil did not, however, strike Hawaii's residents as a solution to their energy conundrum, and they had essentially outlawed construction of nuclear generating plants. The possibility of importing liquefied natural gas (LNG) to fuel electricity generation in Honolulu had been discussed on and off over the years but was largely dismissed due to concerns over price volatility and also, public safety risks associated with a possible terrorist strike at an LNG facility in the urbanized, densely populated area surrounding the port of Honolulu.

Estimates are that Hawaii exports between $6 and $7 billion annually to purchase oil, equivalent to perhaps 10 percent of gross state product.[15] Instead of looking to perpetuate dependence upon fossil fuels to secure its energy future, the leaders and people of Honolulu and Hawaii decided that their best approach was in accelerating a transition to clean renewable energy and increasing the efficient use of electricity. The result was the Hawaii Clean Energy Initiative (HCEI), unveiled by Governor Linda Lingle to the public in January 2008. Although HCEI is essentially simply an agreement, rather than official government regulations or policy, and lacks the force of law, HCEI seeks to serve as a major focal point and guidance document to drive a fundamental and sustained transformation in the way in which energy resources are planned, developed, paid for, and used.[16]

HCEI is a collaborative partnership bringing together the state of Hawaii, HECO, and the U.S. Department of Energy. Although the HCEI is a statewide effort, the main focus of HCEI is of course, Honolulu, where the majority of Hawaii's electricity is consumed. To achieve the oil reduction goal, the state and HECO have committed to "having 70 percent of its energy use come from clean energy sources by 2030."[17]

In 2009, the aspirations embedded in the HCEI were translated into law when Governor Lingle signed Act 155. The act requires that, by 2030, 40 percent of all electricity consumed in Hawaii must be generated from renewable energy resources, including wind and solar energy, marine energy including ocean wave generation, and geothermal energy. In addition, Act 155 calls for accelerated energy efficiency measures that will reduce overall energy consumption by an additional 30 percent from the amount of electricity that would otherwise be projected to be consumed in Honolulu in 2030.

HCEI involves dozens of other initiatives, including a commitment by HECO and the island's other electric utilities to add approximately 1,122 megawatts of additional new renewable energy resources throughout Hawaii by 2030. The focus of the balance of this chapter is upon the regulatory changes and technology investments that Hawaii will need to embrace if the goals of the Clean Energy Initiative, "among the most ambitious in the world," according to the *Wall Street Journal*, are to be realized.[18]

Regulatory Changes

Attainment of the HCEI renewable energy goals requires several types of regulatory changes to the system by which Hawaii has traditionally regulated HECO and the other investor-owned utilities that supply electricity to Hawaiians. Historically, Hawaii's approach to electric utility regulation has been to rely upon a standard model that has evolved over the last century. Under this model, electric utilities have an obligation to serve all customers in their service territories. Utilities generate or purchase from third party "merchant" power developers electricity needed to serve their customers and in return are protected from competition from other utilities. Rates are determined by regulatory proceedings based upon the concept that utilities are entitled to recover their reasonable costs of providing service and a reasonable rate of return on their invested capital. In practice, this has meant that utilities had an incentive to sell increasing amounts of power since they earned revenue based upon the total number of kilowatt-hours they sold. This approach has traditionally worked well in ensuring an adequate supply of power to consumers. However in recent years, deregulation, inflation, increases in oil prices, increased construction costs, and a variety of other factors have caused rates to rise. While Hawaii's involvement in deregulation has been limited, its electric rates have historically been extremely high because of its dependence on imported oil as a fuel source. Moreover, because Hawaii is not interconnected to the adjacent electric grids of other utilities, it is unable to import inexpensive generation that is available elsewhere during nonpeak periods—generally times other than normal workweek hours.

HCEI renewable energy goals required a departure from this historical model by decoupling electricity sales by HECO and Hawaii's other electric utilities from the amount of revenue received by the companies. As noted, the traditional model of utility regulation provided HECO an incentive to sell an increasing amount of electricity to consumers. The result is to undervalue investment in low-cost energy-efficiency measures that could reduce the demand for electricity. In February 2010, the Hawaii Public Utilities Commission issued an order requiring that HECO and the island's other utilities use a different method for calculating how they will earn their revenues. Under the new, decoupled method, the PUC will set a revenue level for HECO based upon a level of electricity services that it authorizes the company to deliver to Honolulu's consumers. The actual rates HECO can charge for the electricity it sells will be adjusted based upon varying sales levels. Under this decoupled regulatory regime, HECO will be allowed to recover the costs it incurs in supplying electricity, "but not earn additional profit from higher sales. This model provides greater support for energy efficiency and conservation and achievement of Hawaii's clean energy goals."[19]

A second area of regulatory change pertains to the state's Renewable Portfolio Standard (RPS). Traditionally utilities have been free to generate or purchase power from whatever source they sought. Because they were monopolies protected from competition, utilities often lacked an incentive to minimize costs. Beginning in the 1980s, regulatory authorities nationwide began requiring utilities to employ what is called integrated least cost planning as a way of accelerating investments in energy efficiency into the utility fuel mix. The RPS can be seen as an extension of least cost planning in that it requires utilities to procure a certain amount of their generating mix from renewable energy resources. While least cost planning often emphasizes energy efficiency measures as the least expensive way of adjusting energy demand to supply, RPS directly targets renewable energy resources.

Under Hawaii's RPS, HECO and other electric utilities must by statutory requirement acquire specific percentages of electrical energy from nonfossil fuel energy resources.[20] Hawaii first established a voluntary RPS in 2001 under which the state's utilities were encouraged to supply 9 percent of the electricity they sold to consumers from renewable energy resources. In 2004 the RPS was made mandatory, with the goal raised so that 20 percent of the state's electricity had to be generated from renewable sources by 2020. With passage of Act 155, the RPS goal was raised again to 10 percent of net electricity sales from renewable energy by 2010, 15 percent by 2015, 25 percent by 2020, and 40 percent by 2030.[21]

Hawaii's RPS allows utilities to count energy savings toward attainment of the renewable energy goal until 2015. Electric utilities can satisfy the RPS requirements not only via renewable electrical energy but also through use of energy-efficiency measures that reduce the amount of electricity consumed. Hawaii's RPS also includes a penalty of $20 for each megawatt hour the utility falls short of the RPS. The penalty may be waived, however, under certain circumstances deemed to be outside the utility's control. Hawaii's RPS provides one leg of the regulatory framework that will guide the state during its anticipated twenty-year transition to a 70 percent clean energy sector by 2030.

A third regulatory leg upon which Hawaii aims to construct its clean energy future is in the form of a feed-in-tariff, or FIT. A FIT is an innovative policy mechanism that has been demonstrated to spur development of renewable energy. A FIT consists of a set of standardized, published purchased power rates, terms, and conditions that set the amount a utility is required to pay to renewable energy developers who construct and operate wind farms, solar arrays, and other renewable energy generating technologies.[22] FITs have been established in seventy-five countries, states, and provinces around the world and are responsible for 75 percent of all solar photovoltaic and 45 percent of all wind-generating capacity developed worldwide.[23] FITs provide renewable energy developers and investors assurance that they will receive a predetermined, fixed price for the electricity they sell to the utilities. This provides a degree of certainty to the investors who finance renewable energy development because their revenue stream becomes predictable in what would otherwise be a potentially volatile energy market.

Although the price has been coming down in recent years, at the present time it still generally costs more to generate renewable energy than to generate energy from traditional fossil fuels. In part, this is due to the unpredictability surrounding the availability of wind and sunshine to generate renewable energy from these technologies. According to the U.S. Energy Information Administration projections, it will cost an estimated $104 to generate a megawatt-hour of electricity from coal in 2016, when measured in 2008 prices.[24] The comparable figure for generating electricity from the burning of natural gas is estimated at between $83 and $123. For onshore wind energy, the figure is $149 and for photovoltaic solar, $396.[25] The FIT blends the cost of adding renewable energy to a power grid into the cost of other, lower cost generating resources. The effect is to "level the playing field" by lowering the net cost of renewable generation to consumers. Although FITs have been controversial in some areas they have been used in Europe extensively, particularly in Germany and Spain, where they have contributed to significant expansion in the amount of wind and solar energy being generated. Hawaii is among the first states in the United States to adopt a FIT. Combined with Hawaii's RPS, the FIT aims to provide the regulatory and price stability and predictability to underwrite development of new renewable energy generation in Honolulu and on Oahu's neighboring islands.

Climate Change and Energy Transformation

High oil prices are undoubtedly the principal driving force behind the HCEI. However, HCEI is also in part driven by the need to address how climate change will affect Honolulu's unique environmental, cultural, and economic resources. As in other parts of the world, global warming is influencing the climate in Honolulu and the Hawaiian Islands. Global warming is expected to lead to increased air temperature, decreased rainfall and stream flow, increased storm intensity, a higher sea level and surface temperatures, and ocean acidification.

Sea level rise is of particular concern to Honolulu, which extends to the water's edge and includes Waikiki's famed shoreline. The changing climate is causing the global mean sea level to rise in two ways: warmer ocean waters take up greater volume, and melting glaciers and ice fields increase the amount of water in the oceans. University of Hawaii scientists have concluded that the sea level has risen in Hawaii at approximately 0.6 inches per decade during the last century. Waikiki, a key economic driver of Honolulu and the state, may be particularly vulnerable to the economic impacts of rising sea levels. Coastal erosion is also a significant related concern. A function of rising sea levels, ocean waves and currents, and human alteration of the natural environment, coastal erosion threatens the loss of valuable beachfront property in Honolulu. It threatens buildings, roadways, public services, and community infrastructure. Faced with chronic erosion, shoreline property owners in Honolulu often resort to construction of seawalls, which further aggravates beach loss. It is estimated that approximately 25 percent of Oahu's beaches have been lost to seawall construction and 72 percent of the neighboring island of Kauai's beaches are chronically eroding.[26]

In 2007, declaring that climate change poses a serious threat to the economic well-being, public health, natural resources, and the environment of Hawaii, the

Hawaii legislature passed major climate change legislation known as Act 234.[27] Act 234 does not specify enforceable limits on emissions but instead grants a broad mandate to the State of Hawaii Department of Health to adopt adminis-trative rules to achieve the emissions limit. These rules are to be developed by a greenhouse gas emissions reduction task force comprising members from the government, business, academic, and environmental sectors. Act 234 took effect in July 2007, making Hawaii among the first states in the nation to pass a law with a greenhouse gas emissions reduction limit. The act's emissions limit is con-sistent with the limit established by the Kyoto Protocol and climate change laws adopted by California, Washington, New Jersey, and Florida. Key provisions of Act 234 have been codified in Chapter 342B, Hawaii's air pollution control law. These climate change–related amendments to Chapter 342B are subject to its existing enforcement provisions, including civil and administrative penalties. Also authorized are lawsuits by private individuals against companies in violation of greenhouse gas emissions limits and against state agencies for failing to en-force the law.

In June 2010 a broad coalition of elected officials and community leaders from Hawaii issued a call for the federal government to adopt legislation to limit atmospheric green house gas emissions. Summing up the concerns of many Hawaiians was Henk Rogers, a local entrepreneur and founder of the Honolulu-based clean energy advocacy group Blue Planet Foundation. Speaking on World Oceans Day, Rogers said he and others involved "are committed to ending fossil fuel use in Hawaii." While it cannot be said that climate change was the primary impetus to Hawaii's embrace of the HCEI, laws passed to address climate change may act as a further spur development of a clean energy future for Honolulu.[28]

Big Wind and Undersea Transmission Cable

One of the most important initiatives to accelerate renewable energy develop-ment to meet electricity demand in Honolulu is the wind farms contemplated for the islands of Molokai and Lanai. These islands lie to the southeast of Oahu, separated by a strait that at its narrowest is twenty miles across. Both islands are a part of Maui County and are subject to strong trade winds that blow from the southeast across the northern Pacific Ocean. The U.S. Department of Energy uses a seven-point scale to rate the wind energy potential of any given part of the United States. Whereas some selected portions of Oahu are rated highly, these are located along the island's mostly urbanized south coast or on protected lands and not suitable for large-scale wind farm development. In contrast, there are sections of sparsely inhabited western and southern Molokai and Lanai that are rated at six or seven—outstanding or superb—on the wind power classification rating scale.[29] Wind turbines can be interspaced on the island's agricultural lands. Current plans call for construction of wind farms with a generating capacity of 200 megawatts on each island, with 100 megawatts being enough to power an average of 20,000 homes in Honolulu.[30]

The so-called Big Wind agreement arising out of the HCEI aims to transmit wind-generated electricity from Molokai and Lanai to meet demand in Honolulu. This will require construction of an undersea cable across the more than twenty-mile ocean strait that separates the neighboring islands from Oahu. Undersea electric transmission cables are a mature technology and have been constructed elsewhere. The longest currently in operation spans 360 miles between Norway and the Netherlands, and plans have been announced to install a cable under the North Sea that would transmit hydroelectricity from Norway to Britain.[31] Work began on an environmental impact statement for the Hawaii cable in June of 2010. Current estimates are that construction of the first phase of the cable could begin in 2012 at a cost of as much as $1 billion. The start date may be an overly ambitious estimate. The environmental review will involve a multitude of federal agencies and must comply with Hawaii's strict environmental laws. A significant potential for delay exists for any complex environmental review process involving multiple agencies. A similar cable was considered to carry geothermal electricity from the Big Island to Oahu in the 1980s but failed due to technical problems, high cost, and public opposition. Nonetheless, if all goes according to plan, construction of the cable would involve a later extension to the island of Maui, to tap the significant wind power potential of that island. Construction of the cable would, for the first time, tie several of the Hawaiian islands into a single interconnected electrical transmission system.

One outstanding issue that has not been completely resolved regards the construction of the wind farms themselves. In March 2009 it was announced that two investor-owned wind power developers had agreed to build wind farms on Molokai. Beginning in 2006, one of the merchant wind developers, First Wind, began discussing its plans to build a wind farm on homestead lands owned by native Hawaiians, who comprise a larger proportion of the population on Molokai than on any of the other Hawaiian Islands. The homestead lands were created by the federal government in 1921 through the Hawaiian Homes Commission Act, which set aside land for homesteading by native Hawaiians. However, First Wind concluded available homestead sites were inadequate for large-scale wind farming and subsequently shifted its attention to what is known as the Molokai Ranch. Owned by an Asian financial concern, Molokai Ranch occupies about one-third of the island and has been historically used for cattle farming. A resort hotel has also been operated on the property. The ranch's future has been subject to a contentious battle for some time. The property owner's attempts to develop upscale housing and hotels have evoked sharp opposition from island residents. During the 1990s, protesters destroyed five miles of pipes that served the ranch and engaged in other acts of vandalism. In the face of persistent opposition to its development plans, the property's owner announced in 2007 that it would close down the ranch's lodge.

In 2008, First Wind announced that it was committing $50 million to the Ho'i I Ka Pono (To Restore Righteousness) campaign on Molokai. Under this arrangement, the Molokai Ranch property would be placed in a land trust. First Wind would lease portions of the property for wind farm construction and operation.[32] However, in July 2010 the owner of Molokai Ranch announced that it had rejected the $50 million offer to purchase the property, which the owner said was worth $300 million. The property owner also stated that any property sale would be contingent upon an expression of community support for wind farming on the property. While local organizations such as the Molokai Community Service Council have supported the effort to build the wind farms on Molokai Ranch, other preservationists on the island have objected on the grounds that they do "not want to see wind turbines mar the beauty of the land in their backyards."[33]

Whether Molokai Ranch will prove to be the location of First Wind's wind farm remains uncertain. It's possible that plans to construct and operate wind farms needed to attain the HCEI goals might be embroiled in the sort of conflicts that have divided cultural preservationists and environmentalists over plans to build renewable energy farms elsewhere. An example can be found in Massachusetts where plans to construct the Cape Wind offshore wind farm in Nantucket Sound have been delayed by conflicts over aesthetics and cultural considerations. Likewise, plans to construct concentrated solar power farms in the Mojave Desert of California have been stymied by opposition from environmentalists concerned about the effects of these projects on endangered species.[34] As the *Economist* has written, "the odd thing about conflicts over wind is that, usually, each side claims to be greener than the other."[35] It is an irony of the movement to create a renewable energy future that it often creates tension among environmentalists and other sympathetic community groups in seeking both to reduce the nation's dependence upon fossil fuels and at the same time, preserve sensitive land and wildlife in appealing aesthetic settings.

Another unresolved issue that surrounds the plan to build wind farms on Molokai pertains to the price at which power generated there will be sold to consumers on Honolulu. HECO has announced that it will purchase the electricity that First Wind generates on Molokai and distribute this to its Honolulu consumers. However, the cost of this energy to the consumer has yet to be determined. This will depend upon the rates that HECO will pay it under long-term power purchase agreements. Initially at least, Hawaii's FIT will pertain only to renewable energy projects of five megawatts of generating capacity or less. Although the large wind projects planned for Molokai are therefore likely to be excluded from the initial FIT program due to their size, the rates obtained through power purchase agreements may well be influenced by the outcome of the FIT proceeding before the Hawaii Public Utility Commission. In September 2009 the PUC issued an order that created a FIT. However it did not establish the actual rates at which HECO would be required to purchase renewable energy from renewable energy generators. Several issues divide the parties involved in the FIT proceedings, which include, in addition to HECO, the state's Department of Business, Economic Development, and Tourism and the state's Division of Consumer Advocacy of the Department of Commerce and Consumer Affairs. Included among these issues is the cost HECO should have to pay to purchase renewable energy and accordingly, how these costs would be passed on to consumers. While progress has been made in efforts to connect Honolulu to the potential for wind generation on neighboring islands, questions remain with regard to the undersea cable, the siting of the wind farms, and at what cost the wind generated electricity will be sold to Honolulu's households and businesses.

Electric Vehicles

In January 2010, a new electric vehicle arrived in Honolulu. The Nissan Rogue that arrived is a hand-built automobile whose unveiling was aimed at showcasing plans to place up to 50,000 electric vehicles on Honolulu's roads by 2020 and up to 200,000 by 2030.[36] The latter figure is equal to about 20 percent of all vehicles on Honolulu's roadways today.[37] The vehicle's arrival is part of an initiative that brings together HECO and Better Place, a Palo Alto, California–based, investor-owned venture. Better Place does not actually build or sell vehicles but builds and operates battery swap stations. Car buyers would purchase the electric vehicles with installed battery packs owned by Better Place. When a vehicle's battery began to run down, the driver would pull into a battery swap station shaped like a car wash. The old battery would be removed for recharging and subsequent installation in another vehicle and a new fully charged battery would be installed.

Although the demonstration vehicle unveiled in January 2010 was built at a cost of $200,000, electric vehicles offered for sale in Honolulu are expected to cost significantly less. Better Place has already initiated battery swap service in Israel and has entered into an agreement with French automaker Renault for production of 100,000 battery swap vehicles expected to sell for about $20,000 apiece. The company is involved in negotiations to install the battery swap stations with the City and County of Honolulu, some of which may be placed on municipally owned properties.

Battery swap technology is not the only electric vehicle technology being considered to reduce Honolulu's reliance upon imported oil. In 2009, Governor Lingle signed into law a requirement that all public and private parking facilities having 100 parking spaces or more designate 1 percent of the parking spaces exclusively for electric vehicles and install technology to allow these vehicles to be charged. Hawaii is the first state in the nation to enact such a law. Also, in July 2010, HECO filed for permission from the Hawaii PUC to begin a small-scale pilot project under which owners of plug-in electric vehicles who charge their batteries during off-peak hours would be charged a lower electricity rate than if they charge their vehicles during peak electrical use hours.

Honolulu's efforts to accelerate the market for electric vehicles would appear to hold promise. Drivers tend to prove reluctant to purchase electric vehicles until they are assured that an adequate recharging network is in place. At the same time, charging network providers tend to be reluctant to make the investments needed to install charging stations until a sufficient number of electric vehicles are on the road to create demand and generate revenue. Most of the driving on the island of Oahu is within the highly urbanized core of Honolulu. Only drivers in New York, Rhode Island, Alaska, and the District of Columbia average fewer miles driven per year than Hawaii's drivers. The length of Oahu's shoreline is only 227 miles, reducing the expense of installing charging stations at a density needed to assure drivers that they will not find themselves stranded with a dead battery.

If the electric vehicle program is successful, increased use of electric vehicles in Honolulu will not only reduce oil consumption but also create demand for electricity planned to be generated by renewable technologies, providing further impetus to development of the wind farms on Oahu's neighboring islands. It's too early to gauge the success of efforts to accelerate electric vehicle use in Honolulu. Despite the program's relatively small scale, among the supporters of the filing HECO made to offer incentives for those who charge their electric vehicles during off-peak hours was the Hawaii Automobile Dealers Association, which hailed HECO's filing as an "extraordinary announcement."[38] Whereas the U.S. automobile industry has often proved in the past to be resistant to efforts to expand the nation's fleet of electric vehicles, in Honolulu, at least, it appears that the move toward greater electric vehicle use is gaining widespread support.

Honolulu Sea Water Air Conditioning

Another key component of the plan to make Honolulu more energy independent lies in sea water air conditioning. Known as SWAC, plans call for forty of the largest commercial office buildings totaling 12.5 million square feet in Honolulu's downtown core to have their air conditioning connected to a system that will reduce the amount of generated electricity needed to cool these buildings.

The SWAC will involve extending pipes as far as 4 miles from Honolulu's beaches into the Pacific Ocean to a depth of more than 1,700 feet to access water at a temperature of 44 degrees (see figure 7.1). The cool water will be drawn ashore to lower the amount of energy needed to chill fresh water to 44 degrees, the temperature at which conventional chilled water air conditioning systems run. The air conditioning systems of the buildings will not need to be replaced. They will simply be connected to the SWAC system via heat exchangers. Approximately 35 to 45 percent of the energy used in Honolulu's downtown commercial towers is used for air conditioning, and the SWAC is expected to reduce the need for as much as 14 megawatts of new electrical generating capacity, equivalent to a full year of future load growth projected for HECO in the absence of SWAC construction.[39]

The SWAC is similar to district heating systems that have been used elsewhere in which excess heat from industrial cogeneration, or combined heat and

FIGURE 7.1. Computer rendered image illustrating how the deepwater inflow pipe will serve the Sea Water Air Conditioning district system planned for downtown Honolulu.

power systems, are used to supply heat to commercial and residential buildings. The largest district heating system in the world is currently in operation in Vienna, Austria. The largest system in the United States operates in St. Paul, Minnesota. Large-scale district cooling is less common. Cornell University operates a system to air condition campus buildings, and a system operates in Toronto. Once operating, Honolulu's SWAC would be the largest deep sea water air conditioning system in the world.

The idea for installing SWAC in Honolulu first emerged during the 1990s. With adoption of HCEI, in 2008 the state authorized nine companies to issue up to $392 million in tax-exempt revenue bonds to support clean energy projects. Included was Honolulu Sea Water Air Conditioning LLC, the developer of the SWAC project, which was authorized to issue up to $100 million in tax exempt bonds. In July 2008 it was announced that HSWAC had raised $10.75 million in independent funding, with more than half this amount coming from local Hawaii-based investors. However, tightening credit conditions stemming from the economic downturn have led to difficulties in raising additional capital. In February 2009, the *Pacific Business Journal* reported that none of the bonds for which the tax-exempt financing had been authorized had yet been sold. Meanwhile the cost of the SWAC project has escalated from an initial estimate of $152 million to $200 million and may potentially rise to as much as $240 million.[40] Plans call for construction of the SWAC to begin in late 2011 but this now looks unlikely. By the same measure that volatility in oil markets has given Honolulu the highest electricity prices in the United States, the investment needed to propel the transition to a clean energy future appears contingent upon the willingness of capital market to finance projects such as HSWAC and fluctuations in the U.S. and global economies.

Energy Efficiency and Green Buildings

As noted earlier, reaching Hawaii's goal of a 70 percent clean energy economy by 2030 will require that new renewable energy generating technology is accompanied by improvements in the efficient use of energy. Act 155 directs the PUC to create a statewide Energy Efficiency Portfolio Standard (EEPS).[41] The PUC commenced proceedings aimed at designing the EEPS, including how it will be financed, in March 2010. Under Hawaii's RPS, progress toward reducing the use of oil for electricity generation is measured in terms of new renewable energy generation added to Honolulu's power grid. The EEPS is similar in concept in that it will likely set a mandatory statewide electricity-use reduction target. The EEPS aims to achieve energy savings by ensuring that new buildings are constructed to incorporate technologies that increase energy efficiency and that existing buildings are retrofitted to increase their efficient use of energy. The aim is for Hawaii's EEPS to save 4,300 gigawatt hours of electricity by 2030, equivalent to 30 percent of total projected electricity load in the same year. The U.S. Department of Energy's National Renewable Energy Laboratory has estimated that it could cost as much as $4.1 billion in energy efficiency investments to reach the 2030 target with much of the costs to be incurred in improving efficient energy use in the many high-rise commercial, hotel, and apartment buildings that populate Honolulu's urban core. NREL has concluded that achieving this level of investment will likely require that incentives be provided to private property owners to encourage them to install needed energy efficiency improvements.[42] Determining how and by whom the cost of providing these incentives will be paid will be a central issue for the PUC as it moves ahead with its EEPS design process.

Most state government buildings in Hawaii are located in Honolulu and new state buildings standards have been adopted in an attempt to bring them into compliance with the EEPS goals. A Green Building Law signed into law in May 2006 requires that all new state government buildings constructed in Honolulu and elsewhere be built to LEED (Leadership in Energy and Environmental Design) Silver green building rating standards. As an incentive for private builders, the City and County of Honolulu and the other county governments must give priority in reviewing applications for projects to be built to LEED Silver specifications. In February 2006, the City and County of Honolulu adopted an ordinance requiring that any buildings of 5,000 gross square feet or larger constructed by the municipality must also be built to LEED Silver requirements.[43]

Similar measures apply to residential construction. For example, the Green Building Law also requires that, beginning in 2010, all newly constructed single family homes must incorporate solar water heaters. The steps being taken to improve the energy efficiency of buildings are not limited to adaption of technologies, however. For example, state law governing community associations has been revised so associations may not prohibit the hanging of clotheslines in sunny areas of association properties. As this example suggests, in Honolulu, both high- and low-technology solutions are being embraced in the effort to speed the transformation to a clean energy future.

Conclusion

The Hawaii Clean Energy Initiative seeks to transform Honolulu, the island state's preponderant population and economic center, from a municipality that depends upon oil-fired electricity generation for almost 90 percent of its electricity generation to one primarily dependent upon renewable energy and more efficient use of energy. The reach of the HCEI extends to almost the entirety of Honolulu's energy infrastructure. HCEI aims to substitute wind and solar power generation for oil by constructing an undersea cable that may for the first time link several of Hawaii's islands into a single, interconnected electrical grid. Honolulu plans to air condition buildings by drawing upon cold waters from beneath the ocean waves that wash upon Oahu's shores and put in place infrastructure that can fuel the widespread expansion of electric vehicle use on Oahu's roads, reducing reliance upon oil for transportation. Underlying the HCEI are regulatory changes that place Honolulu in the forefront of efforts to both increase the supply of clean energy and, at the same time, generate demand for these same clean energy sources.

Honolulu's aggressive efforts at energy transformation are born of historical forces, including its isolation as an island city located at the maritime crossroads between global oil suppliers. With regard to the prospects for success, while Honolulu appears to be embracing highly innovative steps to reduce its dependence upon oil, its experience to date also points to the possibility that its progress may be impeded by financial circumstances beyond local control and be subject to conflicts that have the unfortunate consequence of sometimes pitting environmental advocates at odds with each other. This said, it is a hopeful sign that Honolulu's efforts to transform its energy sector do seem to be benefitting from broadly shared public and political support. The HCEI was championed and signed into law by a Republican governor at the same time that Republican President George Bush was calling for greater reliance upon fossil fuels to meet the nation's energy challenges. Writing in 1932, the late Supreme Court Justice Louis Brandies famously referred to the U.S. states as laboratories of democracy. Honolulu's efforts to transform itself from an oil-dependent to a clean-energy-dependent economy are reflected in HCEI, a statewide initiative. However, Honolulu has striven to go beyond state mandates, as demonstrated by new regulatory requirements pertaining to green building construction and the installation of electric vehicle fueling stations, for example. We can conclude therefore that when it comes to its efforts at energy transformation, among America's cities, Honolulu comprises its own laboratory. Honolulu's experience is one worth watching by other localities that are seeking to reduce their dependence upon fossil fuels and create a more sustainable, energy-independent, and climate-friendly environment.

Notes

1. U.S. Census Bureau, "Honolulu CDP, Hawaii," *State & County Quickfacts*, 2010, http://quickfacts.census.gov/qfd/states/15/1517000.html; State of Hawaii Department of Business, Economic Development and Tourism, *2009 State of Hawaii Data Book*, www.hawaii.gov/dbedt/; and U.S. Bureau of the Census, *Federal-State Cooperative Program for Population Estimates*, release date: March 19, 2009.

2. U.S. Department of Labor, Bureau of Labor Statistics, 2010, www.bls.gov/home.htm.

3. State of Hawaii Department of Business, Economic Development and Tourism, Strategic Industries Division, *Energy and Hawaii: The Need for Options, Strategic Integrated Policies, and Change*, 2005, http://hawaii.gov/dbedt/info/energy/publications/briefing050120.ppt.

4. Hawaii State Constitution, art. XI, sec. 8. http://hawaii.gov/lrb/con/conart11.html.

5. Burl Burlingame, "Happy Hundredth: Despite Debate on Its Birthdates, the City Is Ready to Celebrate," *Honolulu Star-Bulletin*, June 26, 2005, http://archives.starbulletin.com/2005/06/26/features/story1.html.

6. California Department of Conservation, *Oil and Gas Statistics: 2007 Annual Report*, (Sacramento, California, December 31, 2007), ftp://ftp.consrv.ca.gov/pub/oil/annual_reports/2007/0102stats_07.pdf; William H. Frederick and Robert L. Worden, eds. *Indonesia: A Country Study*. Washington: GPO for the Library of Congress, 1993. http://countrystudies.us/indonesia/.

7. Hawaiian Electric Company, "Fuel Oil Use in Hawaii," August 2009, www.heco.com/vcmcontent/StaticFiles/pdf/FuelOilUse_8-2009.pdf; U.S. Department of Energy, Energy Information Administration, "Crude Oil and Total Petroleum Imports" (Washington, D.C., July 29, 2010), www.eia.doe.gov/pub/oil_gas/petroleum/data_publications/company_level_imports/current/import.html.

8. U.S. Department of Energy, Energy Information Administration, "Independent Statistics and Analysis" (Washington, D.C., 2010), www.eia.doe.gov/; *The Ledger.com*, "Unemployment Rate: Hawaii," n.d., www.ledgerdata.com/unemployment/hawaii/1982/august/.

9. Hawaii Natural Energy Institute, "History of HNEI," 2008, www.hnei.hawaii.edu/history.aspat.

10. Puna Geothermal Venture, "History of the Puna Geothermal Venture," 2009, www.punageothermalventure.com/PGV/15/history.

11. *BBC News*, "Oil Price Hits Yet Another Record," July 3, 2008, http://news.bbc.co.uk/2/hi/business/7486764.stm; U.S. Department of Energy, Energy Information Administration, "Independent Statistics and Analysis."

12. State of Hawaii Department of Business, Economic Development and Tourism, *Energy and Hawaii: The Need for Options, Strategic Integrated Policies, and Change* (Honolulu, Hawaii, January 20, 2005).

13. U.S. Department of Energy, Energy Information Administration, "Independent Statistics and Analysis"; Jim Carlton, "Hawaii: The Alternative State," *Wall Street Journal*, June 30, 2008, http://sopogy.com/blog/2008/06/30/wall-street-journal-alternative-state/; U.S. Department of Energy, National Renewable Energy Laboratory, "Energy Imports and High Rates Squeeze the State," September 5, 2008, www.nrel.gov/features/20080905_islands_initiative.html.

14. *CNN*, "Bush Urges More Refineries, Nuclear Plants," April 4, 2005, www.cnn.com/2005/POLITICS/04/27/bush.energy/.

15. Hawaiian Electric Company, n.d., www.heco.com/portal/site/heco/menuitem.20516 707928314340b4c0610c510b1ca/?vgnextoid=c6caf2b154da9010VgnVCM10000053011bac RCRD.

16. State of Hawaii Department of Business, Economic Development and Tourism, *State of Hawaii Energy Resources Coordinator Annual Report 2008*, available at http://hawaii.gov/dbedt/info/energy/publications/erc08.pdf.

17. Office of the Governor of Hawaii, "State and Hawaiian Electric Strike Sweeping Agreement for Hawaiian Energy Future," October 20, 2008, www.heco.com/portal/site/heco /menuitem.508576f78baa14340b4c0610c510b1ca/?vgnextoid=195aca9d24c2d110VgnVCM 1000005c011bacRCRD&vgnextchannel=c6caf2b154da9010VgnVCM10000053011bacRC RD&vgnextfmt=default&vgnextrefresh=1&level=0&ct=article.

18. Jim Carlton, "Hawaii: The Alternative State."

19. Interstate Renewable Energy Council, "Hawaii PUC Approves Method of Electric Rate Decoupling," March 2010, http://irecusa.org/2010/03/hawaii-puc-approves-method-of -electric-rate-decoupling/.

20. See Haw. Rev. Stat. ch. 269, Part V, et seq.

21. Database of State Incentives for Renewable Energy, 2010, www.dsireusa.org/.

22. Hawaiian Electric Company, "Energy Agreement Summary of Key Agreements," n.d., available at http://heco.com/vcmcontent/StaticFiles/pdf/HCEI_Summary-Final.pdf.

23. Scientific American. "Feed In Tariffs Responsible for Three Quarters of World's Solar PV," August 12, 2010, www.scientificamerican.com/article.cfm?id=feed-in-tariffs -responsible-for-thr-2010-08.

24. U.S. Department of Energy, Energy Information Administration, "Estimated Levelized Cost of New Generation Resources, 2016" (Washington D.C., 2010), www.eia.doe .gov/oiaf/aeo/electricity_generation.html.

25. Given that with the exception of Hawaii oil is so rarely used for electricity generation in the United States, prices for oil fueled generation are not projected by the U.S. EIA.

26. C. Fletcher, "Hawaii's Changing Climate" (briefing sheet, Center for Island Climate Adaptation and Policy, 2010), 3–4, available at http://nsgl.gso.uri.edu/new/.

27. 2007 Haw. Sess. Laws, Act 234 §1(a); H.B. 226, 24th Leg. (Haw. 2007).

28. Conservation Council for Hawaii, "Hawaii Leaders Call for Climate Change and Clean Energy legislation on World Ocean Day," June 11, 2010, www.pdamerica.org /articles/chapters/hi-2010-06-11-10-01-40-chapters.php.

29. U.S. Department of Energy, National Renewable Energy Laboratory, "Hawaii, 50 meter Wind Power," March 26, 2010, www.windpoweringamerica.gov/images/windmaps /hi_50m_800.jpg.

30. Solar Energy Industries Association, "Solar Tax Policies Can Add 200,000 New Jobs, Nearly 10,000 Megawatts of Solar Installation," May 19, 2010, http://seia.org/galleries/pdf /Solar_Factsheet_EUP_Full_Study.pdf.

31. *Skyscraper City*, "Longest Undersea Cable in the World," July 9, 2009, www .skyscrapercity.com/showthread.php?t=975420.

32. First Wind, "Hawaii Electric Company Agrees to Buy Energy from First Wind's Molokai Wind Farms," March 17, 2009, www.firstwind.com/aboutFirstWind/news.cfm?ID= 272cced1-b603-4ca2-8581-7e206c1c3103&test.

33. *Hawaii Free Press*, "Molokai Ranch: Protesters to Cash in with Takeover Plan," March 22, 2008, www.hawaiifreepress.com/main/ArticlesMain/tabid/56/articleType /ArticleView/articleId/1711/Molokai-Ranch-Protesters-to-Cash-in-with-Takeover-Plan.aspx.

34. Matthew I. Slavin, "Where the Wind Blows and Sun Shines: A Comparative Analysis of State Renewable Energy Standards," *Renewable Energy World North American* (May/June 2010), 1–4.

35. *Economist.com*, "Wind Energy and Politics: Not on My Beach, Please," August 19, 2010, www.economist.com/node/16846774?story_id=16846774.

36. Nanea Kalani, "Hawaii Electric Car Initiative Will Begin With Infrastructure," *Pacific Business News*, January 10, 2010, http://pacific.bizjournals.com/pacific/stories/2010/01/25/focus2.html.

37. Honolulu Advertiser. "Hawaii Vehicles Nearly Match State's Population." June 25, 2007, http://the.honoluluadvertiser.com/article/2007/Jun/25/ln/FP706250359.html.

38. Nanea Kalani, "HECO to Offer Electric Car Owners Discounted Rates," *Honolulu Civil Beat*, August 13, 2010, www.civilbeat.com/articles/2010/07/28/3143-heco-to-offer-electric-car-owners-discounted-rates/.

39. Honolulu Sea Water Air Conditioning LLC, "The Honolulu Sea Water Air Conditioning Project," December 9, 2008.

40. Peter Myers, "Investors Fund US $10.75 M for Honolulu Seawater Air Conditioning," *Renewable Energy World.com*, July 9, 2008, www.renewableenergyworld.com/rea/news/article/2008/07/investors-fund-us-10-75-m-for-honolulu-seawater-air-conditioning-53000; *Pacific Business Journals.com*, "Revenue Bonds Go Unused as Credit Market Tightens in Hawaii," February 20, 2009, http://pacific.bizjournals.com/pacific/stories/2009/02/23/story8.html.

41. 2009 Haw. Sess. Laws, Act 155, Part VI.

42. U.S. Department of Energy, National Renewable Energy Laboratory, "Hawaii Clean Energy Initiative Existing Building Energy Efficiency Analysis, November 17, 2009–June 30, 2010," NREL/SR-7A2-48318, June 2010.

43. U.S. Green Building Council, "Summary of Government LEED Incentives," March 2009, www.usgbc.org/ShowFile.aspx?DocumentID=2021.

Chapter 8

Clean Waters, Clean City: Sustainable Storm Water Management in Philadelphia

Lynn Mandarano

Two hundred years ago, Philadelphia became famous for many things, one of which was our water system and another, its Greene Country Towne. It is with great pride that I can say that we are now returning to our forebears' understanding of the connection between a green city and clean water.

Howard Neukrug, Director, Office of Watersheds,
Philadelphia Water Department[1]

The city of Philadelphia has historically been among the leaders in urban water management in the United States and abroad. Philadelphia was not only the first city to provide water as a public utility, but it has also pioneered new technologies—such as distributing its water supply through a centralized system, using hydropower for pumps, and installing disinfection systems—that fueled the revolution of water and sanitation services in the United States.[2]

The early motivation to embark on a challenging path to create a secure water supply source for the city's current and future demands stemmed from the

157

need to address stresses to the existing source of water from a series of yellow fever outbreaks, a growing population, and expanding industrial development. Beginning in the early 1800s with construction of a reservoir along the Schuyl-kill River at the outskirts of town and then with the addition of pumping stations, the city created Fairmount Water Works, the first centralized water distribution system in the world. "By the 1830s Fairmount had become the proto-type of a water-supply system for growing urban areas in the United States and abroad."[3] The city's efforts to provide a secure water supply and to protect drinking water quality eventually led the Philadelphia Water Department (PWD) to recognize the link between water quality and land use, which in turn led to purchase of land upstream of the Fairmount Water Works to protect it from industrial development and thus, protect drinking water quality. The initial purchase of the Lemon Hill estate in the mid-1800s was followed by a succession of additional land acquisitions resulting in the creation of Fair-mount Park, at more than 9,200 acres, the largest landscaped park in the United States. The park system has been established along watershed corridors with the specific intent of protecting the city's water sources and is the founda-tion of Philadelphia's watershed protection heritage.[4] For more than 100 years, recognition of the linkage between land use and water quality has served as a basic underlying principle of PWD's approach to urban water resources management.

This chapter traces the path of how Philadelphia built on this heritage of watershed protection and on its understanding of the relationship between land-use development and water quality. The history begins with a bold commitment to a watershed management approach in its 1997 Combined Sewer Overflow program Long-Term Control Plan, which resulted in the formation of seven wa-tershed partnerships—consortiums of environmental organizations, community groups, government agencies, businesses, residents, and other stakeholders.[5] Through these and other local partnerships, PWD undertook highly visible demonstration projects, developed innovative storm water policies and regula-tions, and initiated a host of other initiatives to further protect the drinking water supply and foster sustainable storm water management in the nation's sixth most populous city. The chapter concludes with Philadelphia's most recent commit-ment to green infrastructure instead of traditional gray infrastructure to meet fed-eral Clean Water Act (CWA) requirements.

Urban Water Resources Management

Like many cities in the United States, the city of Philadelphia is faced with the complex problem of trying to provide an affordable and safe drinking water supply and collect and treat wastewater and storm water while meeting the multiple challenges presented by increasingly more stringent and costly environmental regulations, an aging infrastructure, changing demographics, degraded rivers and streams, climate change, flood protection, and the like. This situation gets more complicated in older cities like Philadelphia that have combined sewer systems. In combined sewer systems, storm water—rainwater that runs off impermeable surfaces, for example, streets, parking lots, sidewalks, and roofs—is comingled with wastewaters from homes, businesses, industries, schools, and other sources. The combined sewer systems collect these waters and convey them to a wastewater treatment plant for treatment prior to being released into a surface waterway. However, during moderate to heavy rain events the flow of storm water into combined sewer systems exceeds the carrying capacity resulting in a combined sewer overflow (CSO) of a mixture of storm water and wastewaters into wetlands, lakes, streams, and rivers. CSOs in some communities pose major water quality problems and risks to both aquatic species and public health due to the amount of untreated wastewater introduced into surface waters.

Historically, the mindset influencing the municipal management of storm water and wastewater alike was one that focused on removing water from the built environment as quickly as possible. Impacts to the receiving waters were not a concern. It wasn't until creation of the National Pollutant Discharge Elimination System (NPDES) program, established as a result of the 1972 amendments to the Clean Water Act (CWA), that a national permit program was established to regulate and reduce the discharge of pollutants to lakes, rivers, and streams. NPDES regulates the discharges for municipal and nonmunicipal point sources such as discharges from publically owned treatment plants, industrial plants, and urban storm water runoff. While the CWA and subsequent amendments have realized a steady improvement in water quality, by the early 1990s the United States Environmental Protection Agency (EPA), the scientific community, and its regulated stakeholders realized a different approach was needed to address the problem of CSOs. Hence, the EPA convened a national advisory committee, which resulted in the development of the EPA's CSO Control Policy.

The 1994 CSO Control Policy established guidelines to control and reduce CSOs through NPDES permits.[6] The first milestone required municipalities to implement "nine minimum controls" by January 1, 1997. The nine minimum controls are technology-based solutions including:

1. Proper operation and regular maintenance programs for the sewer system and the CSOs
2. Maximum use of the collection system for storage
3. Review and modification of pretreatment requirements to assure CSO impacts are minimized
4. Maximization of flow to the publicly owned treatment works for treatment
5. Prohibition of CSOs during dry weather
6. Control of solid and floatable materials in CSOs
7. Pollution prevention
8. Public notification to ensure that the public receives adequate notification of CSO occurrences and CSO impacts
9. Monitoring to effectively characterize CSO impacts and the efficacy of CSO controls[7]

In addition, the policy required municipalities to prepare for EPA approval under NPDES permit program long-term control plans. The CSO Control Policy provides municipalities the flexibility to propose programs specific to their CSO needs and financial capabilities. The long-term control plans typically outline municipalities' plans to characterize their combined sewer systems, monitor the impacts of CSOs on waterways, and propose infrastructure projects for CSO control.

In EPA's 2003 Report to Congress Low Impact Development (LID) was added as one of the technologies used to control the timing and volume of storm water discharges.[8] LID techniques included green roofs, bio-retention, porous pavement, and conservation. The EPA notes that while implementation of LID techniques are becoming more mainstream land-use development techniques, their use as a CSO control is limited and more appropriate for use in separate storm water sewer systems. It was not until 2007, when the EPA formed a collaborative effort resulting in the publication of the *Green Infrastructure Action Strategy*, that the EPA embraced green infrastructure as a means to reduce and control CSOs.[9],

In a 2001 report to Congress, the EPA estimates that implementation of the CSO Control Policy has reduced the volume of CSOs from 1.46 trillion gallons per year to a range of 1.26 to 1.29 trillion gallons per year, which represents a 12 to 14 percent reduction. Although a comprehensive database of the cost of implementing CSO controls does not exist, a tally of the costs to forty-eight communities highlights how expensive compliance with the CSO Control Policy is to affected communities. The total cost incurred by the forty-eight communities is $6 billion, with a range of $134,000 to $2.2 billion per community in 2002 dollars.[10] A 1996 needs survey conducted by the EPA estimated the cost to communities to meet the CSO Control Policy goals would be $44.7 billion. However, communities responded that this amount underestimates the cost to comply with water quality standards.[11] A discussion of the comparative costs of CSO controls and more traditional LID techniques is addressed later in this chapter.

Philadelphia's Water Resources

The city of Philadelphia is located at the confluence of two major rivers, the Delaware and the Schuylkill. William Penn, the founder of Philadelphia, chose this location because the waterways provided an abundant source of pristine water and avenues for commerce. Four tributaries also define the local geography (see figure 8.1). This city's three drinking water plants and intakes are situated on the banks of the Delaware and Schuylkill. Because the city sits at the lower end of these waterways with headwaters located in upstream communities outside of the city's jurisdiction, Philadelphia has limited control over the quality of its source waters.

The city of Philadelphia's water resources are managed by the PWD. The drinking water infrastructure consists of three water treatment plants, eighteen reservoirs, and more than 3,000 miles of mains, serving a municipal population of approximately 1.5 million people. The key components of the city's wastewater collection and treatment system include approximately 3,000 miles of pipes, manholes, storm drains, and control chambers; seventeen pump stations; and three wastewater treatment plants. Unsurprising for a city that was already well developed at the time of the Revolutionary War, Philadelphia's water and wastewater infrastructure has aged. Water mains are an average of 78 years old, sewer lines average 100 years, and the average age of the PWD's water plants is 100 years with wastewater plants somewhat newer, having been constructed in

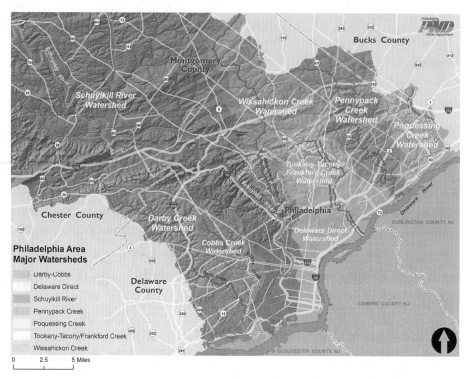

FIGURE 8.1. A contoured map illustrating regional watersheds in the Philadelphia area (Philadelphia Water Department).

the range of 60 to 90 years ago.[12] Maintaining and upgrading this infrastructure is very expensive and one of the main challenges faced by PWD.

The reduction of storm water flows and control of CSOs are of particular concern to the city. Philadelphia was founded in 1682 and incorporated as a city in 1701. At one time, it was the second largest city in the British Empire behind only London. The older areas of the city, comprising roughly 60 percent of the area of the city served by sewers, have combined sewer systems. There are 164 CSOs along the Delaware and Schuylkill Rivers and the Cobbs, Tacony-Frankford, and lower Pennypack Creeks.[13] More important, the city's drinking water intakes are located on the Delaware and Schuylkill Rivers, which are two of the five waterways into which CSOs directly discharge. The CSO discharges are located downstream of the water intakes. The potential threat these CSOs pose to source water quality combined with the city's location at the tail end of these waterways has been critical motivators for Philadelphia's innovative water resources management programs.

Starting in the late 1970s, decision makers assessing the complex water resources problems that transcended political and administrative boundaries started to experiment with watershed management approaches and collaborative partnerships as exemplified by the Chesapeake Bay Program.[14] This new approach to water resources management emerged as a result of dissatisfaction with traditional top-down regulatory approaches that were not capable of addressing multiple water management issues simultaneously. In contrast, a watershed approach focuses on all water concerns simultaneously and uses hydrology rather than governmental jurisdictions to define the geographic planning area. In addition, the watershed approach is multidisciplinary, engaging experts in all aspects of the problem, and is collaborative in that it engages public and private entities from multiple political jurisdictions in the planning and management of shared water resources. By the mid-1990s the EPA realized that "watershed approaches are likely to result in significant restoration, maintenance, and protection of water resources in the United States."[15] While it encouraged and supported the formation of watershed approaches, the EPA did not require engagement in watershed management at the time. However many localities moved ahead on their own and by the late 1990s, organizations had formed numerous informal watershed partnerships for which at least six U.S. states provided financial support.[16]

Among localities that embraced watershed planning early, Philadelphia was one of the first municipalities to make a formal commitment to comprehensive watershed planning and management. This was expressed in PWD's 1997 CSO Program Long-Term Control Plan (LTCP). In addition to outlining a capital program to comply with the EPA-mandated nine minimum controls, and to implement CSO improvements identified by the PWD, the PWD made a substantial commitment to watershed planning and management. In the LTCP, the PWD defined a $4 million comprehensive watershed-planning program to conduct analyses in order to identify additional priority actions to improve water quality. The LTCP defined a comprehensive watershed planning initiative for Philadelphia as having three distinct phases: preliminary reconnaissance survey, watershed assessment and plan, and watershed plan implementation. Phase 1 involves the review of existing information to gain a good, nonquantitative understanding of the physical, chemical, and biological conditions of the water bodies, to understand the character of the watershed land uses that will drive wet weather water quality conditions, and to build a common understanding of these factors among all stakeholders. Phase 2 builds on this understanding and involves detailed monitoring, modeling, mapping, and analytical work to meet the specific needs of the watershed and to supply information needed to develop an effective management plan. Phase 3 involves implementation of the recommended actions identified in the plan by all responsible parties. Integral to this approach is convening groups of stakeholders representative of public and regulatory agencies, businesses, industries, universities, neighborhood groups, environmental groups, and other parties. The PWD prioritizes the formation of watershed partnerships for each of its seven regional watersheds based on the impact of CSOs, storm water discharges, and other water-quality concerns.[17]

Office of Watersheds

In January 1999, the commissioner of Philadelphia's PWD created the Office of Watersheds, making the PWD the first utility in the nation to create a division dedicated to watershed management. The Office of Watersheds is housed within the Planning and Engineering division of the PWD and combines previously separate programs including Combined Sewer Overflow, Storm Water Management, Source Water Assessment, Drinking Water Protection, and Regulatory Affairs. The objective of this unit is to take an integrated approach to optimizing the resources allocated to controlling the city's sewer discharges and drinking water protection in ensuring compliance with regulatory requirements.

Within its first year of operation, the Office of Watersheds prepared a strategic plan to document its vision and to outline how its efforts would transition from traditional regulatory compliance to integrated watershed management.[18] The Office of Watersheds' vision—"Clean Water—Green City"—is to unite the city with its water environment, creating a green legacy for future generations while incorporating a balance between ecology, economics, and equity.[19] Through the integration of three traditionally separate water programs, the Office of Watersheds seeks to maximize existing resources being expended to meet various regulatory mandates such as a national pollution discharge elimination system, combined sewer overflow, storm water, total maximum daily loads under the CWA, and the source water protection program under the Safe Drinking Water Act (SDWA).

In addition to the forming of seven regional watershed partnerships, the Office of Watersheds has, since it inception, worked with its partners to implement dozens of demonstration projects, develop innovative storm water policies, engage in extensive public outreach and education, and, most recently, commit to implementing a green infrastructure program in its 2009 update to the LTCP. The PWD has received widespread acknowledgment for its innovative approach to storm water management including, in 2007, receipt of the Pennsylvania Resources Council, Inc.'s Leader in Sustainable Design and Development award.[20]

Watershed Partnerships

The six watershed partnerships PWD has formed since 1999 range in size from the Poquessing watershed of 21.5 square miles and encompassing four municipalities, to the Delaware River watershed, an area of more than 13,539 square miles and 838 separate municipalities. However, when the PWD formed the Delaware Direct partnership, it limited the planning area to only the portion of the watershed within the city's municipal boundaries. The primary reason the PWD decided to focus its efforts on the local portion of the Delaware watershed is because the Delaware River Basin Commission, a federal, multistate commission, is responsible for establishing water quality standards and monitoring and managing water resources for the entire watershed. The original motivation for initiating the first partnership in 1999, the Darby-Cobbs Creek partnership, stemmed from the PWD's commitment under LCTP to integrate regional watershed planning to identify long-term improvements (not limited to additional CSO controls), which would result in improved water quality and future attainment of water quality standards.[21]

The aim of each watershed partnership is to engage diverse stakeholders in developing an Integrated Watershed Management Plan (IWMP). The planning process involves forming watershed partnerships that have education outreach, and technical advisory committees. Each education and outreach committee consists largely of watershed organizations, educators, residents, and educational nonprofits. The technical advisory committees consist of representatives from local, state, and federal government agencies. This committee is responsible for reviewing technical documents produced by PWD and its consultants. During the development of the plan, the PWD conducts extensive field assessments to document and understand the watershed's biological, chemical, and physical conditions.

The watershed partnerships initiated by PWD employ a consensus-based decision-making process to seek agreement on each plan's goals, issues and recommendations. Third-party professional facilitators facilitate the planning process. The process to develop an IWMP takes an average of four years with average costs near $1 million. Participation at partnership meetings typically ranges from fifteen to thirty stakeholders. Organizations active in watershed partnerships are responsible for implementing the recommendations and the range of projects identified in each plan. The watershed partnerships themselves tend to disband after finalizing plans to allow PWD to redeploy its resources to meeting new watershed challenges as PWD has limited resources to support ongoing permanent watershed partnership organizations and develop watershed plans for all of the watersheds at the same time.

Demonstration Projects

One of the early outgrowths after forming the first watershed partnership was a deluge of interest from willing partners to implement storm water demonstration projects and restoration projects on publically owned land. "A perfect storm of interest, partners and funding," is how Marc Cammarata, manager of Watershed Engineering for the Office of Watersheds at PWD, described the early days of initiating demonstration projects.[22] The first demonstration project implemented by the PWD had nine partners and more than thirty volunteers. PWD and its partners implemented a stream corridor restoration project and planted a meadow on the banks of the Schuylkill River to deter roughly 100 geese from depositing 25 tons per year of fecal matter into the river just upstream of the city's Belmont water treatment plant intake.[23] This high-visibility demonstration project led to the creation of other partnerships notably with the Pennsylvania Horticultural Society and Fairmount Park Commission, both of which were involved in the demonstration project.

In 2001, Philadelphia's former Mayor John Street initiated a Neighborhood Transformation Initiative to address the more than 31,000 vacant lots dispersed throughout the Philadelphia landscape. To support this program the PWD partnered with the Pennsylvania Horticultural Society's (PHS) Philadelphia Green program, one of the nation's oldest urban greening initiatives, to create and implement the project models of storm water management on reclaimed vacant lands in North Philadelphia. Formed in 2003 and funded with a grant from the Pennsylvania Department of Environmental Protection (PADEP), the goal of the partnership was to stabilize five vacant sites using green infrastructure, which included clearing the land of debris, regrading the surface to create trenches and berms, and planting vegetation. It is estimated that the sites will retain a total of more than 90,000 gallons per year of storm water; water that, once retained, will not contribute to the potential for overflow of PWD pipeline conveyance and treatment system facilities.[24] PWD has now partnered with PHS on many other storm water projects using LID best management practices. Work with PHS has enabled the PWD to connect with many parks' friends groups, with which the PHS already had built strong relationships, and to implement demonstration projects in neighborhood parks. For example, the project at Cliveden Park includes a bio-infiltration swale that diverts storm water from two city blocks into a series of stepped pools and then into a rain garden. Other project partners include the Friends of Cliveden Park and the Department of Recreation. The $210,000 project cost was funded by the PWD and a grant from the PADEP.[25] The PWD and PHS partnership worked with the Northern Liberties Neighborhood Association to incorporate storm water management in the master plan of the Liberty Lands Park located in northeastern Philadelphia. A lined rain garden acts as a cistern providing water for site irrigation, with funding for this project provided in part by a $300,000 grant from the PADEP and Pennsylvania Department of Conservation and Natural Resources (PADCNR).[26]

In 2005, PWD and PHS started to work on implementing storm water improvement projects at Philadelphia schools. The Philadelphia School District projects include a range of storm water management practices including rain gardens, pervious pavement, and bio- and infiltration swales. To date the partners have implemented projects at six schools and are currently are working with another seven schools. One project at the Springtide School involves a traffic circle rain garden and received a Source Water Protection Award from the Schuylkill Action Network in 2008.[27] This project also includes an environmental art installation. Innovative rain gutter artwork installed as a part of the project is called the Water Web and was designed by environmental artist Stacy Levy along with Springside school students. The Water Web circulates water from the roof gutters through loops of tubing before discharging into a rain garden.[28] The partnership between the PWD and PHS has led to a host of other projects community groups and friends of parks associations as well.

In 1999, the Fairmount Park Commission's (FPC) Natural Land Restoration and Environmental Education Program completed, with the assistance of the Academy of Natural Sciences, an inventory of the park system's watershed corridors to identify areas in need of restoration. This led to the creation of a partnership in which the PWD provided the technical expertise and the FPC provided land and volunteers to implement several of the restoration projects identified in the inventory. One of the earliest projects to emerge from this partnership in 1999 was the restoration of nearly 900 linear feet of streambank and relocation of a sewer line in the Darby-Cobbs watershed portion of Fairmount Park. Another key project is the city's first storm water treatment wetland, a 0.7-acre wetland in Saylor Grove Park, which is located in the Wissahickon Watershed portion of Fairmount Park. The latter was funded by a $150,000 grant from the PADEP and more than $450,000 from the PWD.[29]

Storm Water Policies

Through the early alliances that PWD formed with local and upstream stakeholders and in response to changing regulations, the PWD began in 2004 to concentrate on watershed policy issues. Through enacting new policies the PWD has embraced several regulatory strategies. These range from "command and control" regulatory requirements and post-construction storm water management regulations to a softer carrot and stick approach with a revamped storm water management service charge.

As an outgrowth of the watershed partnerships, the city enacted new storm water regulations for post-construction storm water management in January 2006. The new storm water regulations meet state and federal requirements and mesh with the efforts of upstream municipalities to revamp their regulations. The regulations apply to any new development or redevelopment that results in an area of earth disturbance greater than or equal to 15,000 square feet. The regulations have the following three components:

- A water quality requirement stipulates management of the first one inch of runoff from all directly connected impervious areas (DCIA) within the limits of earth disturbance. The water quality requirement is designed to recharge the groundwater table and to improve water quality for storm water runoff but provides other benefits as well, including increased stream base flows, restoration of more natural site hydrology, reduction of pollution in runoff, and reduced combined sewer overflows. The requirement must be met by infiltrating the water quality volume unless infiltration is determined to be infeasible or where it can be demonstrated that infiltration would cause property or environmental damage.

- A channel protection requirement stipulates the detention and release of runoff from DCIA at a maximum rate of 0.24 cubic feet per second per acre in no less than 24 hours and no more than 72 hours for the 1-year, 24-hour storm event. This requirement is designed to reduce the rate of stream bank erosion from storm water runoff from development. Other benefits include protection of fish habitat and man-made infrastructure from the influences of high stream velocity erosive forces and reduction of the quantity, frequency, and duration of CSOs.
- A flood control requirement is designed to prevent flooding from extreme events in areas downstream of the development site with the additional benefit of reducing the frequency, duration, and quantity of overflows in combined sewer sheds. The city of Philadelphia is divided into management districts that require different levels of storm water flood control. The flood control requirement is based upon Act 167, the Pennsylvania Storm Water Management Act, and requires planning studies to delineate flood management districts for controlling peak rates of runoff. In general, a development project is required to meet peak rates of runoff post-development equal to predevelopment conditions.[30]

In addition to developing the new storm water regulations, the PWD has worked with other city agencies to revise the development process. The revised protocol calls for developers to submit conceptual storm water management plans to the PWD for approval prior to submitting site designs for zoning permit approvals. This additional step aims to ensure that developers are aware of the storm water regulations prior to site design and to prevent costly site redesigns.[31] In brief, the regulations require developers to return land to a state more aligned with preconstruction natural state conditions and encourage developers to use green infrastructure/LID techniques such as green roofs to meet storm water management requirements. As a result of this and other initiatives discussed below, Philadelphia has already become number two in the nation behind the city of Chicago in terms of the number of installed green roofs in a locality.[32] PWD's Marc Cammarata estimates that "the new storm water regulations have resulted in approximately 1 billion gallons per year of onsite storm water runoff management citywide. This includes all projects constructed, designed and proposed since the regulations were enacted in 2006."[33] In support of the new regulations, the PWD also created the Storm Water Management Guidance Manual to assist developers in meeting regulatory requirements.[34] The manual provides guidance for the entire site design process and tools such as flowcharts, worksheets, and checklists to aid the development of a storm water management plan.

A new storm water management service charge, commonly referred to as parcel-based billing and enacted by the PWD in 2009, responds to recommendations from the Storm Water Charge Allocation Citizen's Advisory Committee (CAC). [35] Historically, the PWD charged customers a prorated storm water fee based upon the size of their water meters. This practice led to inequities. For example, hotels without surface parking in the dense urban core paid higher storm water fees than car dealerships and malls with extensive impervious areas. In addition, roughly 40,000 customers did not pay a storm water fee at all because they did not have water meters. The CAC tasked the PWD with creating a revenue-neutral program and a storm water charge based on land-use characteristics. The fee includes a gross area rate multiplied by the gross area square footage plus an impervious area rate multiplied by the area of impervious property. The new storm water charge, to be phased in between 2010 and 2014 for nonresidential properties, is based upon the ratio of impervious surface area to gross property area. Properties with a higher ratio could see substantial increases in their storm water charges, which the PWD is hoping will translate into an incentive to implement green infrastructure projects such as porous pavement and green roofs, which would result in a credit to the property's storm water service charge. This parcel-based billing policy was made possible in part by advances in technology. With improvements to aerial photography and geographical information system (GIS) mapping techniques, the PWD is able to assess for each city parcel the amount of pervious and impervious land areas necessary to implement a parcel-based storm water billing program. Although the new fee is designed to be more equitable, the policy generates clear winners and losers. Now, the urban businesses that were overpaying historically will see a reduction in their bill, but on the other hand, the historically underpaying customers will see a dramatic increase in their bill. To help customers that would be impacted the greatest, the PWD has initiated an outreach program offering free conceptual design services and cost-benefit analyses.

Green Programs

In addition to partnering with communities at the watershed scale, the PWD is partnering with local communities through its community-based Green Programs planning initiative. In January 2009, the PWD initiated the Model Neighborhood program with the goal of transforming the neighborhoods of Philadelphia into communities that manage storm water through innovative ways. The PWD works closely with local nonprofit community-based organizations (CBOs) to raise the level of awareness of the need for green storm water management solutions.

The initial step in the Model Neighborhoods program was to implement Green Street storm water management controls to highlight their effectiveness and social benefits. The Green Streets program was modeled on innovative green storm water management techniques similar to those implemented by Seattle and Portland, Oregon, to capture and reduce runoff from city streets. Such infrastructure projects include infiltration tree pits, sidewalk trenches and planters, vegetated sidewalk extensions, and porous pavement to capture and infiltrate storm water that would otherwise flow into the combined sewer system. "Streets and sidewalks are by far the largest single category of public impervious cover, accounting for roughly 38 percent of the impervious cover within the combined sewer service area."[36] Retrofitting streets to include a variety of these projects not only allows streets to act as natural storm water management features but also provides benefits to the community. The addition of trees and wetland-like vegetation will enhance community aesthetics, provide shade, reduce the urban heat-island effect, and calm traffic.

To facilitate the grassroots effort of the CBOs to educate the public on the benefits of Green Streets, the PWD and its partners have developed a range of educational materials, including a Model Neighborhoods brochure and informational handouts.[37] The PWD also generated photo simulations to demonstrate what a storm water planter, tree trench, or other green infrastructure facility would look like on specific neighborhood blocks. In addition, the FPC developed a series of neighborhood tree walks. The educational campaign has been so successful that it has resulted in more Green Street petitions than the PWD has capacity to implement.

The number of CBOs partnering with the PWD on the Green Streets initiative is growing. A partnership between PWD, PHS, and the Passayunk Square Civic Association resulted in the city of Philadelphia's first sidewalk storm water detention planters. The planters are along the sidewalks adjacent to Columbus Square Playground, which is located in an area in South Philadelphia prone to overflows that cause basement flooding. Because infiltration of storm water was not feasible in this location, the planters are designed to capture one inch of runoff and slowly release it into the combined sewer system.[38] In addition to working with community groups, the PWD has been working closely with the Streets Department to prepare design standards to retrofit streets to incorporate green infrastructure as a standard practice when street permits are issued for new development, utility installation, and other types of construction.

The next phase of the community-based planning initiative will be to initiate a Green Homes program. While city agencies are prohibited from spending public dollars on residential improvements, residents who understand the benefits of rain gardens, infiltration planters, and the like are interested in learning how to implement these and other green infrastructure elements. Green roofs are among the LID techniques included in the Green Homes program and present a significant means of storm water management in Philadelphia, as residential roofs make up 20 percent of the impervious surfaces within the city. The PWD is currently seeking external funding to work with community-based organizations and residents to design a protocol to leverage public and private investment to transform a neighborhood through the implementation of a complete system of green storm water management solutions.

Green City—Clean Waters: Long-Term Control Planning

The update to the city of Philadelphia's combined sewer overflow control program, the Long-Term Control Plan Update (LTCPU) issued in September 2009, also referred to as Green City—Clean Waters, builds on the city's commitment to comprehensive watershed planning and the success of its green infrastructure initiatives.[39] Through the LTCPU, the city commits to creating the nation's largest green infrastructure program.

> At the close of this 20 year implementation period, the PWD will have invested approximately $1.6 billion ($1.0 billion in 2009 dollars) to initiate the largest Green Storm Water Infrastructure Program ever envisioned in this country, thereby providing for the capture of 80 percent of the mixture of sewage and storm water that would otherwise flow into portions of the Schuylkill and Delaware Rivers, and the Tacony, Frankford, and Cobbs Creeks, every time it rains.[40]

The LTCPU evaluates five alternatives to reduce and control CSOs and meet CWA requirements. The PWD developed the alternatives based on goals estab-

lished by each watershed partnership, extensive characterization studies, com-
putational models, data processing, and public participation. The five alternatives are briefly described as follows:

1. Complete Sewer Separation. The main components of this option in-
    clude new sanitary sewer infrastructure, conversion of combined sewers
    to separate storm sewers, and the associated disconnection and reconnec-
    tion of sewer laterals and sidewalk and street repairs.
2. Green Storm Water Infrastructure with Targeted Traditional Infrastruc-
    ture. This alternative would include a range of land-based or green infra-
    structure techniques. The targeted traditional infrastructure includes the
    rehabilitation of interceptor sewers and bypass of secondary treatment at
    the water pollution control plants during wet weather events.
3. Green Storm Water Infrastructure with Increased Transmission and
    Treatment Capacity. This alternative combines the large-scale green
    storm water infrastructure proposed above with increased interceptor
    transmission capacity and increased wet weather treatment capacity.
4. Large-Scale Centralized Storage. This option primarily relies on the tra-
    ditional deep tunnel storage system for combined sewer flows.
5. Large-Scale Satellite Treatment. This alternative includes new consoli-
    dated sewers with the treatment and disinfection of combined sewer
    flows before discharge into creeks, streams, or rivers.

In an innovative example of using the sort of triple bottom line methodology
referred to elsewhere in this book, to evaluate the sustainability of storm water solutions PWD examined the five alternatives to fully understand the economic,
environmental, and social costs and benefits of each.[41] The triple bottom line
analysis places the city's CSO program within the broader vision of the city outlined in Greenworks Philadelphia, the city's first sustainable development plan,
which sets the ambitious agenda aimed at transforming Philadelphia into the
greenest city in America.[42] In addition, the PWD used a traditional engineering
cost performance analysis, which revealed a factor of 10 difference between the
most and least expensive alternatives. The most expensive was complete sewer
separation with a cost of $16 billion, whereas the least expensive was the green
infrastructure with targeted traditional infrastructure alternative with a cost of
$1.6 billion. Other alternatives had starting costs in the $4 to $5 billion range.[43]
Comparative cost curves of the triple bottom line analysis and traditional

engineering cost performance analysis were used to identify the alternative that "represents the best balance among performance, cost, affordability, sustainability, social/environmental benefits, public support, and practical factors such as constructability."[44]

The selected alternative, green storm water infrastructure with targeted traditional infrastructure, was the only one that met all of the evaluation criteria across environmental, social, and economic dimensions. John Capacasa, director of water protection, EPA Region III, believes that the Philadelphia LTCPU is groundbreaking "because it's the largest-scale commitment to use these techniques by a larger city and to use them for regulatory compliance, as well as for community quality-of-life issues."[45] The three main elements of this program include converting 34 percent of the combined sewer system drainage area to greened acres using green storm water infrastructure techniques, implementing stream corridor restoration and preservation projects and upgrading the water treatment plants to handle larger wet weather flows. This Green—City Clean Waters approach begins to provide benefits immediately and greater cumulative benefits because many small scale projects are continuously added throughout the twenty-year implementation period. In addition, the total net social benefits of the proposed Green City—Clean Waters plan add up to $2.2 billion.[46] One of the greatest socioeconomic benefits of the green infrastructure approach is the reduced spending associated with a projected decrease in heat stress mortality.

The PWD plans to achieve its goal of converting the impervious surfaces in the combined sewer system areas into green infrastructure through a series of Green Programs. The Green Programs are based on the prior decade of successful storm water demonstration projects and include Green Streets; Green Schools; Green Public Facilities; Green Public Open Spaces; Green Industry, Institutions, Commerce, and Business; Green Driveways and Alleys; Green Parking; and Green Homes. Table 8.1 highlights how each of these programs targets specific impervious areas of the city. Implementation of this program will require not only "partnering with the environment" but a range of partnerships and outreach. Howard Neukrug, director of the Office of Watersheds, PWD, recognizes that the PWD cannot implement this plan in a vacuum, and that Philadelphia's sustainability framework will be the key to incorporating green infrastructure programs in other city departments and agencies.[47] While the new storm water regulations require green infrastructure for new development and major renovations and the new storm water fee to incentivize private property

TABLE 8.1.
Percentage of Impervious Surface by Green Program

Impervious Surface/Green Program	Percent of Total Impervious Surface
Streets*	38%
Homes	20%
Industry, Business, Commerce, Institutions	16%
Public Open Space*	10%
Alleys, Driveways, Walkways	6%
Parking	5%
Public Facilities	3%
Schools	2%

* The "streets" category does not include streets adjacent to public open space; these streets are included in the impervious surface percentage associated with Public Open Space (Lynne Mandarano).

owners to retrofit the landscape and include green infrastructure solutions, these incentives will only achieve a percentage of the plan's goals. The city will need to partner with public agencies as well.

The PWD is fortunate that current Mayor Michael Nutter's vision to transform the City of Brotherly Love into the greenest city in America has been followed by practical steps such as forming a Zoning Code Commission to rewrite codes that make the implementation of sustainable practices difficult. Coordination between the Zoning Code Commission and the PWD to facilitate implementing development aligned with the goals of the Green City—Clean Waters plan will be one of the critical next steps to realizing its outcomes. Collaborating with others is not new to the PWD, as demonstrated by its experience with forming watershed partnerships to create watershed management plans and multiple partnerships to implement and array of demonstration projects. One of the key lessons learned from the successful implementation of such projects is that "collaboration is a must," according to Glen Abrams, manager of Watershed Planning for the Office of Watersheds, PWD.[48]

According to Dr. Robert Traver, director of the Villanova University's Center for the Advancement of Sustainability in Engineering, PWD faces other challenges as well. One is "how to gain approval in a regulatory environment developed around structural approaches and second to develop an adaptive management approach that includes all properties—including highways, and incorporates maintenance and replacement."[49] Although the PWD submitted its LTCPU to the EPA in September 2009, the EPA has not approved the plan yet. The EPA's biggest concern is that the city's LTCPU only calls for capturing 80 percent of the overflows, but regulations require 85 percent capture. The EPA and PWD currently are in negotiations and approval is anticipated. In the interim, the PWD is moving forward with implementing its Green City—Clean Waters approach to meeting its combined sewer overflow obligations.

The Vision: Green City Clean Waters

The LTCPU establishes an ambitious vision and green infrastructure program for the city of Philadelphia and sets a strong precedent for other city departments to use vision set forth in Greenworks Philadelphia as a guiding principle for long-term planning. Becoming a model of twenty-first century sustainability will require a transformation of all city departments in order to align the city government on a path to becoming a more livable and sustainable city. The Green City—Clean Waters approach not only will be a critical element in achieving the goals outlined in Greenworks Philadelphia but a model for other city agencies to follow.

Philadelphia's Green City—Clean Waters approach also holds promise for other cities. Of particular importance is the fact that LID technologies are up to ten times cheaper than, and offer comparable performance to, traditional gray infrastructure projects such as large-scale storage tunnels. This argument becomes more compelling when the societal benefits revealed through the PWD's triple bottom line analysis are factored in.

Notes

1. Neukrug, Howard. *Testimony of Howard Neukrug to the U.S. House of Representatives Transportation and Infrastructure Committee. Subcommittee on Water Resources and Environment*. Washington, D.C.: U.S. House of Representatives Transportation and Infrastructure Committee. Subcommittee on Water Resources and Environment. 2009, 1.

2. Kramek, Niva, and Lydia Loh. *The History of Philadelphia's Water Supply and Sanitation System: Lessons in Sustainability for Developing Urban Water Systems*. Philadelphia: Philadelphia Global Water Initiative. 2007, 9.

3. Gibson, Jane Mork. *Fairmount Water Works*. Philadelphia Museum of Art Bulletin, 39. 1988, 27.

4. AWWA Research Foundation, and American Water Works Association. 2001. *Guidance to Utilities on Building with Watershed Stakeholders*. Denver, CO: AWWA Research Foundation and American Water Works Association. 2001, 240.

5. Philadelphia Water Department. *Long-Term Control Plan*. Philadelphia: Philadelphia Water Department. 1997.

6. U.S. Environmental Protection Agency. 1994. *Combined Sewer Overflow Control Policy*, edited by Office of Water. Washington, D.C.: Federal Register.

7. The EPA's publication *Guidance for Nine Minimum Controls* provides definitions for each of the elements and suggestions on how to identify their causes and measures available to address each control. Combined Sewer Overflows, *Guidance for Nine Minimum Controls*. Washington, D.C.: U.S. Environmental Protection Agency, 1995. www.epa.gov/npdes/pubs /owm0030.pdf.

8. U.S. Environmental Protection Agency. 2004. *Report to Congress. Impacts and Control of CSOs and SSOs*, edited by Office of Water. Washington, D.C.: U.S. Environmental Protection Agency.

9. U.S. Environmental Protection Agency. 2008. *Managing Wet Weather with Green Infrastructure: Action Strategy*, edited by Office of Water. Washington, D.C.: U.S. Environmental Protection Agency.

10. U.S. Environmental Protection Agency. 2004. *Report to Congress: Impacts and Control of CSOs and SSOs*.

11. U.S. Environmental Protection Agency. 2001. *Report to Congress: Implementation and Enforcement of Combined Sewer Overflow Control Policy*, edited by Office of Water. Washington D.C.: U.S. Environmental Protection Agency.

12. Philadelphia Water Department 2010, Office of Watersheds website. www .phillywatersheds.org.

13. Philadelphia Water Department 2010, Office of Watersheds website. www .phillywatersheds.org

14. For more information on the Chesapeake Bay Program, visit the EPA Region 3's website at www.epa.gov/region3/chesapeake/ or the program website at www.chesapeakebay.net/.

15. U.S. Environmental Protection Agency. 1994. *Combined Sewer Overflow Control Policy*, edited by Office of Water. Washington, D.C.: Federal Register.

16. Sabatier, P.A., W. Focht, M. Lubell, Z. Trachtenberg, A. Vedlitz, and M. Matlock, eds. 2005. *Swimming Upstream: Collaborative Approaches to Watershed Management*. Cambridge, MA: MIT Press.

17. Philadelphia Water Department.1997. *Long-Term Control Plan*. Philadelphia: Philadelphia Water Department.

18. Mandarano, Lynn A. 2000. *Office of Watersheds Strategic Plan*. Philadelphia: Philadelphia Water Department Office of Watersheds.

19. Mandarano, Lynn A. 2000. *Office of Watersheds Strategic Plan*. Philadelphia: Philadelphia Water Department Office of Watersheds, 2.

20. Neukrug, Howard. *Testimony of Howard Neukrug to the U.S. House of Representatives Transportation and Infrastructure Committee*. Subcommittee on Water Resources and Environment. Washington, D.C.: US House of Representatives Transportation and Infrastructure Committee. Subcommittee on Water Resources and Environment. 2009.

21. City watersheds for which CSOs are a concern include Darby-Cobbs Creek, Tacony–Frankford Creeks, Pennypack Creek, Delaware River, and Schuylkill River. Watersheds with separate sewer systems (MS4's) only include the Poquessing and Wissahickon Creeks. It is important to note that only the tidal portion of the Pennypack Creek, a tributary to the Delaware River, has combined sewers. For planning purposes the PWD includes the

Pennypack's tidal drainage area in the Delaware Direct watershed. Hence, the Pennypack watershed partnership's planning area is an MS4 watershed.

22. Cammarata, Marc. 2010. Interview. Philadelphia, PA, March 24.

23. Philadelphia Water Department 2010, Office of Watersheds website. www .phillywatersheds.org.

24. Temple-Villanova Sustainable Storm water Initiative. 2010. Regional BMP Projects. Temple-Villanova Sustainable Storm water Initiative 2009 [cited June 7 2010]. Available from www.csc.temple.edu/t-vssi/BMPSurvey/vacant_lands.htm.

25. Temple-Villanova Sustainable Storm water Initiative. 2010. Regional BMP Projects. Temple-Villanova Sustainable Storm water Initiative 2009 [cited June 7 2010]. Available from www.csc.temple.edu/t-vssi/BMPSurvey/vacant_lands.htm.

26. Buranen, Margaret. 2010. "Philadelphia: Going Green to Manage Stormwater." *Stormwater* (January–February), www.stormh2o.com/january-february-2010/philadelphia -going-green-1.aspx.

27. Springside School. 2010. Inside Springside School. Springside School ND [cited June 17, 2010]. Available from www.springside.org.

28. Temple-Villanova Sustainable Storm Water Initiative. 2010. Regional BMP Projects. Temple-Villanova Sustainable Storm Water Initiative, 2009 [cited June 7 2010]. Available from www.csc.temple.edu/t-vssi/BMPSurvey/vacant_lands.htm.

29. Temple-Villanova Sustainable Storm water Initiative. 2010. Regional BMP Projects. Temple-Villanova Sustainable Storm water Initiative 2009 [cited June 7 2010]. Available from www.csc.temple.edu/t-vssi/BMPSurvey/vacant_lands.htm.

30. Philadelphia Water Department. 2010. Office of Watersheds. Philadelphia Water Department [cited June 16 2010]. Available from www.phillywatersheds.org. Also see Philadelphia Water Department. 2006. "Philadelphia Water Department Regulations." In chapter 6 of *Stormwater Management*, City of Philadelphia. Philadelphia, PA: City of Philadelphia.

31. Center for Watershed Protection. 2006. "Spotlight on Superior Storm Water Programs." In *Philadelphia, Pennsylvania: A Watershed Approach to Water Quality Management*. Ellicott City, MD: Center for Watershed Protection.

32. Neukrug, Howard. Testimony of Howard Neukrug to the U.S. House of Representatives Transportation and Infrastructure Committee. Subcommittee on Water Resources and Environment. Washington, D.C.: US House of Representatives Transportation and Infrastructure Committee. Subcommittee on Water Resources and Environment. 2009.

33. Cammarata, Marc. 2010. Interview. Philadelphia, PA, March 24.

34. Philadelphia Water Department. 2010. Office of Watersheds. Philadelphia Water Department [cited June 16 2010]. Available from www.phillywatersheds.org.

35. City of Philadelphia. 2010. Philadelphia Water Department. City of Philadelphia ND [cited June 7, 1010 2010]. See also Crockett, Chris. 2010. *Parcel Based Billing for Stormwater*. Philadelphia PA: American Society of Civil Engineers Philadelphia Section.

36. Philadelphia Water Department 2009, "Green City Clean Waters. Long-Term Control Plan Update. Summary Report," p. 25.

37. Additional information on the PWD's Green Streets program in available on the Office of Watershed's website's Community Partnerships link: www.phillywatersheds.org /what_were_doing/community_partnerships/programs/model_neighborhoods.

38. Buranen, Margaret. 2010. "Philadelphia: Going Green to Manage Stormwater." *Stormwater* (January–February), www.stormh2o.com/january-february-2010/philadelphia -going-green-1.aspx.

39. Philadelphia Water Department 2009, "Green City Clean Waters: Long-Term Control Plan Update."

40. Philadelphia Water Department 2009, "Green City Clean Waters: Long-Term Control Plan Update," 10–12.

41. The PWD's triple bottom line analysis, Volume 2, of the 2009 CSO Long-Term Control Plan Update is available to download from the PWD Office of Watershed's website: www .phillywatersheds.org/what_were_doing/documents_and_data/cso_long_term_control_plan.

42. Philadelphia, City 2009, "Greenworks Philadelphia." Also see Philadelphia Water Department 2009, "Green City Clean Waters: Long-Term Control Plan Update. Vol 2: Triple Bottom Line Analysis."

43. Philadelphia Water Department 2009, "Green City Clean Waters. Long Term Control Plan Update."

44. Philadelphia Water Department 2009, "Green City Clean Waters. Long Term Control Plan Update," 10–11.

45. Original quote appeared in DiFilippo, Dana. 2010. "Philly Seeks Answers Down the Drain." *On Earth*, www.onearth.org/article/phillywater.

46. Philadelphia Water Department 2009, "Green City Clean Waters. Long Term Control Plan Update."

47. Neukrug, Howard. Testimony of Howard Neukrug to the U.S. House of Representatives Transportation and Infrastructure Committee. Subcommittee on Water Resources and Environment. Washington D.C.: US House of Representatives Transportation and Infrastructure Committee. Subcommittee on Water Resources and Environment. 2009.

48. Abrams, Glen. 2010. "Philadelphia Water Department: Sustainable Stormwater Program." Paper read at Sustainable Communities, March 10, at Dallas, TX.

49. Traver, Robert. Personal Communication. June 27, 2010.

Chapter 9

Toward a Sustainable New York City:
Greening through Urban Forest Restoration

P. Timon McPhearson

The city, suburbs, and the countryside must be viewed as a single, evolving
system within nature, as must every individual park and building within the
larger whole. . . . Nature in the city must be cultivated, like a garden, rather
than ignored or subdued.

—Anne Whiston Spirn, *The Granite Garden*, 1984

On Earth Day 2007, New York City Mayor Michael Bloomberg announced PlaNYC, a long-term vision for making New York City more
sustainable by 2030.[1] PlaNYC creates a long-term urban-planning mission for NYC that has sustainability at its core with a triple bottom line set of
goals: to simultaneously improve the urban environment, economy, and overall
quality of life. The ambitious 127 initiatives range from revamping aging infrastructure to making sure that all city residents live within a ten-minute walk of a
park to cutting greenhouse gas emissions by 30 percent by 2030. One of the most
visible initiatives is MillionTreesNYC, a plan to add 1 million trees to city streets,
parks, and private land by 2017.

PlaNYC has gained tremendous attention both nationally and internationally
since its inception and has been acknowledged around the world as one of the

most ambitious—and most pragmatic—sustainability plans anywhere. However, it remains to be seen how much of the plan will ultimately be enacted and whether the planned environmental, economic, and social benefits will be fully realized. This chapter will explore the sustainability goals and predicted environmental risks for NYC with a focus on the potential solutions provided through one of the most publicly visible and successful of PlaNYC's sustainability initiatives, MillionTreesNYC.[2]

Greening New York City

Despite NYC's towering buildings, congested streets, and often questionable air quality, the Green Apple is still one of the most sustainable cities in the country.[3] NYC's current status as a relatively green city is primarily due to its high density, walkability, and extensive transit system. Its age and restricted coastal geography have helped to generate a dense, compact living environment. While New Yorkers will be the first to tell you that the city has a long way to go to become truly green, the city's per-capita emissions are a third of those in the rest of the country and its famous subway transit system is at a fifty-year high in ridership. In fact, NYC trails only Tokyo, Seoul, and Moscow's subways in annual ridership, and easily carries more passengers than all other rail mass transit systems in the United States combined.[4] Cleaner energy supplies are aggressively being planned and built, tax credits for solar power are some of the best in the country, and the mayor has recently been pushing for installation of offshore wind turbines. And with PlaNYC, these and many other urban improvements are now captured within a unifying plan for the city.

Efforts to improve the sustainability of New York City did not begin with PlaNYC. In the 1950s and 1960s, pioneering New Yorkers and other urbanites began outlining the ways in which NYC could encourage healthier, cleaner, and more sustainable modes of living. New York City owes its current sustainability vision to the foundations laid by works such as William Whyte's seminal book, *The Exploding Metropolis*, Jane Jacobs's *The Death and Life of Great American Cities*, and Ian McHarg's *Design with Nature*. Since then, a small but growing minority has continued to vocalize the need for greening NYC. Modern threats such as climate change have only served to rally a larger and larger citizenry to lobby, protest, and work diligently to build the kind of future plan for the city that is embodied in the best of PlaNYC's intentions.

In addition to government action, the city boasts a number of grassroots and neighborhood organizations working to green the city. Indeed, in a recent study by the U.S. Forest Service, researchers found well over 2,000 NYC-based civic environmental groups that describe themselves as actively involved in stewardship.[5] Sustainable South Bronx is one of the most successful and well known of these. The group, centered in a low-income borough of the city, is helping to revitalize parks, improve greenways, install green roofs, and provide green job training. Other nonprofits like the Lower East Side Ecology Center, Solar One, the Hudson River Foundation, New York Restoration Project, and many others are working to improve both the terrestrial and aquatic environment in the city. Current efforts include urban farming programs to increase the local food supply, painting roofs white to decrease the urban heat island effect, green roof installations, expanding farmer's markets through the Green Market program, revitalizing local oyster populations through ecological restoration, and a host of environmental education programs throughout the city.[6]

New York City's relatively high position in the hierarchy of "green" cities is due to another important piece of history. Specifically, this is Frederick Law Olmsted's transformation of the city into urban parkland through signature works such as Central Park in Manhattan and Prospect Park in Brooklyn. These and many smaller parks provide the city with the rich green infrastructure resources upon which further greening continues today. The country's largest metropolitan area is a highly complex human ecosystem. The city has a wide variety of natural environments and habitats, including 29,000 acres of parkland—11,000 acres of which are still natural—ranging from beaches and rocky shorelines to freshwater wetlands, salt marshes, meadows, and forests.[7] It also has a large urban forest, including trees growing in city parks, on private land, and along city streets. It is crucial that the city efficiently uses and expands ecological amenities like these as it seeks to meet the environmental, economic, and social challenges confronting it.

Urban Climate Challenges

New York City faces a number of modern environmental challenges, some of which affect cities generally and others that are unique to the NYC metro region. The increased heat in the urban core—otherwise known as the urban heat island effect (UHI)—is a challenge in most cities and can be dramatic, with temperatures between the urban cores and their surrounding suburban areas differing from 2 to 22°F. The UHI occurs when the city is significantly warmer than its surrounding rural areas and is usually most pronounced at night.[8]

Trees and other types of green infrastructure are well known tools for offsetting the UHI. Figure 9.1 demonstrates the strong correlation between cooler temperatures and the presence of trees in NYC. The cooling effect of the extensive tree canopy cover in the surrounding areas and in the parkland within NYC can, of course, be measured, but it can also be *felt* when compared to the intense heat capture of the pavement and buildings in downtown Manhattan. It is now standard procedure for cities to plant trees and install green roofs to mitigate urban heat.[9] For example, Los Angeles, Chicago, Denver, and Austin all have city-wide programs to plant a million trees, similar to the NYC initiative. Chicago in particular has been a national leader in the use of green roofs for urban cooling. The flagship green roof there is the 20,300 square foot rooftop garden atop Chicago's City Hall that has more than 20,000 herbaceous plants of more than 150 varieties including 100 woody shrubs, 40 vines, and 2 trees.

Global climate change provides a significant challenge that is already beginning to threaten parts of the city. Formed by New York Mayor Michael Bloomberg in 2008, the New York City Panel on Climate Change issued a report in 2009, which shows that the city is vulnerable to rising sea levels, flooding from increased precipitation, and more extreme weather events such as heat waves.[10] A comparison of global climate model simulations for NYC shows that climate change is extremely likely to bring warmer temperatures to the city and the surrounding region, causing more hot days, hotter summers and warmer winters, higher sea levels, more frequent and intense coastal flooding, and more frequent and intense heat waves.

It is possible that the predicted effects of climate change are already being felt. Urban forests in NYC recently suffered from a couple brief but intense storms of the type described in the recent climate risk analysis. In August of 2009, a fierce rainstorm with high winds tore through the city, toppling more than 100 trees in Central Park and damaging many others. Adrian Benepe, the city parks commissioner, said "It created more damage than I've seen in thirty years of working in the parks."[11]

Just eight months later in April 2010, after days of steady rain saturated the ground across the region, a brief but heavy windstorm with hurricane-force winds blew through the metro area. The effects were so severe in some places

FIGURE 9.1. Urban Trees Mitigate Urban Heat: The potential mitigating effect of the urban forest on the urban heat island is shown in these two comparison satellite images measured by NASA's Landsat ETM+ on August 14, 2002, one of the hottest days in New York City's summer. The Landsat ETM+ satellite also collected thermal infrared data for heat and vegetation data at the same time. The coolest areas during this heat wave correspond to areas with the most vegetation. The top map shows temperature, with cooler temperatures appearing in darker shading and hotter temperatures appearing in lighter shading. The bottom image shows vegetation, with lighter shading indicating sparse vegetation and darker shading indicating dense vegetation. The maps show a correlation between dense vegetation and cool temperatures and between sparse vegetation and high temperatures. Maps were created by Robert Simmon of NASA Earth Observatory, using data from the Landsat Program, and can be accessed at http://earthobservatory.nasa.gov/Features/GreenRoof/greenroof2.php.

that it looked as if a tornado had touched down. The local power company officials at ConEdison said that the storm damage was the worst in thirty years. Kevin Law, president of the Long Island Power Authority, said that the storm was "among the top five or six weather events that have impacted Long Island in the last forty years."[12]

In the days following the April storm, the city parks department found that more than 1,100 street trees had fallen or split and 25 city parks crews had to be dispatched to investigate reports of trees crashing into 117 homes. By the time the worst of the weekend storm was over, at least six people were killed, countless vehicles and homes were smashed, scores of roadways were left impassable, and more than 500,000 homes had lost power (many of which stayed without power for weeks). Recent data from global climate models suggest that NYC will be in for more of these intense storms, which likely means more havoc to manage for the NYC Department of Parks and Recreation and more destruction to the critical green infrastructure of the city. The recent economic downturn and budget cuts across the city have affected the parks department right when it is in need of *increased* resources to manage the needed ecological infrastructure upon which so much of PlaNYC and the city's future depends.

In the last few years the general public has become increasingly aware that rising sea levels, caused primarily by glaciers melting globally and rising ocean temperatures causing them to expand, pose a serious potential threat to the economy and ecology of NYC. More than 62 percent of the city's population lives in marine coastal counties. The Northeast Climate Impacts Assessment conducted by the Union of Concerned Scientists in 2007 concluded that as seas rise, beaches and bluffs will suffer increased erosion, severe flooding and storm damage will increase, low-lying areas will become inundated with potential for saltwater to infiltrate into surface waters and aquifers, and sewage and septic systems as well as transportation infrastructure will be at risk of flooding and erosion.[13]

Globally, sea levels are currently rising on average about one tenth of an inch per year. In the New York–New Jersey Harbor area, sea level is projected to rise up to 12 inches by 2050. In addition, droughts may also become more severe, which could affect urban ecosystems and the services they provide to New Yorkers. These types of short-duration climate hazards can pose particular threats to both built infrastructure and natural ecosystems . . . and they will affect every New Yorker.

r reviewing the climate-risk information, Mayor Bloomberg declared cli-
1ange the "biggest challenge of all" facing the city. To develop responses,
both mitigating and adapting to climate change, we need to ensure that we plan
the city in ways that increase our climate resilience. PlaNYC is relying heavily
on green infrastructure such as NYC's urban forest to protect local waterways
from stormwater runoff while utilizing "green streets" and new storm water capture designs beneath green traffic islands to reduce the predicted increases in
runoff. If PlaNYC is to be successful, it must dramatically transform the city to
mitigate our impact and adapt to these threats.

PlaNYC 2030

One of the primary motivations for PlaNYC is the realization that by 2030 an additional nearly 1 million people will reside within city boundaries, growing from
8.36 million today to roughly 9.1 million in 2030. New York is already the largest
and most dense metropolitan area in the United States.[14] Planning for this challenge requires NYC to build new affordable housing while it also goes through a
serious rezoning effort to further direct growth. The challenge of addressing
threats from climate change and other environmental issues while accommodating a growing population is what led the Bloomberg administration to set the
ambitious goals in PlaNYC. The PlaNYC 2030 goals include seeking to:

- Create homes for almost a million more New Yorkers while making hous-
  ing more affordable and sustainable
- Ensure that all New Yorkers live within a ten-minute walk of a park
- Clean up all contaminated land in New York City
- Open 90 percent of waterways to recreation by preserving natural areas
  and reducing pollution
- Develop critical backup systems for the aging water network to ensure
  long-term reliability
- Improve travel times by adding transit capacity for millions more residents,
  visitors, and workers
- Reach a full "state of good repair" on New York City's roads, subways, and
  rails for the first time in history
- Provide cleaner, more reliable power for every New Yorker by upgrading
  the energy infrastructure

• Achieve the cleanest air quality of any big U.S. city
• Reduce global-warming emissions by more than 30 percent

Successes so far include a 2.5 percent reduction in citywide greenhouse gas emissions between 2005 and 2007, conversion of 15 percent of the taxi fleet to hybrid vehicles, and construction on the largest UV disinfection plant in the northern hemisphere to treat more than 2 billion gallons of drinking water a day. The city has also installed 141 miles of bicycle lanes and 1,211 new bicycle-parking racks, part of a bike master plan to provide 1,800 miles of bike paths throughout the city.[15] One of the most visible successes of the plan is the planting of hundreds of thousands of trees, including tens of thousands of street trees—especially in low-income and poor-health neighborhoods—through the MillionTreesNYC campaign.

However, issues such as air quality remain a challenge in NYC. Poor air quality is increasingly recognized as a major public health threat. Despite decades of progress, the New York City metropolitan area is still rated one of the most polluted cities for exposure to fine particulate matter, ozone, and other air pollutants.[16] Air pollutants exacerbate respiratory and cardiovascular illness and contribute to hundreds of premature deaths annually. Improving air quality relies on reducing emissions but also on finding ways to absorb pollutants. Planting trees is a relatively low-cost tool for dealing with air pollution, while simultaneously investing in the physical green infrastructure that provides a host of other aesthetic and social benefits to urban dwellers.

Benefits of Trees

The list of ecological, economic, and social benefits that urban trees provide cities is quite long. Indeed, many of the city's plans to offset urban contributions to climate change count on the urban forest growing, maturing, and sequestering an increasing amount of carbon while cooling the city via thermoregulation. Trees can regulate local surface and air temperatures by reflecting solar radiation and shading surfaces, such as streets and sidewalks, that would otherwise absorb heat. Decreasing the heat loading of the city and thereby mitigating the urban heat island effect is probably the most important ecological service trees provide to cities. Trees also provide cooling to cities through evapotranspiration of water. Evaporated water leaves the plant as water vapor, absorbing heat as it evaporates and rises, thus cooling the air in the process. A single mature, properly watered oak tree can evapotranspire up to 40,000 gallons of water a year.[17] If an urban area like New York City eventually adds 1 million additional trees to its urban forest, the total cooling effect could decrease the heat of the city by a full degree or more.[18]

Urban trees provide a direct ecological service to cities by reducing urban surface and air temperatures through both shading and evapotranspiration, yet the indirect effects of trees are just as important. For example, a cooler city leads to substantial reductions in energy use for air conditioning. The U.S. Forest service found that New York City's street trees provide an estimated $27 million a year in energy savings through shading buildings.[19] As decreased energy use translates into fewer emissions from energy supply sources, it could also improve stability in the energy supply during peak uses, such as summer heat waves. Trees also provide shade for roads and parking lots, which would otherwise become very hot during the day and which store heat for later release at night. Shading of vehicles in parking lots can reduce evaporative emissions from gasoline, which contributes to increased levels of urban ozone.

Urban trees, like all trees, help offset the root causes of global climate change by capturing and storing atmospheric carbon dioxide in their leaves, stems, and roots. The U.S. Forest Service (USFS) has been actively studying the benefits of urban forests and found that NYC's trees store about 1.35 million tons of carbon valued at $25 million. In addition, NYC's trees remove another 42,000 tons of carbon each year. The soils that support trees also remove carbon dioxide from the atmosphere and absorb water. Similarly, urban trees capture rainfall on their leaves and branches and take up water through their roots, acting as natural storm water capture and retention devices. Storm water capture is a major issue in cities, and one of the major goals of PlaNYC is to improve it in order to prevent pollution loading to local waterways. Street trees in NYC intercept almost 900 million gallons of storm water annually, or 1,500 gallons per tree on average. The total value of this benefit to New York City is more than $35 million each year.[20]

Improving air quality by removing dust and other pollutants from the air is another primary benefit of urban trees. In fact, one tree can remove 26 pounds of carbon dioxide from the atmosphere annually, the equivalent of 11,000 miles of car emissions. NYC trees remove about 2,200 tons of air pollution per year, valued at $10 million annually.[21] There is growing evidence that trees help reduce air pollutants that trigger asthma and other respiratory illnesses. To find out how air quality relates to human health the Department of Health and Mental Hygiene (DOHMH) launched the New York City Community Air Survey (NYCCAS) in December 2008 to measure the variation in concentrations of street-level pollutants at 150 locations during every season of the year.[22] Though links between human health and air quality are still being studied, Million-TreesNYC has targeted its initial tree plantings in areas with high asthma rates, the expectation being that spending money on trees could be one of the highest-return investments in public health. Trees also provide about 60 percent block-age from the sun's rays, thus reducing overexposure to UV radiation, the primary environmental risk factor in the development of skin cancers and other diseases.

Economically, trees provide an important return on the significant invest-ment cities make in their care and planting. In NYC, trees provide approxi-mately $5.60 in benefits for every dollar spent on tree planting and care, dollars that would otherwise be spent on energy for cooling and storm water retention services.[23] They also increase property values, as homes are worth more when they are next to parks, green belts, or other green spaces. Additionally, the green-ing of business districts can increase community pride and positive perception of an area, drawing customers to the businesses.

MillionTreesNYC

The potential for the urban forest to simultaneously reduce the effects of cli-mate change and mitigate the urban heat island effect, while also improving the quality of life of New Yorkers, eventually made it obvious to city officials to put significant resources toward increasing the green infrastructure of NYC. MillionTreesNYC (MTNYC), a campaign to plant 1 million trees in NYC by 2017, is regularly lauded as one of the most important and most successful ini-tiatives in PlaNYC. At the beginning of the campaign, the Department of Parks and Recreation initiated a strategy of full-block planting to rapidly green entire neighborhoods, with a target in the first years on low-income areas with few trees and high asthma rates (*Trees for Public Health*).[24]

MTNYC intends to fill every available street tree opportunity in New York City. To achieve these ambitious goals, the parks department allocated $400 mil-lion to the MTNYC campaign over ten years and developed a public-private partnership with the local nonprofit New York Restoration Project (NYRP). The ultimate goal is for the city to add 220,000 street trees and 380,000 park trees in a massive forest restoration effort that will expand the city's forest by 2,000 acres, while NYRP coordinates planting 400,000 trees, working with private organizations, homeowners, and community organizations. In total, MTNYC will add 20 percent more tree canopy cover to the city.[25]

Since the launch of MTNYC in 2007, NYC has, through the New York City Department of Parks and Recreation, added 112 acres of new parkland, as well as improved access and amenities at existing parks and open spaces. Now in its third year, MillionTreesNYC has added to this effort by planting 350,000 trees, more than 35,000 of which are newly planted street trees (see figure 9.2 for a map of MTNYC tree plantings to date). Public, private, and nonprofit organizations have together rallied nearly 4,000 citizen volunteers to plant trees across the city in what has become an unprecedented tree-planting campaign and citywide environmental movement. But what will this extra tree canopy do for New Yorkers, other biological species, and the climate? Is the ecological pulse of

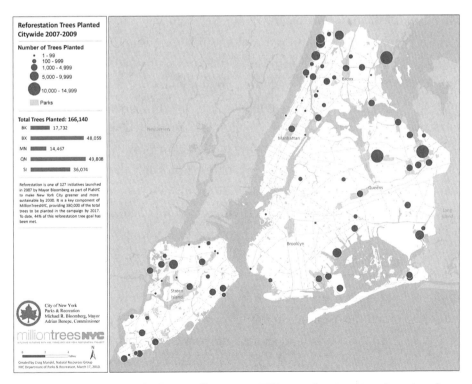

FIGURE 9.2. Recent results from MillionTreesNYC tree planting in parks, privately held land, along streets, and other areas around the city between 2007 and 2009. The image is taken from the MTNYC website at www.milliontreesnyc.org/.

added trees in a citywide tree-planting campaign sufficient to measurably increase long-term resilience and, therefore, sustainability in New York City's ecosystems? In the case of enlarging and restoring urban forests to make NYC more sustainable, many of the expected benefits of trees will not be felt until well after 2017 because trees need significant time to grow and mature. Indeed, it is not yet clear that planting trees will achieve the ambitious goals set forth in PlaNYC. The 1 million new trees must first survive the early years of city life in order to function as intended.

The Need for More Research

It is clear that trees are not simply landscaping agents in the city. Rather, they are major structural and functional elements in human terrestrial ecosystems. Trees are also homes to birds, mammals, invertebrates, and microbes, all of which perform additional important ecological services. However, urban environments are notoriously difficult places to live for many biological species. Urban trees suffer from a vast array of damaging pollutants, from acid rain washing over their leaves to being doused with bleach water as part of morning sidewalk cleaning routines. Road-salt application in the winter and prolonged heat spells in the summer can create extreme drought-like conditions for trees living in city streets. Street trees are particularly susceptible to stress due to the small spaces in sidewalks where they are forced to grow, their highly compacted and acidic soils, and the many injuries they suffer from living in such close proximity to urban life.

Young urban trees (less than 5 years old) are probably the most at risk with often-high mortality rates in New York City largely due to common urban stressors of heat, salt, and pollution, but also from lack of individual care during the first five years of their lives.[26] Forest restoration tree plantings in city parks and on degraded or existing parkland are typically small two-gallon container trees that are one half to one meter tall and one to two centimeters in diameter. MTNYC volunteers and contractors strategically plant these susceptible trees in the fall and spring months to avoid harsh drought conditions in the summer. However, expectations are that without adequate care, many of these trees will fail to survive the first year. With climate change predicted to increase the frequency of extreme heat events in NYC, newly planted young trees may ultimately fail to perform ecologically, economically, and socially as intended. Can the urban forest reliably function at the level urban sustainability campaigns such as PlaNYC expect and predict? What are the best planting strategies to maximize the many functional demands being placed on trees as urban environmental cleanup machines? These questions are still unanswerable, primarily because the study of urban ecosystems is new and as yet has not been able to provide adequate data for managers. We simply do not know what tree species will best meet the challenges of urban environments, or how best to design green spaces to maximize both desired ecological functions such as carbon sequestration and human functions including aesthetics and recreation. Similarly, it is difficult to know whether the current management practice of chemically and physically removing invasive species from city parks and planting trees in their place will ultimately change the structure of urban forests from invasive-dominated systems to multistory forests.

Ecologists, urban planners, and designers alike are asking: How do we simultaneously accommodate more urban dwellers and design cities as functional sustainable ecosystems? Clearly, there is a need for increased research in human-dominated ecosystems, New York City included. Though city officials and park managers are aware that evaluation of existing planting strategies and site designs are critical to the long-term success of the MTNYC campaign, providing mechanisms, incentives, and opportunities for research has been slow, even though the motivation exists among city government personnel. This is not surprising given the pressure put on small, often understaffed departments to deliver results, such as ambitious annual planting goals (~100,000 trees/year), in short periods of time.

At the beginning of the campaign, MTNYC created a Research and Evaluation Subcommittee of their advisory board. In conjunction with collaborators, including the New School, Cornell University, New York University, the U.S. Forest Service, and a nonprofit SoundScience, a workshop was hosted, MillionTreesNYC, Green Infrastructure, and Urban Ecology: Building a Research Agenda.[27] The workshop brought together nearly 100 researchers and practitioners to help MTNYC develop research priorities for evaluating the effects of MTNYC on the city ecosystem. One of the outcomes of this research workshop was a critical examination of the goals of MTNYC and the management strategies currently employed to meet them. The primary consensus from symposium participants was articulated in terms of a pressing need to understand urban ecosystems much better than we do. New York City, as such a system, is no exception.

The Study of Human Ecosystems

Though the study of urban ecosystems is still a relatively new pursuit in ecology, the contemporary ecological paradigm now recognizes that humans are an integral part of ecosystems, exerting direct and/or subtle influence on their functioning.[28] Though social scientists began contributing to a broader view of ecosystems that included humans during the 1950s along a continuum from wilderness to urban areas, cities remain an open frontier for socio-ecological research.[29] The need to understand the intricacies of urban systems is made obvious by the fact that an increasing proportion of humanity call cities home and also from the disproportionate impact cities have on regional and global systems. Among the many human activities that cause habitat loss, urban development produces some of the greatest local species extinction rates and can frequently eliminate a large majority of native species.[30] It is also clear that the increased energy use by humans in and around cities is another significant driver of changes in the way ecosystems function. At the same time, densely populated cities like NYC can be a net benefit to global ecosystems because they provide efficiencies that can limit the human impacts of more dispersed, resource-intensive settlement patterns such as sprawling suburbs. Ecosystem services, such as carbon uptake and thermoregulation by vegetation, can be promoted and managed in urban settings. These facts and more point to the need for a different manner of urban living and a more nuanced understanding of urban ecosystems in order to improve and adaptively use a combined socio-ecological theory to explain and predict urban ecosystem dynamics.

Urban ecology was first pioneered in Europe with the study of the succession of vegetation on ruins following World War II bombing sites in Berlin and other cities. Later ecologists began to study energy flow and nutrient cycling at the scale of whole cities in the 1970s.[31] The first on-the-ground research in the United States of cities as human ecosystems arguably began in NYC with the establishment of a long-term Urban-Rural Gradient Ecology (URGE) program in the late 1980s by Mark McDonnell and Steward Pickett.[32] It has taken the last couple of decades to develop the supporting theory and for different disciplines to learn to dialogue and collaboratively share data. Urban ecology has proceeded significantly in recent years primarily due to funding by the National Science Foundation (NSF) of two long-term ecological research (LTER) sites, Baltimore, Maryland, and Phoenix, Arizona, which are now producing important empirical observations of the cities as ecosystems.[33] Though these two cities now dominate the current field of urban ecology in the United States, it remains to be seen whether the findings from these studies can be generalized and are applicable to other cities like NYC. Similar studies elsewhere could yield important advances in urban ecosystem theory while significantly adding to the growing empirical understanding of the dynamic interplay of patterns and processes that influence the functioning of urban ecosystems generally.

What We Still Need to Know

There is a high demand for research and testing in urban ecosystems, not only with respect to the ecological conditions of cities, but also in terms of putting into practice ecological knowledge in urban planning. We still need to know what it is exactly that we need to know.[34] Although in cities like NYC there are extensive databases of various sorts including infrastructure data layers in GIS, past vegetation studies scattered around the city, and weather data from local weather stations, most data are not of direct importance to ecologically oriented urban planning. Therefore, one clear need is for model projects to establish a framework, stating which data are essential and in what forms they should be made available. Likewise, we need to effectively measure the success, failure, and efficiency of planning efforts such as MillionTreesNYC. Only by actually analyzing goals, techniques, and results can we be sure that the guidelines for ecologically oriented urban development such as PlaNYC can be implemented in an optimum way. The above needs can really only be satisfied through long-term research, such as the ongoing studies in Baltimore and Phoenix.

Ecosystem science has historically dealt with non-urban areas, and many of the accepted ideas that dominate ecosystem science are not easily applied in urban settings. The need for testing of current theory is paramount to identifying the future research directions in urban ecology. This is also true of urban forest ecology. The urban forest ecosystem includes all flora and fauna (including humans) in a defined urban area.[35] This means that management of an area, such as an urban forest ecosystem has to plan for the sustainable interaction between human and nonhuman components of the system. The ecosystem approach employed in Baltimore and Phoenix has finally taken hold, and city managers are beginning to embrace an adaptive management approach that includes an underlying view of cities as human ecosystems. NYC Parks and Recreation, for example, is working to employ an adaptive management approach through the various parks it is actively restoring and the ongoing ecosystem research it supports.

Ecological restoration, urban forestry, and greenspace management are all efforts that require not only technical information but also a comprehensive and integrated approach that fully accounts for the spatial and temporal distribution of benefits and costs of different actions. Any action in the system will affect the operation, or function, of the system, and various states will generate different spatial-temporal distributions of benefits and costs. MillionTreesNYC will therefore logically affect the urban forest ecosystem and, by extension, the entire human ecosystem of NYC. The Human Ecosystem Framework, originally developed by Gary Machlis, Jo Ellen Force, and William Burch, provides an entry point for integrating the human and nonhuman components of the city in a way that allows hypothesis generation regarding the interaction of these components.[36]

Urban Ecosystem Research in NYC

New York City is just beginning to initiate empirical urban ecosystem research that is large in scale and interdisciplinary—that joins the sociological and ecological study of the city as an ecosystem. A year after the symposium to set a research agenda for MTNYC, the New School hosted another symposium, the MillionTreesNYC, Green Infrastructure, and Urban Ecology Research Symposium, in 2010, sponsored by MTNYC and multiple partners.[37] More than 200 attendees joined more than 60 national and international presenters during two days to present research results and discuss new pathways toward designing more sustainable cities. The event provided an important platform for networking, generating new collaborations between attendees, and, we hope, will generate novel research both in NYC and other urban ecosystems.

A collaborative effort bringing together Columbia University, New Jersey's Science and Technology University, the U.S. Forest Service, NYC Parks Department, the New School's Tishman Environment and Design Center, and others began examining the dynamics of forest stewardship activity and its impact on urban ecosystems. Funded by the National Science Foundation (NSF) in 2009, the study is part of the NSF ULTRA-Ex, or Urban Long-Term Research Areas Exploratory Award program.[38] Sixteen other studies in cities across the United States were also funded by NSF ULTRA-Ex for a total investment of nearly $5 million into urban ecosystem research, which provides an encouraging step toward furthering our understanding of urban systems and potentially provides a basis for city-to-city comparisons.

Academic researchers joined forces with NYC Parks in 2008 through the MTNYC Advisory Board's Research and Evaluation Subcommittee to begin to assess the ecological outcomes of MTNYC. This resulted in a partnership among NYC Department of Parks and Recreation's Natural Resources Group; the New School's Tishman Environment and Design Center; Columbia University's Department of Ecology, Evolution, and Environmental Biology; and Yale University's School of Forestry and Environmental Studies to assess the short- and long-term impacts of MTNYC's forest restoration efforts on the structure and functioning of NYC urban forest ecosystems. Some of the questions the research will address over the next years in order to provide baseline scientific data to inform adaptive forest management in NYC include:

- What planting strategies should NYC park managers employ to maximize particular ecosystem functions in urban forests?
- How will newly forested urban land affect invasive species dynamics at the scale of the park, city, and the region?
- Will current forest management practices affect biodiversity?
- How long will it take for the forest canopies to close under different management practices?

Researchers were able to leverage the MTNYC campaign to reorganize volunteer tree-planting events into a structured long-term experimental study of plot treatments. By studying vegetation and soil dynamics in a large number of heterogeneous sites across the city, researchers will build a more comprehensive picture of the ecological dynamics of forests in NYC. Long-term study of forest restoration and regeneration such as this is critical to understanding NYC as a human ecosystem, because so much of the system is forested. The plot-based, ground-scale approaches will help evaluate the ecological outcomes of the reforestation of the city, but will also provide recommendations for future design and forest management strategies at multiple scales.

Conclusion

PlaNYC is an ambitious effort to make NYC more sustainable by the time it is expected to exceed 9 million residents in 2030. MillionTreesNYC, one of the

PlaNYC initiatives, has already achieved some success, planting more than 300,000 trees in less than three years. Whether or not planting trees succeeds in generating the kinds of ecological, economic, and social benefits that are expected remains to be seen. To judge the effectiveness of the urban sustainability improvements projected in PlaNYC requires well-designed scientific research. Urban ecological research in New York City must take a front seat in the challenge to make the city more sustainable. This will require government and private foundations to sponsor research over short and long time frames in order to provide the fundamental science that policy makers, managers, and practitioners need in order to make decisions that can achieve the noble sustainability goals set forth in PlaNYC. Urban planners and designers alike will need to commit to making use of available ecological science.

Urban ecology is most useful when it is applied to the problems it was originally designed to address. Urban ecosystem research, well demonstrated in the Baltimore Ecosystem Study, has the potential to provide important data on how best to maximize various functions urban dwellers desire from the green infrastructure of the city, but only if urban planners commit to doing the hard work of understanding and incorporating ecological research results into their creative enterprises.[39] Similarly, urban ecologists must commit to interdisciplinary dialogues that make use of the storehouse of knowledge designers and practitioners working in urban areas already have. As global climate change, urban population growth, economic upheaval, and other threats provide new challenges to New Yorkers, transforming NYC into an "ecological city" depends on building a strong coalition of sustainability minded city officials, urban planners, green infrastructure managers, academic researchers, and motivated citizens to leverage the limited resources we have now to create a sustainable future New York City.[40]

Notes

1. More detail on PlaNYC 2030 can be found at www.nyc.gov/planyc2030.

2. Information on MillionTreesNYC is accessible at www.milliontreesnyc.org/.

3. Owen, D. 2009. *Green Metropolis: Why Living Smaller, Living Closer, and Driving Less are the Keys to Sustainability*. Riverhead Books, NY.

4. American Public Transportation Association Factbook accessible at: http://apta.com /resources/statistics/Documents/FactBook/APTA_2010_Fact_Book.pdf.

5. View a description of the U.S. Forest Service's mapping of stewardship organizations, called STEW-MAP, at http://nrs.fs.fed.us/nyc/focus/stewardship_mapping/. A recent article

describing STEW-MAP is: Svendsen, E. S. and L. K. Campbell. 2008. "Urban Ecological Stewardship: Understanding the Structure, Function and Network of Community-Based Urban Land Management." *Cities and the Environment*, 1(1): 4, accessible at http:// escholarship.bc.edu/cate/vol1/iss1/4/.

6. See the chapter by Cohen and Obadia in this volume.

7. For more information on NYC's green infrastructure see the NYC Parks and Recreation's Natural Resources Group at: www.nycgovparks.org/sub_about/parks_divisions/nrg/nrg _home.html.

8. The U.S. Environmental Protection Agency provides an overview of the urban heat island effect at: www.epa.gov/heatisld/.

9. For a concise overview of the mitigation possibilities for the UHI in NYC see Cynthia Rosenzweig, William Solecki, Lily Parshall, Stuart Gaffin, Barry Lynn, Richard Goldberg, Jennifer Cox, and Sara Hodges. 2006. "Mitigating New York City's Heat Island with Urban Forestry, Living Roofs, and Light Surfaces." Presentation at 86th American Meteorological Society Annual Meeting, Jan. 31, 2006, Atlanta, Georgia. Article is available at: www.giss .nasa.gov/research/news/20060130/103341.pdf.

10. The New York City Panel on Climate Change, which consists of climate change and impacts scientists, and legal, insurance, and risk management experts, was charged by NYC Mayor Michael Bloomberg with serving as the technical advisory body for the mayor and the New York City Climate Change Adaptation Task Force (the "Task Force") on issues related to climate change, impacts, and adaptation. The full Climate Risk Information report can be accessed at: www.nyc.gov/html/om/pdf/2009/NPCC_CRI.pdf.

11. The *New York Times* article describing the 2009 storm more fully is available at: http://cityroom.blogs.nytimes.com/2009/08/19/storm-topples-scores-of-trees-in-central-park /?scp=2&sq=new%20york%20storm%20trees%20down%202010&st=cse.

12. The *New York Times* article describing the 2010 storm more fully is available at: www.nytimes.com/2010/03/15/nyregion/15storm.html?scp=8&sq=new%20york%20storm %20trees%20down%202010&st=cse.

13. For more on sea level rise in NYC, view the Union of Concerned Scientists full report at: www.climatechoices.org/assets/documents/climatechoices/new-york_necia.pdf. The Sea Level Rise Task Force for NYC is studying the effects of predicted sea level rise and how to adapt at: www.dec.ny.gov/energy/45202.html. To view a simple map-based simulation for sea level rise in NYC, go to: www.climateatlas.org/nycslr.html or a global map is available at: http://flood.firetree.net/. See also NASA's website for predicted sea level in NYC at: www .nasa.gov/mission_pages/hurricanes/archives/2006/sealevel_nyc.html.

14. U.S. Census Bureau, accessible at: www.census.gov/population/www/censusdata /density.html.

15. PlaNYC 2010 Progress Report, available at: www.nyc.gov/html/planyc2030/down loads/pdf/planyc_progress_report_2010.pdf.

16. American Lung Association 2010 report accessible at: www.stateoftheair.org/2010 /city-rankings/most-polluted-cities.html.

17. US Geological Survey Water Cycle and Evapotranspiration page: http://ga.water .usgs.gov/edu/watercycleevapotranspiration.html.

18. For details on the analysis of the of the city's forest using the U.S. Forest Service's Urban Forest Effects Model (UFORE, now called iTREE), see Grove, J. M., J. P. M.

O'Neil-Dunne, K. Pelletier, D. J. Nowak, and J. Walton (2006). A Report on New York City's Present and Possible Urban Tree Canopy. Prepared for Fiona Watt, Chief of the Division of Forestry & Horticulture. New York City's Department of Parks & Recreation, Northern Research Station, USDA Forest Service. Also see the iTREE urban forest analytical software available at: .www.itreetools.org/.

19. Nowak, D. J., R. E. Hoehn, D. E. Crane, J. C. Stevens, and J. T. Walton. 2007. Assessing urban forest effects and values, New York City's urban forest. Resource Bulletin NRS-9. U.S. Department of Agriculture, Forest Service, Northern Research Station, Newtown Square, PA.

20. Nowak, D. J., R. E. Hoehn, D. E. Crane, J. C. Stevens, and J. T. Walton. 2007. Assessing urban forest effects and values, New York City's urban forest. Resource Bulletin NRS-9. U.S. Department of Agriculture, Forest Service, Northern Research Station, Newtown Square, PA.

21. Nowak, D. J., R. E. Hoehn, D. E. Crane, J. C. Stevens, and J. T. Walton. 2007. Assessing urban forest effects and values, New York City's urban forest. Resource Bulletin NRS-9. U.S. Department of Agriculture, Forest Service, Northern Research Station, Newtown Square, PA.

22. Information on the New York City Community Air Survey is accessible at: www .nyc.gov/html/doh/html/eode/nyccas.shtml.

23. STRATUM, an early model developed by researchers at the University of California at Davis and the U.S. Forest Service to assess the economic value of trees is now part of the iTREE software suite. Information on STRATUM is available at: www.fs.fed.us/psw /programs/cufr/stratum.shtml.

24. Trees for Public Health priority planting areas for MTNYC can be viewed at: www .milliontreesnyc.org/html/million_trees/neighborhoods.shtml.

25. For more information, see the MillionTreesNYC website at: www.milliontreesnyc .org/.

26. NYC Street Tree Mortality Study results were presented at the 2010 Million-TreesNYC, Green Infrastructure, and Urban Ecology Research Symposium by NYC Parks scientists. The abstract is available here: http://milliontreesnyc.org/downloads/pdf /symposium_research_abstracts.pdf.

27. You can download the full 2009 workshop report at: www.milliontreesnyc.org /research.

28. Egerton, F. N. 1993. "The History and Present Entanglements of Some General Ecological Perspectives," pp 9–23. In McDonnell, M. J. and S. T. A. Pickett (eds.). *Humans as Components of Ecosystems: The Ecology of Subtle Human Effects and Populated Areas*, Springer-Verlag, New York, NY; McDonnell, M. J. and S. T. A. Pickett. 1993. *Humans as Components of Ecosystems: The Ecology of Subtle Human Effects and Populated Areas*. Springer-Verlag, New York, NY; Holling, C. S. 1994. "New Science and New Investments for a Sustainable Biosphere," pp. 57–97. In A. Jansson (Ed.). *Investing in Natural Capital: The Ecological Economics Approach to Sustainability*. Island Press, Washington, D.C.; Cronon, W. 1995. "The Trouble with Wilderness; Or, Getting Back to the Wrong Nature," pp. 69–90. In Cronon, W. (Ed.). *Uncommon Ground: Toward Reinventing Nature*. Norton, New York, NY.; Alberti, M., J. M. Marzluff, E. Shulenberger, G. Bradley, C. Ryan, and C. Zumbrun-

nen. 2003. "Integrating Humans into Ecology: Opportunities and Challenges for Studying Urban Ecosystems." *Urban Ecology* 53(12): 1169–79; Turner, W. R., T. Nakamura, and M. Dinetti. 2004. "Global Urbanization and the Separation of Humans from Nature." *Bioscience* 54: 585–90.; Pickett, S. T. A., M. L. Cadenasso, J. M. Grove, C. H. Nilon, R. V. Pouyat, W. C. Zipperer, R. Costanza. 2001. "Urban Ecological Systems: Linking Terrestrial Ecological, Physical, and Socioeconomic Components of Metropolitan Areas." *Annual Review of Ecology and Systematics* 32: 127–57; Pickett, S. T. A., and J. M. Grove. 2009. "Urban Ecosystems: What Would Tansley Do?" *Urban Ecosystems*, 12: 1–8.

29. Hawley, A. 1950. *Human Ecology: A Theory of Community Structure*. Ronald, New York; Duncan, O. D. 1961. "From Social System to Ecosystem." *Sociol. Inq.* 31:140–49; Duncan, O. D. 1964. "Social Organization and the Ecosystem." In *Handbook of Modern Sociology*, ed. REL Faris, pp. 37–82. Rand McNally, Chicago; Burch, W. R., Jr., and D. De Luca, 1984. *Measuring the Social Impact of Natural Resource Policies*, Albuquerque, University of New Mexico Press; Machlis, G. E., J. E. Force, and W. R. Burch, Jr. 1997. "The Human Ecosystem. 1. The Human Ecosystem as an Organizing Concept in Ecosystem Management." *Society and Natural Resources* 10(4):347–67.

30. Collins, J. P., A. Kinzig, N. B. Grimm, W. F. Fagan, D. Hope, J. Wu, and E. T. Borer. 2000. "A New Urban Ecology." *American Scientist* 88: 416–25; Grimm, N. B., M. Grove, S. T. A. Pickett, and C. L. Redman. 2000. "Integrated Approaches to Long-Term Studies of Urban Ecological Systems." *Bioscience*, 50: 571–84; Pickett, S. T. A., M. L. Cadenasso, J. M. Grove, P. M. Groffman, L. E. Band, C. G. Boone, W. R. Burch, C. S. B. Grimmond, J. Hom, J. C. Jenkins, N. L. Law, C. H. Nilon, R. V. Pouyat, K. Szlavecz, P. S. Warren, and M. A. Wilson. 2008. "Beyond Urban Legends: An Emerging Framework of Urban Ecology, as Illustrated by the Baltimore Ecosystem Study." *Bioscience* 58(2):139–50; Berube, A., and B. Forman. 2001. "Living on the Edge: Decentralization within Cities in the 1990s." *Living Cities Census Series* 2002: 1–11; Elvidge C. D., C. Milesi, J. B. Dietz, B. T. Tuttle, P. C. Sutton, R. Nemani, J. E. Vogelmann. 2004. "U.S. Constructed Area Approaches the Size of Ohio." *EOS: Transactions of the American Geophysical Union* 85: 233–40; McKinney, M. L. 2002. "Urbanization, Biodiversity, and Conservation." *BioScience* 52: 883–90; Luniak, M. and B. Pisarski. 1994. "State of Research into the Fauna of Warsaw (Up to 1990)." *Mem. Zool.* 49:155–65.

31. For more on the history of urban ecosystem research, see Sukopp, H. 2002. "On the Early History of Urban Ecology in Europe." *Preslia Prahs*, 74: 373–93, reprinted in Marzluff, J. M.; Shulenberger, E.; Endlicher, W.; Alberti, M.; Bradley, G.; Ryan, C.; ZumBrunnen, C.; Simon, U. (eds.) 2008. "Urban Ecology: An International Perspective on the Interaction between Humans and Nature" Springer.

32. For more on the URGE program, see McDonnell, M. J. and S. T. A. Pickett. 1990. "Ecosystem Structure and Function along Urban-Rural Gradients: An Unexploited Opportunity for Ecology." *Ecology*, 71: 1232–37; McDonnell, M. J. and S. T. A. Pickett. 1993. *Humans as Components of Ecosystems: The Ecology of Subtle Human Effects and Populated Areas*. Springer-Verlag, New York, NY; McDonnell, M. J., S. T. A. Pickett, P. Groffman, P. Bohlen, R. V. Pouyat, W. C. Zipperer, K. Medley, et al. 1997. "Ecosystem Processes along an Urban-to-Rural Gradient." *Urban Ecosystems*, 1: 21–36.

33. For summaries of recent findings from the LTER studies in Baltimore and Phoenix,

see Collins, J. P., A. Kinzig, N. B. Grimm, W. F. Fagan, D. Hope, J. Wu, and E. T. Borer. 2000. "A New Urban Ecology." *American Scientist* 88: 416–25; Grimm, N.B., M. Grove, S.T.A. Pickett, and C. L. Redman. 2000. "Integrated Approaches to Long-Term Studies of Urban Ecological Systems." *Bioscience*, 50: 571–84; Pickett, S. T. A., M. L. Cadenasso, J. M. Grove, P. M. Groffman, L. E. Band, C. G. Boone, W. R. Burch, C. S. B. Grimmond, J. Hom, J. C. Jenkins, N. L. Law, C. H. Nilon, R. V. Pouyat, K. Szlavecz, P. S. Warren, and M. A. Wilson. 2008. "Beyond Urban Legends: An Emerging Framework of Urban Ecology, as Illustrated by the Baltimore Ecosystem Study." *Bioscience* 58(2):139–50.

34. Wittig, R., J. Breuste, L. Finke, M. Kleyer, F. Rebele, K. Reidl, P. Werner, et al. 1995. "What Should an Ideal City Look Like from an Ecological View? Ecological Demands on the Future City." *Ökologie und Naturschuz*, 4: 157–61, reprinted in Marzluff, J. M., E. Shulenberger, W. Endlicher, M. Alberti, G. Bradley, C. Ryan, C. ZumBrunnen, and U. Simon, (Eds.) 2008. *Urban Ecology: An International Perspective on the Interaction between Humans and Nature*. Springer.

35. Wittig, R., J. Breuste, L. Finke, M. Kleyer, F. Rebele, K. Reidl, P. Werner, et al. 1995. "What Should an Ideal City Look Like from an Ecological View? Ecological Demands on the Future City." *Ökologie und Naturschuz*, 4: 157–61, reprinted in Marzluff, J. M., E. Shulenberger, W. Endlicher, M. Alberti, G. Bradley, C. Ryan, C. ZumBrunnen, and U. Simon, (eds.) 2008. *Urban Ecology: An International Perspective on the Interaction between Humans and Nature*. Springer.

36. For an overview of the Human Ecosystem Framework, often referred to as the HEF Model, see Machlis, G. E., J. E. Force, and W. R. Burch, Jr. 1997. "The Human Ecosystem 1. The Human Ecosystem as an Organizing Concept in Ecosystem Management." *Society and Natural Resources* 10(4):347–67. Pickett, S.T.A., W. R. Burch Jr., S. D. Dalton, and T. W. Foresman, 1997. "Integrated Urban Ecosystem Research," *Urban Ecosystems*, 1, 183–84; Cadenasso, M. L., S. T. A. Pickett, and J. M. Grove. 2006. "Integrative Approaches to Investigating Human-Natural Systems: The Baltimore Ecosystem Study." *Natures, Sciences, Societes*, 14: 1–14.

37. Details on the MTNYC Research Symposium can be found at http://milliontrees nyc.org/research. Also see the journal *Cities and the Environment* at http://escholarship.bc .edu/cate/ for a special journal issue of the symposium, anticipated publication in 2011.

38. The National Science Foundation ULTRA-Ex Program details are accessible at: www.nsf.gov/pubs/2009/nsf09551/nsf09551.htm.

39. For more on the Baltimore Ecosystem Study, see Cadenasso, M. L., S. T. A. Pickett, and J. M. Grove. 2006. "Integrative Approaches to Investigating Human-Natural Systems: The Baltimore Ecosystem Study." *Natures, Sciences, Societes*, 14: 1–14; Pickett, S. T. A., M. L. Cadenasso, J. M. Grove, P. M. Groffman, L. E. Band, C. G. Boone, W. R. Burch, C. S. B. Grimmond, J. Hom, J. C. Jenkins, N. L. Law, C. H. Nilon, R. V. Pouyat, K. Szlavecz, P. S. Warren, and M. A. Wilson. 2008. "Beyond Urban Legends: An Emerging Framework of Urban Ecology, as Illustrated by the Baltimore Ecosystem Study." *Bioscience* 58(2):139–50.

40. For additional readings on the "ecological city" concept, see Platt, R. 2006. *The Human Metropolis*. University of Massachusetts Press, Amherst, MA; Platt, R., R. Rowntree, and P. Muick. 1994. *The Ecological City: Preserving and Restoring Urban Biodiversity*. University of Massachusetts Press, Amherst, MA; Register, R.. 2006. *Ecocities: Rebuilding Cities in*

Balance with Nature . New Society Publishers, Canada; Wittig, R., J. Breuste, L. Finke, M. Kleyer, F. Rebele, K. Reidl, P. Werner, et al. 1995. What Should an Ideal City Look Like from an Ecological View? Ecological Demands on the Future City." *Ökologie und Naturschuz*, 4: 157-161, reprinted in Marzluff, J. M., E. Shulenberger, W. Endlicher, M. Alberti, G. Bradley, C. Ryan, C. ZumBrunnen, and U. Simon. (eds.) 2008. *Urban Ecology: An International Perspective on the Interaction between Humans and Nature*. Springer.

Chapter 10

Greening the Food Supply in New York

Nevin Cohen and Jennifer Obadia

Each step in the food cycle, from the farm all the way to the table . . . has the potential to create jobs, to improve public health, and to preserve our shared environment.

—Christine Quinn, Speaker, NYC Council[1]

New York City's food system, like those of most major cities, offers an abundance of high-quality, low-cost food from all around the world. Food to satisfy diverse tastes is available year round at markets and restaurants throughout the city's five boroughs. Superficially, the system that feeds New Yorkers appears to work wonderfully. Yet, as is apparent to an increasing number of policy makers and advocates, the city's food system is based on an inherently unsustainable and vulnerable foundation. It is rife with inefficiencies that increase costs, cause environmental problems, and inequitably distribute resources so that while many New Yorkers enjoy the best that food has to offer, millions of others lack easy access to healthy, fresh food. During the last several years, individuals have sought to forge policies and develop wide-ranging programs to address these problems, making New York City one of the nation's leaders in sustainable urban food initiatives.

Why Change Was Needed

During the last century, U.S. agricultural policies and international trade agreements have combined with advanced transportation technologies to create a food system based on large-scale, global production and complex and lengthy distribution networks. At the municipal level, reform efforts directed at reducing distribution inefficiencies that were perhaps well intentioned but lacking sufficient foresight caused cities like New York to dismantle their dispersed farmers' markets and build large, wholesale food markets to accommodate the delivery and distribution of food from around the world.[2] At present, the city's primary wholesale food market, and the largest food market in the United States by revenue, is located in the Hunts Point neighborhood of the South Bronx. Unfortunately, the market is outdated and inefficient. As a result approximately 15,000 truck trips are required into and out of the Hunts Point neighborhood each day, creating a nuisance and ecological burden on the community. The market is not cold-chain compliant and lacks sufficient refrigerated storage. Delivery vehicles must therefore run their refrigeration units to keep their cargo fresh and produce is vulnerable to spoilage. The inefficient layout of the market causes such long queues that some Hudson Valley farmers prefer to sell through markets as far away as Philadelphia. Small, local neighborhood-based markets called bodegas in communities like Central Brooklyn and Queens cannot afford to drive back and forth to Hunts Point to buy fruits and vegetables.

Some 3 million New Yorkers live in neighborhoods with few to no grocery stores and supermarkets. As a result they pay higher prices for a narrower selection of poor-quality food at bodegas and convenience stores.[3] One consequence is poorer nutrition and an epidemic of diet-related illnesses, from diabetes to heart disease. A second consequence is the loss of tax revenue and jobs as consumers with automobiles seek alternatives in adjacent suburbs. The New York City Economic Development Corporation has estimated that new supermarkets in New York City would have the potential to capture $1 billion per year in sales now lost to grocers in nearby communities beyond the city's boundaries.[4]

The unmet demand for local food is large and growing. According to a 2005 study, New York's restaurants, supermarkets, and other wholesale purchasers constitute an unmet market of some $866 million worth of locally produced food.[5] Given the rising interest in local food during the last five years, the potential market is likely to be much larger today. Providing the infrastructure to make wholesale sourcing of local food less costly and more convenient would meet this nascent demand and keep dollars circulating in the region's economy. Improving opportunities for local producers to sell wholesale in New York City would also boost farming in upstate communities, including those towns in New York City's rural Catskill-Delaware watershed currently considering alternatives to farming. These alternatives include gambling, natural gas extraction, and suburban home development that threaten the natural environment and the long-term safety of the city's drinking water supply.

There is a large untapped potential for job creation in food manufacturing, which translates into a potential for green job growth in the area. Currently, New York City's food manufacturing industry produces $5 billion worth of products per year and adds approximately $1.3 billion to the city's gross product.[6] Food manufacturing businesses employ 33,800 New Yorkers, mostly immigrants, including 19,200 directly in food manufacturing, 9,100 local jobs in supplier industries, and an estimated 5,500 local jobs induced by employees and owners spending their income.[7] New Yorkers annually consume $2.3 billion worth of locally manufactured food products, and restaurants and bars buy $500 million of food from lo-cal manufacturers.[8] Stimulating the food processing industry in New York City would create jobs for the million new residents anticipated over the next two decades while reducing the costs and impacts of food transportation.

Urban agriculture is a means to increase real estate value and supplement the diets of low-income residents. Furthermore, agricultural production can supplement the food budgets of low-income New Yorkers. A recent study in Philadelphia found that community gardeners produced $4.9 million worth of summer vegetables alone, not including spring and fall plantings or fruits and berries.[9] A similar assessment of New York City gardens is being conducted during the 2010 growing season by a team of researchers. To the extent the city wishes to increase the availability of open space and use of vacant land and brownfields for environmentally beneficial purposes and support a growing entrepreneurial economy of urban agricultural producers, a comprehensive plan is needed to identify land use changes and policies. For example, entrepreneurs are starting innovative urban agriculture projects that use the rooftop space of warehouse and manufacturing buildings for food production, saving building energy and capturing rainwater while creating jobs. At present, however, building codes and zoning do not explicitly encourage the wider productive use of rooftops, inhibiting the expansion of this form of urban agriculture. Other problems are prevalent as well, from the provenance and quality of the 860,000 meals purchased daily for public school students to the lack of a municipal composting system for discarded food that constitutes more than one-fifth of the city's residential waste stream.

Despite the aforementioned problems, over the last few years, New York City has developed a number of public policies and initiatives that have helped to create a more sustainable food supply. The city has helped to expand the number and scale of community gardens and urban farms within the five boroughs. Simultaneously New York has supported farmers in the city's watershed and beyond through financial assistance and the expansion of distribution and marketing opportunities from a wholesale farmers' market to programs that source regionally produced food for public institutions. For low-income New Yorkers, various policies and programs have expanded access to healthy foods in the schools and their neighborhoods. And a multidimensional campaign for healthier diets has improved the nutritional value of city-provided meals and increased the availability of fresh fruits and vegetables in underserved neighborhoods.

New York's effort to use federal and state nutrition dollars to help both small- and medium-scale farmers and provide affordable healthy foods to the most at-risk neighborhoods, such as the Farmers Market Nutrition Program and the use of electronic benefit transfer cards at farmers markets, are innovations that have been replicated nationally. Food advocates have worked with political leaders to develop a number of policy initiatives, including a New York Food Charter and a new legislative initiative to support the development of infrastructure for sustainable food production, processing, and distribution.

Urban and Peri-Urban Agricultural Production

Agricultural production is an important part of the food system, yet it tends to be overlooked in the urban context. Building and population density in urban areas create a challenge for those looking for land on which to produce. However, even in cities as dense as the Big Apple there are numerous pocket parks, vacant plots, and even rooftops that can be converted into agricultural land. This section will explore the three most common types of urban production: community gardens, rooftop farms, and small-scale urban farms. Additionally, we will look at the importance of preserving peri-urban (suburban and exurban) agricultural land in the face of development pressure.

Community Gardens

Community gardens are the primary form of agricultural production in urban centers in the United States. New York City is no exception. Community gardens have long been a part of the landscape throughout the five boroughs. During the last 100 years the number of community gardens has peaked and fallen in relation to war driven food efforts. During both World War I and II the country came together around "liberty gardens" or "victory gardens," growing food to feed the country so that other food sources could be shipped overseas to the soldiers and allies.[10] However, most of these war gardens disappeared as the wars ended and the country returned to more prosperous times.

During wartime, gardens were most sought after for their ability to provide food. However, in the years since, additional benefits have been attributed to community gardens. Some of these include neighborhood improvement, community development, and increased food access.[11] The "back-to-the-land movement" in combination with these benefits led the U.S. Department of Agriculture (USDA) to take a strong interest in community gardens. As a result of the 1976 federal Farm Bill, the USDA established an Urban Gardening Program in six cities across the country, including New York.[12] This program aimed to provide urban gardeners with tools, skills, and technical assistance on issues related to growing food in a major urban center. Under this program there was a great expansion of community gardens throughout the five boroughs. USDA funding of such programs ended in 1993, yet New York City has maintained its effort to support urban gardeners through public and private programs.

Green Thumb is a city-sponsored community gardening program housed in the city's Department of Parks and Recreation. It helps to manage more than 600 community gardens located throughout the five boroughs serving approximately 20,000 city residents.[13] One of the main benefits of New York's community gardens has been the conversion of vacant lots into active areas where community members can congregate.[14] By offering classes and activities for community members to get involved, neighbors have grown to know one another and some evidence suggests that this has even led to crime reduction. Furthermore, research from New York University has shown that community gardens have such a positive influence on a neighborhood that they even improve property values within 1,000 feet of the garden by as much as 9.4 percentage points within five years of a garden's opening.[15] In addition to the Green Thumb program, community gardens are supported by a number of not-for-profit organizations. Grow NYC, Just Food, the New York Restoration Project, and Green Guerillas all provide technical assistance to community gardens. The Trust for Public Land created three nonprofit land trusts to take over the ownership and management of some sixty-four gardens it owned.[16]

Despite the many benefits of community gardens and the institutionalized support that they have received in NYC, many gardens remain at risk of closure. Some gardens were developed on vacant land without official permission from the city. Additionally, in many instances the gardeners have received permission, but the leases allow the city to reclaim the property with advance warning. Due to the uncertainty of land tenure for many gardens there has been a movement to purchase gardens and put them into conservation easements, which would permanently prohibit development on these properties. In the late 1990s the city nearly lost more than 100 gardens due to temporary leasing agreements and the decision by the city to develop the sites.[17] While many gardens were spared as a result of a protracted legal and political battle between gardeners and the city, the fragile lease agreements on which many gardens are established leaves many of them in danger of being destroyed. Newly adopted leasing arrangements would require the city to offer alternative sites to gardens it wishes to develop and subjects the process to the city's land use review procedures, but nevertheless establishes the right of the city to use the gardens for other purposes.

Urban Farms

Somewhat new to the scene of urban agricultural production is the presence of small-scale farms, some nonprofit and others set up as profit-making ventures. These farms tend to provide a variety of services to their communities. Chief among these are the provision of local food and educational programming. While these farms often share similar goals they can take many different forms. For example, in 2000 the New Farmer Development Project (NFDP) was created in collaboration with New York City Greenmarket and Cornell Cooperative Extension. NFDP trains immigrant farmers to be successful in their new environment. Since its inception 130 individuals have completed the ten-week farmer training course. Sixteen of them have gone on to start their own farming businesses in the New York metro area. These graduates sell their products at more than forty farmers' markets in NYC.[18]

Added Value is a 2.75-acre community farm that was established in 2003 with help from New York City Department of Parks and Recreation and Cornell University Cooperative Extension. Together with the community these stakeholders transformed an unused asphalt playground covering an entire city block into a raised-bed farm and center for urban agriculture. With few options for food in the farm's immediate neighborhood of Red Hook, Brooklyn, Added Value opened a farm stand to provide residents with access to fresh produce. Additionally, to address the lack of meaningful educational and job opportunities for area youth, Added Value established a youth job corps in which high school students are paid for their farm labor. The youth also receive training in agricultural production, agriculturally related business development, documentation of the food justice movement, or community mobilization. Since its inception the farm has been a focal point of the community bringing together neighbors around food, economic development, education, and much more.[19]

Schools have also been the location of innovative new urban farms. For example, the business BK Farmyards developed a new farm at the High School for Public Service. Located in Brooklyn, the farm will not only feed many people in the surrounding community, but will also serve as a unique educational tool for high school students.[20]

Rooftop Farms

Rooftop vegetable farms are a relatively new phenomenon. Green roofs, rooftops on which plant life is intentionally grown, have come into fashion as a way to address some of the environmental problems facing cities. For example, a study from the Environmental Protection Agency (EPA) found that a critical mass of green roofs can help to reduce the ambient air temperature by reducing the amount of heat absorbed by buildings and reduce the urban heat island effect.[21] This can lead to energy savings by limiting the need for air conditioning during summer months. Additionally, green roofs can reduce the amount of storm water runoff flowing from rooftops into drainpipes, reducing the occurrence of combined sewer overflows.[22]

Beyond the capacity of green roofs to assist with environmental problems, they have recently been recognized as a way to increase food production in urban areas where land is sparse. One rooftop farm that has been getting a lot of attention is the Eagle Street Rooftop Farm located in Greenpoint, Brooklyn. Just across the East River from Manhattan, this 6,000 square foot farm provides pro-duce directly to the surrounding community. Eagle Street distributes its produce through a community supported agriculture program with an onsite pick-up, through a farmstand, and to area restaurants. In addition to growing food, the farm hosts a series of educational workshops about how to grow food in the city.[23] While Eagle Street is leading the way in rooftop farms, new organizations are starting farms every season (see figure 10.1). In 2010, the Brooklyn Grange, a for-profit rooftop farming venture created an approximately one-acre rooftop farm in Long Island City, Queens.[24]

Peri-Urban Farmland Protection

Like most cities across the country, New York City experienced a pattern of flight from the inner city in the post–World War II era. This period of rapid develop-ment of the peri-urban areas surrounding New York led to the development of a significant amount of productive farmland on Long Island, in Northern New Jer-sey, and in the Hudson Valley. The preservation of farmland in the suburban and urban areas surrounding New York City is of significant importance to the devel-

FIGURE 10.1. Farmer Annie Novack at Eagle Street Rooftop Farm. Photo: Adam Golfer.

opment of a more sustainable food system. The capacity to grow food within the city limits is insufficient to meet the full needs of the city's 9 million residents, so the preservation of nearby farmland is critical for increasing the number of individuals that can be fed from regionally produced food.

Purchase of Development Rights Programs

Since the 1990s, a decade in which more than 2 million acres of farmland were lost to development, great efforts have been made to preserve farmland in both rural and urban contexts.[25] Suffolk County on Long Island was the first county in the country to develop a purchase of development rights (PDR) program to create incentives for farmers to keep their land in agricultural production. PDR programs enable conservation entities, like a land trust, to purchase the development rights from a property owner through a conservation easement that restricts the site to agricultural, recreational, and other uses.[26] PDR programs have similarly been used to preserve farmland in New Jersey. In 1998 a referendum was passed requiring 1 percent of New Jersey's sales tax, up to $98 million, to be allocated to farmland preservation. And in 1999 the Garden State Preservation Trust Act was passed, guaranteeing $1 billion in funding over ten years for farmland and open space preservation.[27] The primary goal of the preservation act is to preserve 1 million acres of open space, including 500,000 acres of farmland.[28] As of June 2003, permanent easements had been placed on 64,739 acres of farmland.[29]

Farm to Institution Purchasing Programs

One strategy to ensure that regional farms remain profitable is to use public purchasing power to support them. Among the institutions that have a large potential to source food from the region's farms is the Department of Education (DOE). DOE wields enormous purchasing power in New York City. It operates the city's roughly 1,400 public schools. School Food, a division of DOE, is the second-largest school food service provider in the United States and ranks behind only the Defense Department in number of meals provided, serving students some 860,000 meals each day.[30] Policy changes in the 2008 Farm Bill made it possible for schools to buy local food. The law establishes a local preference for food purchases and allows schools to specify local in their bids. Through an innovative program called School Food Plus, the DOE provides enhanced meals to some students in an effort to improve nutrition and increase student participation in the school meal program. In support of regional agriculture, the School Food Plus program attempts to purchase some regionally produced ingredients for its meals.

Farmland Preservation in the City's Watershed

New York City has taken a different approach to aiding in the preservation of farmland in the Catskill-Delaware watershed, just 90 miles north of the city. Not only is this area a region dotted with some 250 dairy farms, vegetable farms, and orchards, but it also contains the streams that supply New York City with 90 percent of its drinking water. New York City's Catskill-Delaware reservoirs comprise the nation's largest surface drinking water supply that is still clean enough to safely remain unfiltered. Though federal law requires all surface drinking water to be filtered, the agency responsible for supplying New York's drinking water, New York's Department of Environmental Protection (DEP), made the decision in the 1980s to pursue a waiver from this requirement by demonstrating to the U.S. Environmental Protection Agency that it would implement a broad and aggressive watershed protection program that would ensure that pollutant loading to the reservoirs would be minimized.

On the basis of the city's watershed protection plan and a memorandum of understanding between the city and upstate communities, EPA was willing to grant a five-year waiver from the city's filtration requirement in 1993, which was renewed twice and then renewed for a ten-year period in 2007.[31] The watershed protection plan engages DEP in protecting family farming in the region. As part of the memorandum of understanding, DEP provides whole farm planning services and capital for infrastructure improvements to farmers within the watershed to help them reduce impacts to the streams that are tributary to the reservoirs. The program is a voluntary partnership between the city and farmers to reduce nonpoint, or indirect, sources of agricultural pollution, particularly waterborne pathogens, nutrients, and sediment. By providing this assistance, DEP not only helps farmers to improve the efficiency of their operations, but also enables farmers to comply with increasingly stringent environmental standards and therefore remain operating within the watershed compatibly with an unfiltered water supply for New Yorkers. By helping to maintain farms, DEP's program enables the villages and towns within the Catskills to remain economically viable as agricultural communities. This approach has forestalled larger-scale residential and commercial development that would bring larger populations and more built infrastructure to the watershed, and the accompanying nonpoint source pollution that would deteriorate water quality.

The city's desire to avoid having to build and operate filtration infrastructure has provided an increased incentive for the city to protect the land from commercial and residential development and ensure it is well maintained. DEP has worked with a wide variety of stakeholders to create land-management plans for the communities surrounding the city's watershed so as to prevent surface water contamination. This includes working with farmers to ensure that they are using the most environmentally sound practices.[32]

Policy Changes to Support Urban and Peri-Urban Agriculture

Urban agriculture can be increased with the support of municipal agencies that control vacant public land that can be put into productive use, through land use regulation and by procuring food for various public programs. In New York City, for example, the Department of Buildings (DOB) is responsible for monitoring and enforcing the building code, zoning resolution, and other laws that ensure the safe and permissible use of some 900,000 buildings in New York. To facilitate rooftop farming, DOB will need to develop standards to determine the conditions under which it issues building permits for buildings with integrated food production including rooftop farms, greenhouses, hydroponics, and aquaculture. The Department of City Planning will also need to address whether greenhouses can be placed atop roofs without counting them as interior space for the purpose of determining the allowable building envelope. The Division of Real Estate Services (DRES) oversees the city's commercial real estate portfolio: leasing or buying privately owned properties for city agency use; leasing and licensing city-owned nonresidential property for private use; and selling city-owned real estate through public sales and lease auctions. Thus, DRES has the potential to play a role in the disposition of land for urban agriculture. The New York City Housing Authority (NYCHA) provides affordable housing to 420,000 low- and moderate-income residents who live in 345 housing developments with 180,000 apartments. NYCHA runs one of the country's largest community gardening programs, providing materials and technical support to 1,800 adult residents and more than 2,400 youth and children who cultivate nearly 600 gardens citywide. As NYCHA develops and renovates housing projects it has the capacity to integrate food-related facilities, from supermarkets to vegetable gardens. The Department of Housing Preservation and Development (HPD) is the nation's largest municipal housing agency, developing and helping to manage housing throughout the city. In an innovative low-income housing development in the Bronx, Via Verde, HPD selected a design that incorporates community gardens and an orchard into the core of the project. The School Construction Authority (SCA) is responsible for new school construction and major renovations to older schools. SCA has been working with the Trust for Public Land to redesign asphalt school yards into garden spaces, including food-producing school gardens.

Schools are not the only city institutions that purchase food. Other agencies, from the correctional facilities to senior citizen feeding programs could begin to review and rewrite purchasing specifications to procure food commonly produced within the metropolitan region. In addition, the city could make an investment in the distribution infrastructure to make it more cost-effective for local farmers to sell wholesale through the city's main food market or another specially designated wholesale marketplace, to restaurants, supermarkets, and other wholesale food purchasers.

Increasing Access to Healthy Food

Increasing access to healthy food is the cornerstone of a sustainable city food system. Diet-related illnesses like diabetes and cardiovascular disease are an increasing source of mortality and morbidity, and disproportionally affect low-income individuals. There is increasing evidence that that the food environment of a community, including conveniently located grocers, fruit and vegetable retailers, farmers markets, and community gardens, is associated with the consumption of healthier food and consequently better health outcomes.[33]

In 2008, Mayor Michael Bloomberg issued an executive order creating the Office of Food Policy Coordinator.[34] The mission of the office is to promote the health of New Yorkers by increasing the availability of and access to healthy food in the city. It aims to do so by making the food that agencies buy and serve more nutritious and by getting a higher percentage of qualified low-income residents to avail themselves of federal nutrition support programs, like the Supplemental

Nutrition Assistance Program, formerly "food stamps." The coordinator reports to the deputy mayor for Health and Human Services.

Healthy Food Standards

In July, 2008, New York City issued nutrition standards that apply to all of the meals and snacks the city purchases, prepares, and serves, including both meals and snacks served in schools, senior centers, homeless shelters, child care centers, after school programs, correctional facilities, public hospitals, and parks.[35] The standards require the following:

- An appropriate range of calories, salt, and fiber
- Water available at all meals in addition to any other beverages regularly served
- Juices that are 100 percent fruit juice, with servings limited to 8 ounces
- Two servings of vegetables in every lunch and dinner served
- Five daily servings of fruits and vegetables by agencies that provide three meals a day
- The use of fresh or frozen fruits and vegetables instead of canned products
- The elimination of deep fryers
- No trans fat in the food.

To ensure that these standards are being followed, all city agencies must have a plan for periodic menu review.

Since New York's purchasing power is so large, even modest changes to the nutritional standards can have a large impact on the nutrition of city residents. Given that the city's ban on trans fats sold by restaurants led to the development of foods prepared with healthier oils, the city has hypothesized that compliance with these new standards will result in broader impacts than merely on the quality of the meals served by city agencies. The city believes compliance will change the nature of food served in other institutional settings, as suppliers conform to the new requirements.

"Healthy" Bodegas

In some low-income neighborhoods in New York City 80 percent of the food retailers are bodegas, the term for small convenience stores. These retailers typically carry highly processed, shelf-stable foods and items like sodas and snacks that are high in calories, sodium, and fat and low in vitamins and minerals. Only about a third sell reduced-fat milk, and fewer still sell fresh fruits. According to one survey, only 10 percent of bodegas sell leafy green vegetables.[36]

The Department of Health and Mental Hygiene initiated a "Healthy Bodegas" initiative to persuade bodega owners to carry healthy food, offering technical and marketing assistance. The program initially focused on getting owners to stock low-fat milk, and has since been expanded to include fresh fruits and vegetables. In addition to getting bodega owners to sell these foods, the program works with local organizations in these neighborhoods to encourage consumers to buy these healthier foods.[37]

Approximately 1,000 bodegas were included in the initial milk initiative, half of which were also included in the fruits and vegetables campaign. Approximately 45 percent of bodega managers reported an increase in low-fat milk sales during the program, and after the health department's intervention one fifth of bodegas that had previously sold only whole milk started selling low-fat milk. Bodega owners also reported increases in produce sales, with a third increasing their fruit sales and a quarter reporting an increase in vegetable sales. Approximately half of the owners in the program increased the variety of produce sold in their stores and nearly half increased the quantity carried.[38]

Green Carts

New York City has experimented with an innovative means of increasing the availability of fresh fruits and vegetables in neighborhoods with few or no large grocers and fruit and vegetable stores, by promoting the old fashioned pushcart, re-branded as a "green cart." In 2008, the city enacted Local Law 9, legislation authorizing 1,000 additional pushcart licenses to vendors agreeing to sell only fruits and vegetables, exclusively in designated areas with few healthy food retail establishments.[39] The Department of Health and Mental Hygiene used data on food consumption from its Community Health Survey to identify neighborhoods in each borough in which respondents consumed significantly fewer fruits and vegetables than the citywide average. These were the communities in which holders of the new licenses were authorized to peddle their fruits and vegetables.[40] While it is too early to know whether the presence of green carts has changed food consumption, the number of permits issued continues to grow, and the Department of Health continues to monitor fruit and vegetable consumption in the green cart communities.

Zoning to Encourage Supermarkets

A growing body of evidence suggests that the location and types of food establishments in a community affects the eating habits of its residents with significant nutrition-related health consequences. Simply put, having a supermarket nearby makes it easier to buy healthy foods such as fresh produce.[41] Compared to more affluent neighborhoods, however, communities with lower socioeconomic status have been shown to have fewer large supermarkets and greater distances between residents and the nearest major food store, and therefore less access to the healthy foods that supermarkets typically carry.[42] Instead, low-income communities typically have a higher proportion of small convenience stores, bodegas, and liquor stores to full-service groceries and large supermarkets. Though some low-income neighborhoods have specialty grocers supplying high-quality food at an affordable price, in many communities, small shops and bodegas generally have fewer healthy options and less fresh produce than larger grocery stores and supermarkets located in higher-income neighborhoods.[43]

According to the New York City Planning Department, low-income communities are disproportionately affected by the lack of full-service supermarkets. Some of the barriers to supermarket development include high rents, the lack of suitable sites, and a slow land use review process for uses such as supermarkets. To reduce these barriers, New York City unveiled a Food Retail Expansion to Support Health (FRESH) initiative in 2009, which combines zoning changes and financial incentives to make it less costly for developers to include supermarkets in their projects, and to allow the construction of supermarkets in light manufacturing districts without a special permit. The initiative applies to four areas of the city with the least access to healthy, fresh food: the South Bronx, Upper Manhattan, Central Brooklyn, and Downtown Jamaica (Queens).

The zoning changes allow developers in the four target communities to build larger buildings than otherwise permitted under the existing zoning if they include a neighborhood grocery store on the ground floor. The bonus to the developer is one additional square foot of residential floor area for each square foot of grocery store, up to a maximum of 20,000 additional square feet. The food retailer must have at least 6,000 square feet of selling area for general food and nonfood grocery products, with at least half the square footage devoted to the sale of general food products intended for home preparation and consumption. Thirty percent of the area must be for perishable food, with at least 500 square feet for the sale of fresh produce. The zoning change also reduces the burden of providing parking spaces as an additional incentive.[44] To encourage grocery store development in areas zoned for light manufacturing use (M-1 districts), the proposed zoning would allow large food stores to be permitted as-of-right, which can save a developer time and money. In addition to these zoning changes, the city has assembled incentives for grocers to build, renovate, and equip their stores in low-income neighborhoods. These include real estate tax abatements, mortgage recording tax waivers, sales tax exemptions, and a variety of existing financial incentive programs that grocery store owners can take advantage of.

Policy Changes to Support Increased Access to Healthy Food

A wide range of municipal policies can increase access to healthy food. In our school system, advocates have been pushing for, in addition to more federal dollars to improve the quality of school lunches, a variety of steps that school districts can take. They include increasing the use of fresh ingredients, reducing competitive foods like snacks and soda, reintroducing nutrition education, and expanding access by universalizing school food and removing the stigma associated with eating school food.[45]

Low-income communities can be turned from food deserts into healthy food environments through initiatives like the FRESH program. A healthier food environment can also be encouraged by providing the capacity for all farmers markets to accept food stamp and WIC payments; by providing fresh, healthy food at other government feeding programs, like day care and after school and senior centers; and by supporting innovative transportation planning to enable easy access to large grocers. In New York City, for example, a program by the Department for the Aging, in cooperation with the Department of Education, makes use of the large network of school buses to shuttle seniors between senior centers and naturally occurring retirement communities (NORCs) and supermarkets during the middle of the school day when the buses are idle. The program accomplishes the goal of helping the elderly get access to fresh, healthy food without additional expenditures by the city.

Changes to the Food Policy Environment

Political leaders in New York City have launched a comprehensive plan to address problems in the city's food system. One effort to change the food policy environment was initiated by the Manhattan Borough President Scott M. Stringer, who, in 2008, hosted a conference on the politics of food at Columbia University. It was attended by more than 600 food advocates, community activists, social service providers, and policy makers. The goal of the conference was to develop the elements of a food policy for New York City. The report that emerged from the conference proposed a wide range of policies to support regional and urban food production, distribution and processing infrastructure, food access, and the elements to ensure that food planning is integrated into existing policy and planning processes.[46] Since the release of the report, the borough president has led an effort to develop a "food charter" for the city that would enumerate the policy principles required for a sustainable food system.

In 2009, New York City Council Speaker Christine Quinn announced a five-part food policy called FoodWorks to emphasize the job-creation value to the city of investing in the food system.[47] Legislation to be introduced will, among other things, require government agencies to report data on their role in the food system to the city council, enabling the council to develop specific food-related public policies that will make the food system more environmentally sound and good for the city's economy.

Insights from Other Cities

New York City is among the leaders in transforming the food system, but examples of efforts to address the sustainability of urban food systems can be found across the country. Several examples are presented below.

Turning Abandoned Land into Farmland in Detroit

Proposals advanced by advocates in the city of Detroit provide an example of how urban agriculture might be used to reinvigorate the economy of a post-industrial city. Once home to a robust auto manufacturing industry, Detroit has long experienced job loss and economic decline. This has led to a precipitous reduction in population, leaving the city with half the people it was designed to support. Today Detroit is estimated to have 100,000 to 130,000 vacant plots and as many as 40 square miles of vacant land.[48] Furthermore, in 2007, Detroit became the first major city in the country to have no major supermarket chains, leading to severe food access issues for the city's poor and elderly populations. These bleak conditions are difficult for any city to overcome, but advocates in Detroit are advancing urban agriculture as an economic opportunity to reuse vacant land productively while creating new jobs and providing another source of healthy food. Organizations such as the Fair Food Network have emerged in recent years to help convert vacant land into community gardens and full-scale farms.[49] Market gardens have evolved to teach new urban farmers how to operate as successful businesses. Additionally, a private entrepreneur has proposed two large-scale urban farms, 2,000 acres each, within the city limits.

Detroit is using many models of urban agriculture to provide job opportunities and increase food access in the city. Kathryn Lynch Underwood, a City Planning Commission staff member, has said, "We're going to end up with a lot of different models of urban agriculture in Detroit. There isn't going to be just one, and there shouldn't be."[50] Detroit is learning from its past and using multiple forms of urban agriculture as an opportunity to improve food access while creating new jobs.

Executive Directive to Promote Sustainability in San Francisco

San Francisco has long been a leader in the realm of sustainability, including the development of a sustainable urban food system. There are many factors that contribute to this: the weather, which leads to the availability of local produce on a year-round basis; the plethora of nonprofit organizations working toward this end; and the support of the mayor.

Twenty million tons of food are produced within 100 miles of the Bay Area, and the population consumes only 5.9 million tons of food. Despite the abundance of local food, a quarter of the food consumed in the San Francisco area is imported from abroad. And 40 percent of the food produced in the area is shipped to other parts of the country.[51] To address the issue of local food and the development of a sustainable food system Mayor Gavin Newsom issued an executive order in July of 2009.

The order, Healthy and Sustainable Food for San Francisco, was one of the first of such orders made by mayors in the United States. This order had four main foci to move the city toward meeting the goal of a sustainable food system.

First, a commitment to "safe, nutritious, and culturally acceptable food" was acknowledged as a basic human right. Second, a series of principles were laid out to guide the development of a healthy and sustainable food system. They include education initiatives, reduction of the environmental impact of food production, preservation of farmland, and the promotion of agricultural jobs among others. Next, the San Francisco Food Policy Council was given the authority to monitor and advance all agenda items. Finally, city agencies were ordered to collaborate to conduct research and develop initiatives so as to make the goals of the executive order a reality.[52]

It is too soon to tell whether this executive order will have an impact on the development of a healthy and sustainable food system in San Francisco. However, given the number of obstacles that exist in attempting such a shift in the food system of any U.S. city, efforts to coordinate city agencies in support of a sustainable food system make this initiative an ambitious and innovative effort.

Community Development in Philadelphia

Philadelphia stands out as another leader in the development of a sustainable urban food system. The city currently has more than thirty farmers' markets, forty restaurants, twenty-five specialty stores that serve locally produced products, and more than two hundred community gardens.[53] Like other cities in the development of a sustainable urban food system, Philadelphia aims to improve access to healthy and affordable food and create new jobs. However, Philadelphia is unique in its use of urban agriculture as a tool to facilitate social ties and community development in underserved, low-income neighborhoods.

In Philadelphia urban agriculture has primarily taken the form of community gardens. Most often these gardens are established on vacant lots as a way to beautify blighted blocks. Many join the gardens more for a sense of community rather than necessarily for the food that is produced in the garden.[54] As noted earlier, community gardens often end up acting as an outdoor community center and offer neighbors a chance to organize around common concerns. Typically, community organizing and social ties develop around creation of the garden, or an effort to maintain access to the land on which a garden is located. However, as relationships develop between gardeners and neighbors grow to know each other, the gardens take on new roles and meaning.

The relationships developed between gardeners also tend to bring neighbors together to confront neighborhood safety issues. Research has shown that the more people are outside the less likely crime is to occur. Additionally, the more neighbors know each other the less likely crime is to occur—acts of crime tend to be against strangers, therefore even informal relationships reduce the likelihood of muggings and robberies and increase community safety. Philadelphia has been unique in the urban agriculture movement for recognizing this function and supporting the development of community gardens in low-income neighborhoods.

Multiple Cities Embrace Food Systems Planning

Nearly a decade ago, Pothukuchi and Kaufman documented the extent to which the city planning profession has ignored the food system, despite ample evidence that food production, processing, and retailing have significant local and regional land use, economic development, and public health consequences.[55] Recently, there has been an explosion of interest in urban food systems spurred by a greater appreciation of the consequences for cities: obesity and diet-related health problems, hunger and food insecurity, the loss of peri-urban farmland.

As a result of a growing interest in food, urban planners are beginning to pay increasing attention to food systems, the relationship between food and agriculture and cities, and food's relationship to the urban systems traditionally under the purview of planning departments, such as housing, open space, transportation, and economic development. Within the last few years, professional planning associations in North America and Europe have articulated the importance of food planning in policy directives, reports, and increasingly well-attended conferences on food systems planning.[56] Many states, counties, tribal councils, and cities have also started or supported citizen-based food policy councils to involve stakeholders in setting goals and implementing activities to improve the local food system.[57] Municipalities have conducted assessments, cataloguing sources of food production and retailing or land suitable for food production, developing indicators of food system sustainability, and, in some cases, integrating food into their general plan.

More and more cities have been very proactive at adjusting their local land use policies to promote urban agriculture, food access, and a more sustainable food system. Seattle, for example, declared 2010 the Year of Urban Agriculture, providing city resources and encouraging people to grow food and increase the number of gardens in Seattle. Among many other initiatives, the city is working on implementing a food system plan, expanding its network of community gardens (called the P-Patch program), and working with King County planners to implement a transfer of development rights program to protect farms that provide produce for Seattle's farmers' markets. On June 10, 2010, the Kansas City, Missouri, city council adopted an ordinance to foster urban agriculture by allowing onsite sales of food in urban gardens and farms, enabling local food growers to have apprentices and interns, allowing gardening as a principal or accessory usage of a property, and allowing homeowners to grow produce in their front yard for their own consumption or off-site sales.[58] On March 11, 2010, Georgia's House Committee on Agriculture and Consumer Affairs reported out legislation that would preempt local ordinances so that individuals may grow food crops and raise small animals on private property, covering community or cooperative gardens, coops, or pens as well as individual backyard gardens, coops, or pens.[59] Maryland's House considered legislation authorizing local governments to give a five-year property tax credit for urban agricultural property.

Conclusion

New York is among several cities in the United States that has recognized the importance of developing a sustainable regional food system. As described throughout the chapter many steps have been taken over the last couple of years to begin acting on this recognition. The city has taken an interdisciplinary approach working across many agencies to bring various initiatives to life. Additionally, New York is working to address various aspects of the food system from production to distribution to retail and consumption. This last element is critical to creating a system that works harmoniously and is truly sustainable.

Improved land tenure for garden space and support of both urban farms and rooftop gardens play an important role in improving the local food supply. Additionally, the relationship between New York City and the farmers in the Hudson Valley/Catskill region provides a unique opportunity for close collaboration. The farmers benefit from a lively and prosperous agricultural community, while city residents benefit from both a local food supply and a preserved watershed. In combination, these efforts will continue to strengthen the reliable availability of fresh local food. By upgrading the Hunts Point distribution center so that it is more accessible to smaller scale retailers, New York will drastically impact the number of stores that are able to acquire produce through this channel. Additional renovations can make Hunts Point more accessible to the small- and medium-scale farms that the city is working to develop and preserve throughout its watershed. Finally, a focus on retail has significantly shifted who has the ability to purchase fresh fruits and vegetables. Initiatives like Healthy Bodegas, FRESH, and Green Carts are widening the food options for nearly 3 million New Yorkers who had previously limited access to healthy choices. Further, increasing enrollment in and acceptability of WIC and SNAP (food stamps) at farmers markets throughout the city allows low-income individuals to participate in previously off-limits markets.

All of these initiatives are encouraging. While they are largely new, with limited data to prove their efficacy, there are many reasons to believe that they will be largely successful. However, there is still a great deal of work to do before New York City can boast a sustainable regional food system. Some issues that still need to be tackled are topics like nutrition education and cooking classes, composting and reduced food waste, and increased affordability of healthy food options. Despite the work that stands before New York, the city can still be proud of the initiatives that it has implemented. And they can be assured that they are at least on the right trajectory toward creating a food system that serves all city residents and has a reduced impact on the physical environment.

Notes

1. New York City Council Press Room, "Speaker Quinn Announces 'Food Works New York,'" 2009, *The Council of the City of New York Office of Communications*, http://council .nyc.gov/html/releases/foodworks_12_7_09.shtml (August 5, 2010).

2. Donofrio, Gregory A. "Feeding the City." *Gastronomica* (2007): 30–41.

3. New York City Department of City Planning, "Going to Market: New York City's Neighborhood Grocery Store and Supermarket Shortage," 2008, *Department of City Planning*, www.nyc.gov/html/dcp/html/supermarket/index.shtml (August 5, 2010).

4. Ibid.

5. Market Ventures, Inc. and Karp Resources. "New York City Wholesale Farmers' Market Study." *Market Ventures, Inc. and Karp Resources* (2005): 8.

6. Friedman, Adam. "More Than a Link in the Food Chain: A Study of the Citywide Economic Impact of Food Manufacturing in New York City." *NY Industrial Retention Network and Fiscal Policy Institute.* (2007).

7. Ibid.

8. Ibid.

9. Vitiello, D., and M. Nairn. *Community Gardening in Philadelphia 2008 Harvest Report*. PA: University of Pennsylvania, 2009.

10. Lawson, Laura J. *City Bountiful: A Century of Community Gardening in America*. Berkeley: University of California Press, 2005.

11. Englander, D. *New York's Community Gardens—A Resource at Risk*. The Trust for Public Land. 2001.

12. Lawson, Laura J. *City Bountiful: A Century of Community Gardening in America*. Berkeley: University of California Press, 2005.

13. Green Thumb, "Welcome to Green Thumb," *New York City Department of Parks and Recreation*, n.d., www.greenthumbnyc.org/ (August 5, 2010).

14. Ibid.

15. Voicu, I., and V. Been. *The Effects of Community Gardens on Neighboring Property Values*. NY: New York University, 2007.

16. Conserving Land for People, "Overview of NYC Garden Land Trusts," *The Trust for Public Land*, n.d., www.tpl.org/tier3_cd.cfm?content_item_id=15456&folder_id=631 (August 5, 2010).

17. Englander, D. *New York's Community Gardens—A Resource at Risk*. The Trust for Public Land. 2001.

18. Greenmarket, "New Farmers Development Project," *Greenmarket*, n.d., www.grownyc.org/greenmarket/nfdp (August 5, 2010).

19. Added Value, "About Us," *Added Value*, n.d., www.added-value.org/history (August 5, 2010).

20. BK Farmyards, "About Us," *BK Farmyards*, n.d., http://bkfarmyards.blogspot.com/p/about-bk-farmyards.html (August 5, 2010).

21. Environmental Protection Agency, "Heat Island Effect Research," *Environmental Protection Agency*, n.d., www.epa.gov/heatisland/research/index.html (August 5, 2010).

22. Doshi, Hitesh. *Environmental benefits of green roofs on a city scale: An example of the city of Toronto*. Boston, Green Roofs for Healthy Cities, 2006.

23. Eagle Street Rooftop Farm, "What We Offer," *Eagle Street Rooftop Farm*, n.d., http://rooftopfarms.org/ (August 5, 2010).

24. Brooklyn Grange Farm, "About Us," *Brooklyn Grange Farm*, n.d., http://brooklyngrangefarm.com/ (August 5, 2010).

25. Economic Research Service, "Conservation Policy: Farmland and Grassland Protection Programs," United States Department of Agriculture, n.d., www.ers.usda.gov/Briefing/ConservationPolicy/farmland.htm (August 5, 2010).

26. Veslany, Kathleen. *Purchase of Development Rights: Conserving Lands, Preserving Western Livelihoods*. San Francisco: Trust for Public Land, 2002.

27. New Jersey Department of Environmental Protection, "Green Acres Program," *New Jersey Department of Environmental Protection*, n.d., www.state.nj.us/dep/greenacres/ (August 5, 2010).

28. Ibid.

29. Natural Resources Conservation Service, "FY-2003 New Jersey Farm and Ranch Lands Protection Program," *Natural Resources Conservation Service*, 2003, www.nrcs.usda.gov/programs/frpp/StateFacts/NJ2002.html (August 5, 2010).

30. New York City Department of Education, "School Meals Program," *New York City Department of Education*, n.d. www.opt-osfns.org/osfns/meals/default.aspx (August 5, 2010).

31. U.S. Environmental Protection Agency, "New York City Filtration Avoidance Determination. Surface Water Treatment Rule Determination for New York City's Catskill/Delaware Water Supply System," U.S. *Environmental Protection Agency*, 2007, www.epa.gov/region2/water/nycshed/doc_links.html (August 5, 2010).

32. New York City Department of Environmental Protection, "Watershed Protection," New York City Department of Environmental Protection, n.d., www.nyc.gov/html/dep/html/watershed_protection/index.shtml (August 5, 2010).

33. Story, Mary et al, "Creating Healthy Food and Eating Environments: Policy and Environmental Approaches." *Annual Review of Public Health* no. 29 (2008): 253–72.

34. Office of the Mayor. "Executive Order No. 122. Food Policy Coordinator for the City of New York and City Agency Food Standards," The City of New York, September 19, 2008, www.cspinet.org/new/pdf/nyc_food_standards_executive_order.pdf (August 9, 2010).

35. Ibid.

36. New York City Department of Health and Mental Hygiene, "Physical Activity and Nutrition," *New York City Department of Health and Mental Hygiene*, n.d., www.nyc.gov/html/doh/html/cdp/cdp_pan_hbi.shtml (August 5, 2010).

37. New York City Department of Health and Mental Hygiene. (2010) New York City Healthy Bodegas Initiative 2010 Report.

38. Ibid.

39. Local Law 9 of 2008 amends Section 17-306 of the administrative code of the city of New York to allow additional green cart licenses.

40. New York City Department of Health and Mental Hygiene. (2009) Report to the New York City Council on Green Carts FY 2008–2009. September 2009.

41. Zenk, S.N. et al., "Fruit and vegetable intake in African Americans income and store characteristics." *American Journal of Preventive Medicine*, 2005.

42. Morland, K., Wing, S., and Roux, A.D., "The contextual effect of the local food environment on residents' diets." *American Journal of Public Health*. 2002.; Moore, L. V., and A. Diez Roux, "Associations of neighborhood characteristics with the location and type of food stores." *American Journal of Public Health*, 2006.; Powell, L. M., et al. "Food store availability and neighborhood characteristics in the United States." *Preventive Medicine* 44, no. 3 (2007): 189-95.

43. Graham R., et al., "Eating in, eating out, eating well: Access to healthy food in North and Central Brooklyn.," *New York City Department of Health and Mental Hygiene*, 2006, www.nyc.gov/html/doh/downloads/pdf/dpho/dpho-brooklyn-report2006.pdf (August 9, 2010).

44. NYC.gov, "Food Retail to Support Health Initiative," *NYC.gov*, n.d., www.nyc.gov/html/misc/html/2009/fresh.shtml (August 5, 2010).

45. Poppendieck, Janet. *Free for All: Fixing School Food in America*. Berkeley: University of California Press, 2010.

46. Stringer, Scott M., "FoodNYC: A Blueprint for a Sustainable Food System," NY: *Office of the President of the Borough of Manhattan*, 2010, www.mbpo.org/release_details.asp?id=1496 (August 9, 2010).

47. New York City Council Press Room, "Speaker Quinn Announces 'Food Works New York,'" 2009, *The Council of the City of New York Office of Communications*, http://council .nyc.gov/html/releases/foodworks_12_7_09.shtml (August 5, 2010).

48. Treuhaft, S., M. J. Hamm, and C. Litjens, *Healthy Food for All: Building Equitable and Sustainable Food Systems in Detroit and Oakland*. MI: Michigan State University, 2009.

49. Fair Food Network, "About Us," *Fair Food Network*, n.d., www.fairfoodnetwork.org/ (August 5, 2010).

50. Gallagher, J., "Is urban farming Detroit's cash cow? 2010 may yield profit as efforts reap jobs, tax base," *Free Press*, 2010, www.freep.com/article/20100321/BUSINESS04 /3210433/1318/Is-farming-Detroits-cash-cow (August 5, 2010).

51. Thompson, E. Jr., A. E. Harper, and S. Kraus. "Think Globally—Eat Locally: San Francisco Foodshed Assessment," *American Farmland Trust*. 2008, www.farmland.org /programs/states/ca/Feature%20Stories/San-Francisco-Foodshed-Report.asp (August 5, 2010).

52. Executive Order 09-03 Healthy and Sustainable Food for San Francisco. July 9, 2009. Mayor Gavin Newsom. City & County of San Francisco.

53. Caggiano, C., E. Dowdall, C. Kwan, and A. Wagner. "Farming in Philadelphia? A Proposal for a Sustainable Urban Farm Incubator," *University of Pennsylvania*. 2009, www.design.upenn.edu/files/Panorama09_08_FarmIncubator_Caggianoetal.pdf (August 5, 2010). See also Vitiello, D., and M. Nairn, *Community Gardening in Philadelphia 2008 Harvest Report*. PA: University of Pennsylvania, 2009.

54. Hanna, A. K., and P. Oh. "Rethinking Urban Poverty: A Look at Community Gardens." *Bulletin of Science, Technology and Society*, no. 3 (2000): 207–16.

55. Pothukuchi, K., and J. L. Kaufman. "The Food System: A Stranger to the Planning Field." *American Planning Association. Journal of the American Planning Association*, no. 2 (2000): 113.

56. Mikherji, N., and A. Morales. "Practice: Urban Agriculture." *Zoning Practice*, no. 3 (2010).

57. Community Food Security Coalition, "Food Policy Councils," *Community Food Security* Coalition, n.d., www.foodsecurity.org/FPC/council.html (August 5, 2010).

58. Farris, Emily, "City Council Examines Changes to Urban Agriculture Code: CSAs Top the List of Concerns for Those Unsure of Changes," *KCFreePress*, 2010, www .kcfreepress.com/news/2010/may/05/council-examines-changes-urban-agriculture-code/ (August 5, 2010).

59. Georgia General Assembly, "HB 842—Agriculture; Preempt Certain Local Ordinances; Protect Right to Grow Food Crops," *Georgia General Assembly*, 2010, www.legis .ga.gov/legis/2009_10/sum/hb842.htm (August 5, 2010).

Chapter 11

Where Sustainability Stands Now: Contemporary Trends and Future Prospects

Matthew I. Slavin

Those who cannot remember the past are condemned to repeat it.

George Santayana (1905), *Reason in Common Sense*

Thumbing through a copy of Jane Jacobs's seminal 1961 work *The Death and Life of Great American Cities*, it is surprising how little is said about the relationship between urban growth and development and the larger circle of natural assets upon which life in the city depends. This might possibly be attributed to the formative experiences that led Jacobs to write the book, reflecting her pique with the building predilections of Robert Moses and imbuing *Death and Life* with an inward focus revolving around issues of urban regeneration and neighborhood protection. Of course, the year following publication of Jacobs's formative book saw the appearance of another work that would shape the attitudes of future generations and do as much as anything to ignite the environmental movement in America. This was Rachel Carson's *Silent Spring*, published in 1962. Yet, there has not always been a well-reflected convergence between the views espoused by these two groundbreaking books. The editor's recollection is that early-term graduate students in urban studies and planning found Jacob's book on their reading list while graduate students in environmental studies were directed to Carson. With the urban sustainability movement, the convergence between urban development and the environment has come much more clearly into focus.

What Do American Cities Say about the State of Sustainability Today?

It is the objective of this book to examine not just the announced goals but the mechanics and efficacy of the implementation of contemporary urban sustainability initiatives by U.S. cities. With this in mind, it is now time to turn attention to examining what the contributors to this book have to say about the current status of the movement to create more sustainable cities in the American context.

One conclusion that emerges from this book is that while cities have sought through their sustainability endeavors to mitigate or adopt to carrying capacity constraints and climate change, they have not done so within the context of seeking to "get smaller" but instead, to promote economic development and restructuring and accommodate growth. Evidence from this can be seen in Portland, Phoenix, St. Petersburg, Milwaukee, and, to a certain extent, in Honolulu's efforts to create a clean energy future to forestall the crippling effects oil dependence poses to its economic viability. A city with a long history of public intervention to promote economic development and livability, Portland's climate change initiatives became closely entwined with efforts to promote economic recovery after a particularly grueling downturn, and then more centrally and with some evident success, to promote restructuring and growth by establishing the city as a green economy and industry center. This is not to say that the resources Portland dedicated to mitigating and adapting to climate change were usurped or co-opted. The climate campaign predated the move to more fully embrace the green economy, and by all indications has stood in its own right, maintaining public and political support even amid troubling economic times and bringing together government, business, and environmentalists around common goals.

Phoenix has not developed a reputation as a leader among U.S. cities with regard to efforts to combat global warming. For example, of the fifty largest cities in the nation, SustainLane ranked Phoenix only thirty-second overall in terms of overall sustainability and thirty-fifth in terms of energy and climate care in 2008. However the first decade of the new century did see Arizona's capital city emerge as the focus of an industrial policy aimed at economic restructuring through a university-led consortium aimed at invigorating clean-tech business investment and development around green energy products. A couple of interesting points arise within the context of Phoenix's experience. First, that creating the green economy of tomorrow appears highly contingent upon political support and continuity and available financial resources. When the political winds shifted in Arizona and a progressive Democratic governor was replaced by a more conservative counterpart amid tightening economic conditions, support and investment in efforts to recast the Phoenix area as a leader in sustainable clean-tech business evaporated, leaving the city, traditionally dependent upon the building industries in particular, no clear path forward to economic rejuvenation.

The characterization of the role Arizona State University President Michael Crow played in the attempt to ignite a regional green economy in Phoenix is also instructive. Chapter 4 says little about the personal attributes of Crow in terms of personal ambition and charisma. However, it is clear that he was very committed to the university's green economy initiatives and possessed the vision and political skills needed to build a coalition to generate requisite support and public investment, at least until the political and economic winds shifted. Elsewhere we have seen the drive for city sustainability emerge as a result of a spontaneous rising by activists and through pragmatic coalitions coalesced around common purpose. Activists led a green bicycling insurrection in San Francisco, which reached proportions needed to overcome legal opposition as well as opposition from the city's mayor Willie Brown, a politician with a reputation for "personal magnetism . . . and charisma always evident."[1] There is likewise evidence of the role activism played in widespread mobilization among New Yorkers to plant a million trees in America's largest city in order to offset globally warming emissions. However, in the case of New York and in contrast to San Francisco's experience, activists were responding to a plan introduced by the city's mayor.

The chapters on Philadelphia and Milwaukee point to different pathways to mobilization and participation by institutional stakeholders. In Philadelphia, multiple jurisdictions joined together in a collaborative effort to protect and sustainably manage a watershed vital to all of them. This joining forms a critical component of Philadelphia's ability to implement low-impact development techniques in addressing the need to manage storm water flows for the nation's sixth-largest city. The effort to recreate the Menomonee Valley as a sustainable center of industry and jobs is cast as a highly participatory, collaborative, and consensus-driven initiative bringing together business, government, and nonprofit institutions in an effort to reclaim the city's past within a contemporary environment. Together, these stakeholders leveraged a plan that would promote a level of social and economic equity for those who would work in an environmentally restored Menomonee Valley. This stands in stark contrast to the all too frequent exodus of business from America's urban centers in search of overseas production centers where environmental protections are weak and the cost of employing and the threshold for meeting the other health and welfare needs of employees are much less, if existent at all. The coalitions that came together in the effort to restore the Menomonee Valley into a sustainable business center and sustainably manage Philadelphia's regional watershed were going well beyond the minimum of what would be required by state and federal regulatory requirements.

Endeavors to create more sustainable cities can encounter conflicting visions as to what best makes an area sustainable. The jury is still out, but the possibility exists that Honolulu's endeavors to transform itself into the most energy independent city in the United States by developing renewable wind energy farms in neighboring islands may run into conflicts with land preservationists and native cultures who see the wind farms as a threat to local aesthetics and cultural considerations. By the same measure, however, the urban sustainability movement can be the source of new alignments. Once heavily invested in commercial nuclear generation, the investor-owned Portland General Electric Company has built a respectable record as being among the leading utilities in the United States to invest in renewable energy in meeting the needs of electricity consumers. HECO, Hawaii Electric, which serves Honolulu, may within twenty years become overwhelmingly reliant upon renewable energy and energy efficiency to meet the energy needs of its customers. The investor-owned company has agreed to far-reaching regulatory changes that will further clean energy development and require the company to redraft the way the utility has traditionally done business. In Hawaii, Republican Governor Lingle became a firm supporter of the move to end the state's reliance upon oil for electricity generation and propel the state toward a clean energy future, even while Republican George W. Bush was calling for Americans to further expand domestic oil drilling and refining as a solution to the nation's energy challenges.

Chapter 8 offers food for thought in terms of how local markets can be realigned to better nourish New Yorkers and in the process, spur local economic development efforts by capturing as much as $1 billion per year in food purchase revenues that are currently exported beyond the city's boundaries. New York's effort is also being driven by equity objectives; while conventional food distribution systems do appear to serve the city's affluent, they have not done so well for the city's poor. As with Honolulu's engagement with sustainable energy, the effort to create a more sustainable food production and distribution system in New York City also points to cities entering policy and planning domains in which they have not been extensively involved in the past. By the same measure, the cases of Honolulu and food production and distribution in New York point to the limits upon the autonomy of cities in seeking to make themselves more sustainable. In Honolulu, this is reflected in the principle authority that the Hawaii state government has in regulating electric utilities. New York City required changes in federal farm policy in order to adopt local food purchasing preferences for city schools.

While the case studies in this book point to the great deal of progress America's urban areas are making in sustainable development, progress is to a degree contingent upon cooperation by state and federal governments as well. As federal inaction on climate change legislation makes clear, there is no guarantee that a necessary level of intergovernmental agreement will always be there.

The initiatives profiled in this book point to ample evidence of the role innovative and forward-thinking policy and planning, leadership, stakeholder engagement, and mobilization by coalitions of the willing play in sustainable development in America's cities. But what do they say about technology? Honolulu's clean energy initiative efforts are focused upon developing regulatory provisions to accelerate deployment of electric vehicles and wind farms to generate electricity represent a departure from its historic dependence upon traditional fossil fuels. Through regulatory provisions, Honolulu also seeks to install energy efficiency measures to reduce dependence upon oil for electricity generation.

However, the path to a greener city is not always one that requires highly technical solutions. Honolulu has also enacted regulations to ensure access to sunlight for clothes drying. Philadelphia's approach to regional watershed management incorporates low impact technical solutions to the problem of resolving combined sewer overflow. Indeed, natural capital can be seen as a form of technology in the drive to create more sustainable cities. New York city aims to offset local greenhouse gas (GHG) emissions by planting a million trees. However, natural capitol presents challenges as well, as revealed in chapter 9 regarding the survivability of the trees that are being planted in America's largest city. Clearly, success in creating more sustainable cities will require that technology be effective coupled to effective policy and management.

This becomes clear with regard to LEED green building as well. "LEED is a force to be reckoned with."[2] The number of local governments that in some form or another currently encourage or require LEED certification for new building construction exceeds 200. Chapter 5 points to the success of LEED green building as the product of a convergence of interests between the public and private sectors and the height to which LEED has risen on urban agendas is perhaps the most visible sign of the institutionalization of urban sustainability in the United States. At the same time, there remain challenges to the degree to which the green building rating system can fully achieve its potential. An example is the discrepancy between the energy savings design potential of LEED buildings and the degree to which, once built, these buildings are actually operated in a manner that allows them to achieve their maximum potential. With a *USA Today* headline reporting "Economic downturn pounds commercial real estate market," the wherewithal of building owners to make the investments needed to operate their buildings to maximum efficiency remains open to question.[3] The conclusion to be drawn is that the pathway to a more sustainable future requires commitment to follow through in managing a city's assets and initiatives in an environmentally, socially, and economically sustainable manner over the long term.

What Other Cities Are Doing

There are, of course, other cities engaged in the sustainability movement besides those profiled in this book. A brief look at what some of these cities are doing with regard to sustainability is insightful. The city of Boston has established an Environmental and Energy Services cabinet to oversee a broad menu of sustainability initiatives in that city. A leadership committee was drawn from city agencies, academia, businesses, and neighborhood coalitions to draft a citywide climate plan and has conducted and reported an annual greenhouse gas emissions inventory since 2005.[4] The emissions inventory targets both emissions directly attributable to municipal operations as well as emissions arising from residential, commercial, and industrial sources. The city's sustainability program includes initiatives in renewable energy and energy efficiency, alternative transportation, green building, and waste management. Green jobs are also a part of Boston's sustainable development program. It was noted in the first chapter of this book that cities have found the Obama administration to be more receptive to their sustainable development ambitions than the preceding Bush administration. In 2009, the city received a $300,000 grant from the U.S. Department of Housing and Urban Development for training and hiring high-risk youth and workforce-displaced adults in areas such as recycling and conducting home energy audits.[5] In September 2010 Boston was selected as one of five cities nationwide to receive assistance under the U.S. Environmental Protection Agencies Greening America's Capitals program, to green public and community buildings and urban infrastructure. The other four cities are Charleston, West Virginia; Little Rock, Arkansas; Jefferson City, Missouri; and Hartford, Connecticut.

At an average of 1.8 meters, or 72 inches, above sea level, Miami is one of the lowest-lying cities in the United States. Projections point to Miami being subject to a global warming–induced "sea level rise of at least 18 inches in the next 50 years and 36 to 60 inches by 2100." This projected rise does not take into account the potential melting of the Greenland and arctic ice caps. At a minimum, $400 billion in property is estimated to be at risk due to climate change in the city and the figure could rise to $3.7 trillion by 2070.[6] In light of these projections, the *Wall Street Journal* has raised the question of whether property on Florida's southeast coastal cities will even be insurable in the future.[7] Serious engagement with sustainability in Miami began in late 2003 when a thirty-two-member task force was assembled to offer recommendations on what the city should do to prepare in the face of global warming. The scope of the challenge and the need to innovate were recognized early on, with the panel's chairman noting, "there are no success models to emulate . . . our efforts could well prove to be just such a guidepost for others to follow."[8] The city of Miami completed a greenhouse gas inventory in 2006, and Miami Mayor Manny Diaz, speaking in 2008 as the newly elected head of the U.S. Conference of Mayors, drew attention to progress the city had made by installing photovoltaic solar panels at city hall, perhaps the first city in the country to do so. LEED is also a key component of Miami's sustainability program, and Diaz pointed to the city's new green building law, commenting "The message in the city of Miami is you are either going to build green or you are not going to build at all."[9] Still, it appears more could be done given the severity of the threat. SustainLane ranks Miami-Dade as tied with Phoenix in only thirty-fifth place in terms of energy and climate action among the nation's fifty largest cities.

In contrast to Miami, Denver almost certainly ranks among the U.S. cities least likely to experience flooding from sea level rise. However atmospheric warming is likely to increase snowmelt in the Rocky Mountains with adverse consequences for Colorado's ski industry and potentially as well for Denver's water supply, which is drawn off from Rocky Mountain snowmelt. In 2006, Denver Mayor John Hickenlooper announced a plan to plant 1 million trees in the city by 2025 to offset local CO_2 emissions. In October 2007, Denver's mayor issued an executive order that established a GreenPrint sustainability monitoring and reporting protocol as the city's principal sustainability management tool to tie together initiatives that "can be "tracked, measured, refined, and reported . . . and will position the city as a national leader in a global effort to meet the needs of the present without compromising the ability of future generations to meet their own."[10] The mayor also established a green building policy that requires all buildings constructed with city funds to be built to LEED Silver standards. It's instructive to note that in mid-2010, the Denver area was ranked third by *Site Selection Magazine* on its first ever list of sustainable metropolitan areas.[11] *Site Selection*'s readership mainly consists of industrial location consultants and economic developers. The magazine's sustainability rankings reflect something of a departure from past practice at *Site Selection* whose business climate rankings have been more likely to rank localities in terms of the laxness of local and state environmental and workforce protection standards. Perhaps this is a sign of exactly how far sustainability has come in permeating public as well as business sector consciousness.

It's likewise instructive to note an incident that arose in 2010 when a conservative candidate for election as U.S. senator for Colorado criticized a city of Denver bicycle-sharing initiative as comprising a "well disguised plan . . . for converting Denver into a United Nations community . . . which may not be compatible with (the Colorado) state constitution."[12] If unfortunate, it is perhaps no surprise that formidable business and regional forces have coalesced in opposition to federal climate legislation given the scope that such legislation will have upon the nation. That a bicycle-sharing program should become entrapped in similar political maneuvering suggest that even at the most seemingly benign level urban sustainability initiatives are not immune to the apoplectic disputes that seem to surround almost all aspects of American public policy as the first decade of the twenty-first century draws to a close.

The city of Dallas completed a GHG emissions plan in 2005. Again, green building is a central component of the city's sustainability program, with requirements established in 2003 that all buildings larger than 10,000 square feet financed with city bond revenues be built to LEED Silver standards. In 2005, the city adopted an environmental policy committing he municipality to "implementation of programs and procedures with an intent to meet or exceed all applicable environmental laws and regulations."

Beginning in October 2009, all newly constructed residential and commercial buildings were required to meet energy efficiency and water conservation standards. The city is in the process of developing policy that is anticipated to require all new buildings to meet a comprehensive green building standard beginning in 2011. Energy efficiency measures, bicycle transportation, recycling, and tree planting are also included as part of the city's sustainability efforts.[13]

Like Denver, Minneapolis has also adopted a GreenPrint protocol as the centerpiece of its sustainability efforts. Among the city's initiatives is Homegrown Minneapolis, aimed at fostering expanded markets for locally produced foodstuffs. Minneapolis has created a number of city-sponsored working groups that are working to develop short-, mid-, and long-term strategies for creating and sustaining local food resource hubs. Another objective of the in the city's sustainability plan aims to eliminate combined sewerage overflows, a problem Minneapolis shares with Philadelphia. Sustainability indicators have not been a focus of this book. However, development of indicator metrics with which to measure and track progress are often the first step in any locality's entry into the sustainability milieu Minneapolis's indicators encompass not only such commonplace measures of environmental footprint as GHG emissions and the purchase of renewable energy but also social indicators that target a reduction in asthma hospitalizations and HIV/AIDS and other sexually transmitted disease-related hospitalizations, high school graduation rates, and a reduction in the number of employed residents living in poverty in the city from a 2008 baseline of 10.1 percent to 7 percent by 2014.[14] Minneapolis in particular appears to have developed an expansive set of indicators to assess how the city is fairing in addressing both the environmental, economic, and social dimensions of the triple bottom line concept.

As noted in the introductory chapter, the cities profiled in this book have been selected because, as larger municipalities, they have often had greater resources with which to approach their sustainability endeavors. In the *Boston Review*, Catherine Tumber has written, "Sustainability advocates could be missing the large, strategic, regional and economic advantages smaller cities can offer. . . .

if we temper the metropolitan bias that pervades the sustainable cities movement, green advantages and opportunities distinctive to smaller cities come into focus."[15] As a practical matter, there is not at the current time a great deal in the literature on sustainable development in smaller American cities. However if one considers that all of the cities profiled in this book rank among the fifty most populous in the United States, a brief look at the status of sustainability initiatives in several less populous—if not necessarily small—cities can provide some additional insight as well into the current status of sustainability in America's cities.

Now the nation's ninety-ninth largest city, Akron's path to sustainability differs from many larger cities. Whereas Philadelphia has established the Mayor's Office of Sustainability, Milwaukee city government has created the Office of Environmental Sustainability, and reorganization in Portland, Oregon, created the city Bureau of Planning and Sustainability, Akron has chosen to create a nonprofit corporation to lead its sustainability initiatives. In 2007, shortly after signing on to the U.S. Conference of Mayor's climate protection agreement, the city authorized funding from mandatory street assessments, which together with private donations, provided a $200,000 budget for the nonprofit Keep Akron Beautiful to develop and manage a citywide sustainability plan.[16] Created in 1981 to manage a citywide litter prevention, recycling, and beautification program, the organization has since adopted GreenPrint as its sustainability scorecard. Local initiatives include an incubator to support early-stage, advanced, renewable energy enterprise and various brownfield restoration and land-banking projects.[17]

Boise, Idaho, became a signatory to the mayor's climate protection agreement in 2006. The city has adopted a list of sustainable practices, targeting green building as well as energy conservation, waste reduction, recycling, water conservation, and maintaining parks and open space. But Boise has yet to complete a green house gas inventory, and although at least three LEED-certified buildings have been constructed in the city, including one attaining Platinum certification, the city requires only that LEED be considered when public funds are used for building construction and not that buildings be designed and constructed to LEED standards. For the most part, Boise's list of sustainable practices appears to comprise activities in which the city has been engaged for a number of years and, at least at the current time, sustainability appears more as a vehicle for rebranding existing activities than comprising a new direction in city policy in its own right. Boise did create an advisory committee that provided recommendations in 2008 for changes to municipal building, zoning, and subdivision code changes and measures to improve energy use in support of the municipality's climate protection obligations. However no cost-effectiveness analysis of these recommendations has yet been performed. To their credit, city leaders acknowledge, "More needs to be done."[18] How Boise will proceed in terms of investing in a sustainable future remains, however, undetermined.

With a population of 111,000, Flint, Michigan, has only 56 percent of the number of residents it had in 1960. Once home to more than 75,000 GM employees, deindustrialization has left Flint with a July 2010 unemployment rate exceeding 15 percent, fourteenth highest in the nation among metropolitan areas.[19] Flint is party to the mayor's climate agreement. However no greenhouse gas inventory has been undertaken. City-supported "Green Flint" consists of an Internet site with links to state and nonprofit energy and environmental information centers. Flint's experience must be understood in the context of the perilous state of city finances. Officials in Flint believe that the city needs to contract by as much as 40 percent; more than 1,000 vacant homes have already been demolished by the city with plans for additional demolitions pending.[20] Herbert Girardet and Richard Register, founder of Eco-City Builders, have pointed to the need for cities to decentralize in order to reduce fossil fuel consumption in the face of climate changes. The Brookings Institution has identified fifty U.S. cities that are likely to need to shrink due to population loss accompanied by declining revenues.[21] Included are Detroit, Pittsburg, Baltimore, and Memphis. Plans are already under discussion in Detroit to split the city into small urban centers separated by reclaimed countryside. Less so by reason of a desire to reduce fossil fuel consumption and lighten its footprint upon the earth than due to demographic and fiscal imperatives driving the need to achieve a fiscally sustainable size, Flint may be among the first of U.S. cities headed toward a future characterized by Newman, Beatley, and Boyer as "ruralization."[22]

Future Prospects

If the first decade of the twenty-first century dawned with promise for those seeking to create more sustainable cities in America, the decade appears to be closing on an uncertain note. As the last words in this book were being written, the International City and County Management Association (ICMA) released the results of what may be the first national survey on the status of local government sustainability initiatives in the United States.[23] The survey was sent to more than

8,500 local governments with approximately one-quarter of these responding. The picture painted by the survey is one in which communities across the nation have taken increasing note of sustainability issues. However "while there is near shared agreement in the desire to create more sustainable communities, putting goals into action is a larger challenge." In many localities, specific sustainability plans have been slow to take hold: only 29 percent of local governments responding to the survey had adopted resolutions outlining specific sustainability policy goals, only 27 percent had dedicated staff to sustainability, only 19 percent had developed sustainability benchmarks, and only 16 percent had developed a dedicated sustainability budget. The cities featured in this book have been among the leaders in embracing the urban sustainability movement, and clearly sustainability has taken hold of the agendas of America's cities. However much more work remains to be done.

The recession that beset the United States beginning in the last quarter of 2007 has been followed by a fitful recovery. Municipal finances have been greatly impaired; the National League of Cities projects that the nation's municipal sector will face budget shortfalls of between $56 and $83 billion between 2010 and 2012 due to recession-induced declines in tax revenues and state government transfer payments. According to the NLC,

> City leaders are responding with layoffs, furloughs, and payroll reductions; delaying and canceling capital infrastructure projects; and cutting city services. One in seven cities (14 percent) has already made cuts to public safety services—police, fire, and emergency—a number that will inevitably rise as the municipal budget shortfalls increase.[24]

Amid this economic climate, the degree to which cities will be able to commit resources needed to continue and accelerate sustainable development initiatives is open to question.

LEED has made significant contributions toward making cities more sustainable. However, the economic downturn also casts doubt upon the ability of the commercial real estate sector to continue to invest in green building in the foreseeable future. The U.S. Department of Energy has dedicated $10 million to implement the Solar America Cities program. Under the program, DOE has contracted with ICLEI and ICMA to deliver technical assistance to local governments seeking to accelerate deployment of solar energy technologies in their communities. However another federal program important to advocates of sustainable cities is imperiled. This is PACE, Property Assessed Clean Energy, which would allow local governments to issue bonds and use the proceeds to lower the upfront costs incurred by homeowners in installing clean energy improvements in their homes. Opposition by the Federal Housing Authority to accepting mortgages containing the liens that would be required under PACE has jeopardized the program's future. Local government leaders spent 2009 lobbying Congress for legislation that would override the mortgage entities's opposition; however, a legislative solution to the problem looks beyond reach given the recent upheaval in national housing markets and political paralysis in Washington. The 2008 American Recovery and Reinvestment Act economic stimulus authorized $8 billion to begin planning construction of a number of high-speed rail networks that would connect a number of major metropolitan areas. One line would connect Californians living in Sacramento, the San Francisco Bay Area, Los Angeles, and San Diego. However, recent projections that ridership will be lower than originally estimated, while costs may rise significantly in a state with a 13.5 unemployment rate, makes the rail project's future uncertain as well.

The April 2010 Deepwater Horizon oil platform explosion is a reminder of the risks posed by continued overdependence upon an urban energy and transportation infrastructure reliant upon oil. Nor is the nation's food infrastructure immune from potential catastrophe. August 2010 saw the recall of more than a half-billion eggs contaminated with salmonella due to unsanitary conductions at large "factory" farms in the nation's Midwest.[25] Storm-induced power outages left more than 430,000 customers without electricity in metropolitan Washington, D.C., during July 2010. The Obama administration has successfully raised fuel mileage standards for the nation's automobile fleet; however, there are threats in Congress to strip from the Environmental Protection Agency authority for regulating emissions of globally warming CO_2 emissions. That the EPA is moving toward regulation of CO_2 emissions stems from Congress' failure to pass comprehensive legislation regulating greenhouse gas emissions during 2010. According to the National Oceanic and Atmospheric Administration, 2010 tied with 2005 as the warmest year on record since 1880, when reliable recordkeeping began.[26] In August 2010, an iceberg four times the size of Manhattan calved off into the Atlantic Ocean from a melting glacier in Greenland, a direct consequence of global warming. Yet some commentators believe that with Congress having failed to enact climate change legislation during the warmest year on record, it may be years before comprehensive national legislation to regulate greenhouse gas emissions is considered again.[27]

This book highlights how a select group of large cities have pursued sustainable development through strategies targeting clean energy and climate change mitigation and adaptation, green building, clean-tech economic development and urban revitalization, sustainable transportation and infrastructure, urban forestry, and sustainable food production. It was never going to be easy to create more sustainable cities and, clearly, significant obstacles remain. However some of America's largest cities have shown themselves willing and able to act sustainably in responding to the consequential impacts their urban footprints are having upon environmental carrying capacity, the need to mitigate and adapt to global climate change, and the goal of creating the green economy. This editor is confident that he speaks for all of the book's contributors in concluding that the lessons learned by these cities are cause for optimism if we are to ensure continued progress in the enterprise of creating greener, more sustainable cities in the United States.

Notes

1. Karl Kurtz, "The Pragmatism and Charisma of Willie Brown," *The Thicket at State Legislatures*, March 21, 2008, National Council of State Legislatures, http://ncsl.typepad .com/the_thicket/2008/03/by-karl-kurtz-w.html.

2. Franklyn Cater, "Critics Say LEED Program Doesn't Fulfill Promises," NPR, September 8, 2010. www.npr.org/templates/story/story.php?storyId=129727547.

3. Sue Kirchhoff, "Economic Downturn Pounds Commercial Real Estate Market," *USA Today*, January 12, 2009, www.usatoday.com/money/economy/2009-01-11-commercial -real-estate_N.htm.

4. City of Boston, "Sparking Boston's Climate Revolution: Recommendations of the Climate Action Leadership Committee and Community Advisory Committee," April 2010, www.cityofboston.gov/Images . . . /BCA_full_rprt_r5_tcm3-16529.pdf.

5. CityofBoston.gov, "Boston One of Five Cities Chosen by U.S. EPA Under Greening America Capital Cities Program," September 9, 2010, www.cityofboston.gov/news/default .aspx?id=4752.

6. City of Miami, Office of Sustainable Initiatives, *Climate Action Plan*, June 2008, www.miamigov.com/msi/pages/.

7. Laurence C. Smith, "Unfreezing Arctic Assets," *Wall Street Journal*, September 18, 2010, http://online.wsj.com/article/SB10001424052748703440604575496261529207620 .html?mod=WSJ_hps_LEFTTopStories.

8. Stephen Ursery, "Miami-Dade Studying Climate Change," *American City & County*, December 1, 2003, http://americancityandcounty.com/mag/government_miamidade _studying_climate/.

9. David Adams, "Highlights of the Miami Climate Change Summit #2 from Solar to PHEVs," *TampaBay.com*, June 27, 2008, http://blogs.tampabay.com/energy/2008/06 /highlights-of-t.html.

10. City of Denver, "Sustainability: A Core Value in Denver City Government," *Greenprint Denver*, n.d., www.greenprintdenver.org/about/.

11. *Denver Business Journal*, "Denver 3rd in Site Selection's Sustainability Rankings," July 2, 2010, http://denver.bizjournals.com/denver/stories/2010/06/28/daily66.html; Adam Bruns, "The Green Guide: West Is the Best: Ranking First in Half of Our Eight Criteria, California Tops Site Selection's First Annual Sustainability Rankings," *Site Selection Online*, July 2010, www.siteselection.com/issues/2010/jul/GreenG_SustainRank/.

12. Climate Progress, "CO GOP Candidate Maes Worries Bike-share Program 'May Not be Compatible with State Constitution,'" August 10, 2010, http://climateprogress.org/2010 /08/10/colorado-tea-party-candidate-dan-maes-bike-sharing/.

13. *Green Dallas.net*, "Green Buildings," n.d., www.greendallas.net/green_buildings .html.

14. City of Minneapolis, "Minneapolis Greenprint," 2010, www.ci.minneapolis.mn.us /sustainability/MinneapolisGreenprint.asp.

15. Catherine Tumber, "Small, Green and Good: The Role of Neglected Cities in a Sustainable Future," *Boston Review*, March/April 2009, http://bostonreview.net/BR34.2/tumber .php.

16. Marc Lefkowitz, "Akron Prepares Sustainability Plan," *GreenCityBlueLake*, November 14, 2007, www.gcbl.org/blog/marc-lefkowitz/akron-launches-sustainability-plan.

17. Keep Akron Beautiful, "The Greenprint for Akron," 2010, www.keepakronbeautiful .org/greenprint.

18. City of Boise, "Climate Protection Program," 2010, www.cityofboise.org /Departments/Public_Works/Services/AirQuality/page18402.aspx.

19. U.S. Department of Labor, Bureau of Labor Statistics, "Unemployment Rates for Metropolitan Areas," July 2010, www.bls.gov/web/metro/laummtrk.htm.

20. Tom Leonard, "U.S. Cities May Have to be Bulldozed in Order to Survive," *Daily Telegraph*, June 12, 2009, www.climateactionplans.com/2009/06/us-cities-may-have-to -shrink-to-survive/.

21. Alan Mallach, "Facing the Urban Challenge: Reimagining Land Use in America's Distressed Older Cities—The Federal Policy Role," *Brookings*, May 18, 2010, www.brookings .edu/papers/2010/0518_shrinking_cities_mallach.aspx.

22. Peter Newman, Timothy Beatley, and Heather Boyer. *Resilient Cities: Responding to Peak Oil and Climate Change*. (Washington, DC: Island Press, 2009).

23. SustainableBusiness.com. "Local Governments Slowly Adopting Sustainability Initiatives—Survey," September 23, 2010, www.sustainablebusiness.com/index.cfm/go/news .display/id/21100. The full ICMA survey can be retrieved at http://icma.org/en/icma/ knowledge_network/documents/kn/Document/301646/ICMA_2010_Sustainability_Survey _Results.

24. Christopher W. Hoene, "City Budget Shortfalls and Responses: Projections for 2010–2012," *Research Brief on America's Cities* (Washington, DC: National League of Cities, December 2009), www.nlc.org/ASSETS/5A4EFB8CF1FE43AB88177C808815B63F/BudgetShortFalls_10.pdf.

25. William Neuman, "Second Iowa Producer Recalls 170 Million Eggs," *New York Times*, August 20, 2010, www.nytimes.com/2010/08/21/business/21eggs.html.

26. David A. Farenthold, "So Far, 2010 is the World's Hottest Year on Record, NOAA Data Show," *Washington Post*, August 14, 2010, www.washingtonpost.com/wp-dyn/content/article/2010/08/13/AR2010081306090.html.

27. Brian Merchant, "It's Official: The Climate Bill Is Dead," *Treehugger*, July 22, 2010, www.treehugger.com/files/2010/07/its-official-climate-bill-is-dead.php; Eric Pooley, "In Wreckage of Climate Bill, Some Clues for Moving Forward," *Yale Environment 360*, July 29, 2010, www.energybulletin.net/node/53620.

Abbott, C. 1983. *Portland: Planning, Politics and Growth in a Twentieth Century City*. Lincoln, NE: University of Nebraska Press.

Abrams, G. 2010. "Philadelphia Water Department: Sustainable Stormwater Program." Paper read at Sustainable Communities, March 10, at Dallas, TX.

Achenback, J., and D. A. Farenthold. 2010. "Oil Spill Dumped 4.9 Million Barrels into Gulf of Mexico, Latest Measure Shows." *Washington Post*, August 3. www.washingtonpost.com/wp-dyn/content/article/2010/08/02/AR2010080204695.html?hpid=topnews.

Adams, D. 2008. "Highlights of the Miami Climate Change Summit #2 from Solar to PHEVs." *TampaBay.com*, June 27. http://blogs.tampabay.com/energy/2008/06/highlights-of-t.html.

Added Value. 2010. "About Us," *Added Value*, August 5. www.added-value.org/history.

Adler, S. No date. *Oregon Plans: The Making of an Unquiet Land Use Revolution*. Unpublished manuscript.

Administrative Code of the City of New York, Section 17-306.

Agyeman, J. 2005. *Sustainable Communities and the Challenge of Environmental Justice*. New York: NYU Press.

Alberti, M., et al. 2003. "Integrating Humans into Ecology: Opportunities and Challenges for Studying Urban Ecosystems." *Urban Ecology* 53: 1169–79.

American Public Transportation Association. 2010. *2010 Public Transportation Fact Book*. Washington, DC: American Public Transportation Association.

American Wind Energy Association. 2009. "Wind Energy Grows by Record 8,300 MW in 2008." January 27. www.awea.org/newsroom/releases/wind_energy_growth2008_27Jan09.html.

Arizona Proposition 301 (2000), 2010. www.ballotpedia.org/wiki/index.php/Arizona
    _Proposition_301_%282000%29 (1 July, 2010).

Arizona State University. No date. *New American University.* http://newamericanuniversity
    .asu.edu/(1 July 2010).

Arizona State University Global Institute of Sustainability. No date. "Board of Trustees."
    http://sustainability.asu.edu/about/our-people/our-board-of-trustees.php (1 July 2010).

Association for the Advancement of Sustainability in Higher Education. 2010. "AASHE
    College and University Members." www.aashe.org/membership/members/institutional
    _members.

Association for Pure Water. 2009. "Infrastructure Needs Are Stretching Resources." www
    .americansforpurewater.com/i4a/pages/Index.cfm?pageID=3388.

AtKisson, A. 1996. "Developing Indicators of Sustainable Community: Lessons from Sus-
    tainable Seattle." *Environmental Impact Assessment Review* 16 (4–6): 337–50.

AWWA Research Foundation and American Water Works Association. 2001. *Guidance to
    Utilities on Building with Watershed Stakeholders.* Denver, CO: AWWA Research Foun-
    dation and American Water Works Association.

Battelle Memorial Institute, Technology Partnership Practice. 2010. *Measuring Up: 2010 An-
    nual Report Card on How Arizona's Technology Sector Is Performing and the Contributions
    of Science Foundation Arizona.* Cleveland, OH: Battelle Memorial Institute.

Battelle Memorial Institute, Technology Partnership Practice. 2004. *Positioning Arizona for
    the Next Big Technology Wave: Development and Investment Prospectus to Create a Sus-
    tainable Systems Industry in Arizona.* Cleveland, OH: Battelle Memorial Institute.

Battelle Memorial Institute, Technology Partnership Practice. 2003. *Positioning Arizona and
    Its Research Universities: Science and Technology Core Competencies Assessment.* Cleve-
    land, OH: Battelle Memorial Institute.

BBC News. 2008. "Oil Price Hits Yet Another Record." 3 July. http://news.bbc.co.uk/2/hi
    /business/7486764.stm.

Berube, A., and B. Forman. 2001. *Living on the Edge: Decentralization within Cities in the
    1990s.* Washington, DC: The Brookings Institution.

Betsill, M. M., and H. Bulkeley. 2006. "Cities and Multilevel Governance of Global Climate
    Change." *Global Governance* 12 (2): 141–59.

BK Farmyards. No date. "About Us." *BK Farmyards.* http://bkfarmyards.blogspot.com/p
    /about-bk-farmyards.html (August 5, 2010).

Brinkman, C. 2010. Personal interview with Cheryl Brinkman, president of Livable City, and
    organizer of Sunday Streets. San Francisco. 24 June.

Brook, D. 2004. "Carsharing: Start Up Issues and New Operational Models." Paper presented
    at Transportation Research Board 83rd Annual Meeting, Washington, DC, January
    11–15.

Brooklyn Grange Farm. No date. "About Us." *Brooklyn Grange Farm.* http://brooklyngrange
    farm.com/ (August 5, 2010).

Brugmann, J. 1997. "Sustainable Indicators Revisited: Getting from Political Objectives to
    Performance Outcomes." *Local Environment* 2 (3): 299–302.

Bruns, A. 2010. "The Green Guide: West Is the Best: Ranking First in Half of Our Eight Cri-
    teria, California Tops Site Selection's First Annual Sustainability Rankings." *Site Selec-
    tion Online,* July. www.siteselection.com/issues/2010/jul/GreenG_SustainRank/.

Buettner, R. 2010. "Rain and Wind Created a Deadly Storm." *New York Times*, 14 March. www.nytimes.com/2010/03/15/nyregion/15storm.html?scp=8&sq=new%20york%20storm %20trees%20down%202010&st=cse.

Buranen, M. 2010. "Philadelphia: Going Green to Manage Stormwater." *Stormwater* (January–February). www.stormh2o.com/january-february-2010/philadelphia-going-green-1 .aspx.

Burch, W. R. Jr., and D. R. De Luca. 1984. *Measuring the Social Impact of Natural Resource Policies*. Albuquerque: University of New Mexico Press.

Bureau of Labor Statistics, U.S. Department of Labor. 2010. www.bls.gov/home.htm.

Bureau of Transportation Statistics. No Date. "Table A-10 Distribution of Trips by Mode of Transportation, in Percent." www.bts.gov/publications/highlights_of_the_2001_national _household_travel_survey/html/table_a10.html (20 June 2010).

Burlingame, B. 2005. "Happy Hundredth: Despite Debate on Its Birthdates, the City Is Ready to Celebrate." *Honolulu Star-Bulletin*, June 26. http://archives.starbulletin.com /2005/06/26/features/story1.html.

Burr, A. C. 2008. "CoStar Study Finds Energy Star, LEED Bldgs. Outperform Peers." CoStar Group, March 26. www.costar.com/News/Article.aspx?id=D968F1E0DCF73712 B03A099E0E99C679.

Cabanatuan, M. 2010. "State Bill Offers Twists to Expand Car-Sharing." *San Francisco Chronicle*, 29 April.

Cadenasso, M. L., S. T.A. Pickett, and J. M. Grove. 2006. "Integrative Approaches to Investigating Human-Natural Systems: The Baltimore Ecosystem Study." *Natures, Sciences, Societes* 14: 1–14.

Caggiano, C., E. Dowdall, C. Kwan, and A. Wagner. 2009. "Farming in Philadelphia? A Proposal for a Sustainable Urban Farm Incubator." University of Pennsylvania. www.design .upenn.edu/files/Panorama09_08_FarmIncubator_Caggianoetal.pdf (August 5, 2010).

California Department of Conservation. 2007. *Oil and Gas Statistics: 2007 Annual Report*. Sacramento, CA: California Department of Conservation. December 31. ftp://ftp.consrv .ca.gov/pub/oil/annual_reports/2007/0102stats_07.pdf.

Cammarata, M. 2010. Interview. Philadelphia, PA, March 24.

Campbell, L., et al. 2010. *MillionTreesNYC, Green Infrastructure, and Urban Ecology: Building a Research Agenda*. New York: MillionTreesNYC Advisory Board Research & Evaluation Subcommittee. www.milliontreesnyc.org/downloads/pdf/MillionTreesWorkshop ReportApril2009.pdf.

Capiello, D. 2009. "EPA Releases '07 Climate Document Rejected by Bush Team." *Washington Post*, October 13. www.washingtonpost.com/wp-.dyn/content/article/2009/10/13 /AR2009101303897.html.

Carlton, J. 2008. "Hawaii: The Alternative State." *Wall Street Journal*, June 30. http://sopogy .com/blog/2008/06/30/wall-street-journal-alternative-state/.

CarsharingUS Blog. http://carsharingus.blogspot.com/ (12 June 2010).

Cater, F. 2010. "Critics Say LEED Program Doesn't Fulfill Promises." *NPR*, September 8. www.npr.org/templates/story/story.php?storyId=129727547.

Center for Watershed Protection. 2006. "Spotlight on Superior Stormwater Programs." In *Philadelphia, Pennsylvania: A Watershed Approach to Water Quality Management*. Ellicott City, MD: Center for Watershed Protection.

Cervero, R. 2003. "City CarShare: First-Year Travel Demand Impacts." *Transportation Research Record: Journal of the Transportation Research Board* 1839: 159–66.

Cervero, R., A. Golub, and B. Nee. 2007. "City Carshare: Longer-Term Travel Demand and Car Ownership Impacts." *Transportation Research Record: Journal of the Transportation Research Board* 1992: 70–80.

Cervero, R., and Y. Tsai. 2004. "City Carshare in San Francisco, California: Second-Year Travel Demand and Car Ownership Impacts." *Transportation Research Record: Journal of the Transportation Research Board* 1887: 117–27.

Chan, S., and S. Maslin. 2009. "Storm Topples Scores of Trees in Central Park." *New York Times*, 19 August. http://cityroom.blogs.nytimes.com/2009/08/19/storm-topples-scores-of-trees-in-central-park/?scp=2&sq=new%20york%20storm%20trees%20down%202010&st=cse.

City of Boise. 2010. "Climate Protection Program." www.cityofboise.org/Departments/Public_Works/Services/AirQuality/page18402.aspx.

City of Boston. 2010. "Sparking Boston's Climate Revolution: Recommendations of the Climate Action Leadership Committee and Community Advisory Committee." April. www.cityofboston.gov/Images.../BCA_full_rprt_r5_tcm3-16529.pdf.

CityofBoston.gov. 2010. "Boston One of Five Cities Chosen by U.S. EPA Under Greening America Capital Cities Program." 9 September. www.cityofboston.gov/news/default.aspx?id=4752 .

City of Denver. No date. "Sustainability: A Core Value in Denver City Government." *Greenprint Denver*. www.greenprintdenver.org/about/.

City of Miami, Office of Sustainable Initiatives. 2008. *Climate Action Plan*. June. www.miamigov.com/msi/pages.

City of Milwaukee. 2009a. *TID 53 — Menomonee Valley Shops, Periodic Report*. Milwaukee, WI: City of Milwaukee, Department of City Development.

City of Milwaukee. 2009b. *TID 75 — Reed Street Yards, Periodic Report*. Milwaukee, WI: City of Milwaukee, Department of City Development.

City of Milwaukee. 2006. *Menomonee Valley Industrial Center and Community Park Master Land Use Plan*. Milwaukee, WI: Report prepared by the City of Milwaukee, Redevelopment Authority of the City of Milwaukee, Department of City Development.

City of Milwaukee. 2002. *Menomonee River Valley Brownfields Pilot Project, Interim Report, Redeveloping Milwaukee's Menomonee Valley: Developing an Aqua-shed Framework for Groundwater Regulatory and Remediation Alternatives*. Milwaukee, WI: Report funded by the U.S. Environmental Protection Agency, the City of Milwaukee, the Milwaukee Economic Development Corporation, and the U.S. Geological Survey.

City of Milwaukee. 1998. *Market Study, Engineering, and Land Use Plan for the Menomonee Valley*. Milwaukee, WI: Report prepared for the Department of City Development, City of Milwaukee, by Lockwood Greene Consulting; Fluor Daniel Consulting; Trkla, Pettigrew, Allen, and Payne, Inc.; and Edwards and Associates.

City of Milwaukee. 1975. *Menomonee Valley 1975 Business Needs and Attitudes Survey*. Milwaukee, WI: Report prepared for the City of Milwaukee Department of City Planning by Dun and Bradstreet Inc.

City of Minneapolis. 2010. "Minneapolis Greenprint." www.ci.minneapolis.mn.us/sustainability/MinneapolisGreenprint.asp.

City of New York, Department of Health and Mental Hygiene. 2009. *New York City Community Air Survey*. New York: New York City Department of Health and Mental Hygiene. www.nyc.gov/html/doh/html/eode/nyccas.shtml.

City of New York, New York City Panel on Climate Change. 2009. *Climate Risk Information*. New York: City of New York. www.nyc.gov/html/om/pdf/2009/NPCC_CRI.pdf.

City of New York, PlanYC. 2010. *PlaNYC 2010 Progress Report*. New York: City of New York. www.nyc.gov/html/planyc2030/downloads/pdf/planyc_progress_report_2010.pdf.

City of Philadelphia. 2009. *Greenworks Philadelphia*. Philadelphia: Mayor's Office.

City of Portland. 2007. *Report of the City of Portland Peak Oil Task Force*. Portland, OR. March.

City of Portland. 1993. *Carbon Dioxide Reduction Strategy*. Portland, OR. 10 November.

City of Portland, Bureau of Planning and Sustainability. 2009. "Climate Action Plan." Portland, OR. www.portlandonline.com/bps/index.cfm?c=41896.

City of Portland, Office of Sustainable Development. 2002. *ReThinking Development: Portland's Strategic Investment in Green Building Progress Report: FY 2000–2002*. Portland, OR. www.portlandonline.com/shared/cfm/image.cfm?id=118349.

City of San Francisco. 2010. "Article 1.5: Off-Street Parking and Loading." *City of San Francisco Planning Code*. http://search.municode.com/html/14139/level1/A1.5.html (24 June 2010).

Clean Edge, Inc. 2009. "Clean Tech Job Trends 2009," October. www.cleanedge.com /reports/reports-jobtrends2009.php.

Climate Progress. 2010. "CO GOP Candidate Maes Worries Bike-Share Program 'May Not Be Compatible with State Constitution.'" 10 August. http://climateprogress.org/2010/08 /10/colorado-tea-party-candidate-dan-maes-bike-sharing/.

CNN.com. 2005. "Bush Urges More Refineries, Nuclear Plants." 4 April. www.cnn.com /2005/POLITICS/04/27/bush.energy/.

COG Intergovernmental Green Building Group. 2007. *Greening the Metropolitan Washington Region's Built Environment: A Report to the Metropolitan Washington Council of Governments Board of Directors*. 12 December.

Colaneri, N. 2009. "Army Continues Flexible Display Center Support." *Arizona State UniversityNews Service*. http://asunews.asu.edu/20090129_flexdisplay (1 July 2010).

Collins J. P., et al. 2000. "A New Urban Ecology." *American Scientist* 88: 416–25.

Community Food Security Coalition. No date. "Food Policy Councils." *Community Food Security Coalition*. www.foodsecurity.org/FPC/council.html (August 5, 2010).

Conservation Council for Hawaii. 2010. "Hawaii Leaders Call for Climate Change and Clean Energy Legislation on World Ocean Day." 11 June. www.pdamerica.org/articles /chapters/hi-2010-06-11-10-01-40-chapters.php.

Conserving Land for People. No date. "Overview of NYC Garden Land Trusts," *The Trust for Public Land*. www.tpl.org/tier3_cd.cfm?content_item_id=15456&folder_id=631 (August 5, 2010).

Crockett, C. 2010. *Parcel Based Billing for Stormwater*. Philadelphia, PA: American Society of Civil Engineers Philadelphia Section.

Cronon, W. 1995. "The Trouble with Wilderness; or, Getting Back to the Wrong Nature." In *Uncommon Ground: Toward Reinventing Nature*, ed. W. Cronon, 69–90. New York: Norton.

Daniels, T. 2008. "Taking the Initiative: Why Cities Are Greening Now." In *Growing Greener Cities*, ed. E. Birch and S. Wachter. Philadelphia: University of Pennsylvania Press.

Database of State Incentives for Renewable Energy. 2010. www.dsireusa.org/.

Denver Business Journal. 2010. "Denver 3rd in Site Selection's Sustainability Rankings." Denver Business Journal, July 2. http://denver.bizjournals.com/denver/stories/2010/06 /28/daily66.html.

De Sousa, C. 2008. *Brownfields Redevelopment and the Quest for Sustainability*. London: Elsevier Science/Emerald Group Publishing, Current Issues in Urban and Regional Studies Series, Volume 3.

De Sousa, C., B. Gramling, and K. LeMoine. 2009. "Evaluating Progress toward Sustainable Development in Milwaukee's Menomonee River Valley: Linking Brownfields Redevelopment with Community Quality of Life." In *Community Quality-of-Life Indicators: Best Cases III*, ed. J. Sirgy, D. Rahtz, and R. Phillips, 80–100. Berlin: Springer.

DiFilippo, D. 2010. "Philly Seeks Answers Down the Drain." *On Earth*.

District of Columbia. 2006. *The Green Building Act of 2006*. http://grccn.dc.gov/green/lib /green/pdfs/GreenBuilding_act06.pdf.

Donofrio, G. A. 2007. "Feeding the City." *Gastronomica*: 30–41.

Doshi, H. 2006. *Environmental Benefits of Green Roofs on a City Scale: An Example of the City of Toronto*. Boston: Green Roofs for Healthy Cities.

Dow, K., and T. E. Downing. 2006. *The Atlas of Climate Change: Mapping the World's Greatest Challenge*. Berkeley: University of California Press.

Duncan, O. D. 1964. "Social Organization and the Ecosystem." In *Handbook of Modern Sociology*, ed. R. E. L. Faris, 37–82. Chicago: Rand McNally.

Duncan, O. D. 1961. "From Social System to Ecosystem." *Sociological Inquiry* 31: 140–49.

Dunning, C.P., et al. 2004. *Simulation of Ground-water Flow, Surface-water Flow, and a Deep Sewer Tunnel System in the Menomonee Valley, Milwaukee, Wisconsin*. Denver: U.S. Department of the Interior and the U.S. Geological Survey Scientific Investigations Report 2004–5031 conducted in cooperation with the U.S. Environmental Protection Agency, Region 5, and City of Milwaukee.

Eagle Street Rooftop Farm. No date. "What We Offer." *Eagle Street Rooftop Farm*. http:// rooftopfarms.org/ (August 5, 2010).

Eaton, L. 2009. "Cities Braced for a Prolonged Bout of Declining Tax Revenues," *Wall Street Journal*, 1 September. http://online.wsj.com/article/SB125177344884874971.html.html.

Economic Research Service. No date. "Conservation Policy: Farmland and Grassland Protection Programs." United States Department of Agriculture. www.ers.usda.gov/Briefing /ConservationPolicy/farmland.htm (August 5, 2010).

Economist.com. 2010. "Wind Energy and Politics: Not on My Beach, Please." *Economist*, 19 August. www.economist.com/node/16846774?story_id=16846774.

Egerton, F. N. 1993. "The History and Present Entanglements of Some General Ecological Perspectives." In *Humans as Components of Ecosystems: The Ecology of Subtle Human Effects and Populated Areas*, ed. M. J. McDonnell and S. T.A. Pickett, 9–23. New York: Springer-Verlag.

Elkington, John. 1998. *Cannibals with Forks: The Triple Bottom Line of 21st Century Business*. Stony Creek, CT: New Society Publishers.

Elkington, J. 1994. "Towards the Sustainable Corporation: Win-Win-Win Business Strategies for Sustainable Development." *California Management Review* 36, no. 2.

Elvidge, C. D., et al. 2004. "U.S. Constructed Area Approaches the Size of Ohio." *Transactions of the American Geophysical Union* 85: 233–40.

Englander, D. 2001. *New York's Community Gardens: A Resource at Risk*. The Trust for Public Land.

Environmental Building News. 1997. "DOE Funds USGBC's Development of LEED." *Environmental Building News*, 1 October. www.buildinggreen.com/auth/article.cfm/1997/10/1/DOE-Funds-USGBC-s-Development-of-LEED/.

Environmental Defense Fund. 2009. "Climate Change Hitting Home, Galveston and Houston Residents on Notice." 9 June. http://blogs.edf.org/climate411/2009/06/09/climate-change-hitting-home-galveston-and-houston-residents-on-notice/.

Fairfax County Sustainable Development Policy for Capital Projects. No date. www.fairfaxcounty.gov/dpwes/construction/sdpolicy.pdf.

Fair Food Network. No date. "About Us." Fair Food Network. www.fairfoodnetwork.org/ (August 5, 2010).

Farenthold, D. A. 2010. "So Far, 2010 Is the World's Hottest Year on Record, NOAA Data Show." *Washington Post*, 14 August. www.washingtonpost.com/wp-dyn/content/article/2010/08/13/AR2010081306090.html.

Farris, E. 2010. "City Council Examines Changes to Urban Agriculture Code: CSAs Top the List of Concerns for Those Unsure of Changes." *KCFreePress*. www.kcfreepress.com/news/2010/may/05/council-examines-changes-urban-agriculture-code/ (August 5, 2010).

First Wind. 2009. "Hawaii Electric Company Agrees to Buy Energy from First Wind's Molokai Wind Farms." 17 March. www.firstwind.com/aboutFirstWind/news.cfm?ID=272cced1-b603-4ca2-8581-7e206c1c3103&test.

Fitzgerald, J. 2010. *Emerald Cities: Urban Sustainability and Economic Development*. New York: Oxford University Press.

Fletcher, C. 2010. "Hawaii's Changing Climate." Briefing sheet, Center for Island Climate Adaptation and Policy. http://nsgl.gso.uri.edu/new/.

Frederick, W. H., and R. L. Worden, eds. 1993. *Indonesia: A Country Study*. Washington: GPO for the Library of Congress. http://countrystudies.us/indonesia/.

Friedman, A. 2007. "More Than a Link in the Food Chain: A Study of the Citywide Economic Impact of Food Manufacturing in New York City." NY Industrial Retention Network and Fiscal Policy Institute.

Frumkin, D. 2001. "Urban Sprawl and Public Health." Department of Environmental and Occupational Health, Emory University, December. www.publichealthgrandrounds.unc.edu/urban/frumkin.pdf.

Gallagher, J. 2010. "Is Urban Farming Detroit's Cash Cow? 2010 May Yield Profit as Efforts Reap Jobs, Tax Base." *Free Press*. www.freep.com/article/20100321/BUSINESS04/3210433/1318/Is-farming-Detroits-cash-cow (August 5, 2010).

Gammage, G. Jr. 1999. *Phoenix in Perspective*. Tempe: Herberger Center for Design Excellence, Arizona State University.

Gammage, G. Jr., J. S. Hall, R. E. Lang, R. Melnick, and N. Welch. 2008. *Sun Corridor Megapolitan*. Tempe: Morrison Institute for Public Policy.

Georgia General Assembly. 2010. "HB 842—Agriculture; Preempt Certain Local Ordinances; Protect Right to Grow Food Crops." *Georgia General Assembly.* www.legis.ga.gov /legis/2009_10/sum/hb842.htm (August 5, 2010).

Gibbs, D. C. 2002. *Local Development and the Environment.* London: Routledge.

Gibson, J. M. 1988. "Fairmount Water Works." *Philadelphia Museum of Art Bulletin,* 39.

Girardet, H. 2007. "Creating Livable and Sustainable Cities." In *Surviving the Century: Facing Climate Chaos and Other Global Challenges,* ed. H. Girardet. London: Earthscan.

Girardet, H. 2004a. *Cities People Planet: Livable Cities for a Sustainable World.* Hoboken, NJ: Wiley.

Girardet, H. 2004b. "The Metabolism of Cities." In *The Sustainable Urban Development Reader,* ed. S. Wheeler and T. Beatley. New York: Routledge.

Girardet, H. 1999. *Creating Sustainable Cities.* White River Junction, VT: Chelsea Green Publishing.

Gober, P. 2005. *Metropolitan Phoenix: Place Making and Community Building in the Desert.* Philadelphia: University of Pennsylvania Press.

Gordon, R. 2009. "New S.F. Study: Phase-In Market St. Car Ban." *San Francisco Chronicle,* 10 May.

Gordon, R., and J. Tucker. 2010. "Ruling Paves Way for San Francisco Bike Lanes." *San Francisco Chronicle,* 6 August.

Governor's Advisory Group on Global Warming. No date. "Oregon's Strategy for Greenhouse Gas Reductions." *Oregon.gov.* Salem, Oregon. www.oregon.gov/ENERGY /GBLWRM/Strategy.shtml.

Graham R., et al. 2006. "Eating In, Eating Out, Eating Well: Access to Healthy Food in North and Central Brooklyn." *New York City Department of Health and Mental Hygiene.* www.nyc.gov/html/doh/downloads/pdf/dpho/dpho-brooklyn-report2006.pdf (August 9, 2010).

Greater Washington Initiative. 2010. *Greater Washington Energy Efficiency and Sustainability Industry Report.*

Green Building Density Incentive Policy for Site Plan Projects. 2009. Report presented to County Board of Arlington County, Virginia, 14 March. www.arlingtonva.us /departments/EnvironmentalServices/epo/PDFfiles/file69951.pdf.

Green Dallas.net. No date. "Green Buildings." *Green Dallas.net.* www.greendallas.net/green _buildings.html.

Greenmarket. No date. "New Farmers Development Project." *Greenmarket.* www.grownyc .org/greenmarket/nfdp (August 5, 2010).

Green Thumb. No date. "Welcome to Green Thumb." *New York City Department of Parks and Recreations.* www.greenthumbnyc.org/ (August 5, 2010).

Grimm, N. B., et al. 2000. "Integrated approaches to long-term studies of urban ecological systems." *Bioscience* 50: 571–84.

Grove, J. M., et al. 2006. *A Report on New York City's Present and Possible Urban Tree Canopy.* New York City's Department of Parks & Recreation, Northern Research Station, USDA Forest Service.

Gurda, J. 2003. *The Menomonee Valley: A Historical Overview.* Milwaukee, WI: Report prepared for the Menomonee Valley Partners.

Gurda, J. 1999. *The Making of Milwaukee*. Milwaukee, WI: Milwaukee County Historical Society.

Hardesty, L. 2006. "Phoenix Voters Approve Funding for ASU Downtown Campus." *Arizona State University News Service*. www.asu.edu/news/stories/200603/20060315_phoenix campus.htm (1 July 2010).

Hanna, A. K., and P. Oh. 2000. "Rethinking Urban Poverty: A Look at Community Gardens." *Bulletin of Science, Technology and Society* 3: 207–16.

Hawaiian Electric Company. No date. www.heco.com/portal/site/heco/menuitem.2051670 7928314340b4c0610c510b1ca/?vgnextoid=c6caf2b154da9010VgnVCM10000053011 bacRCRD.

Hawaiian Electric Company. No date. "Energy Agreement Summary of Key Agreements." http://heco.com/vcmcontent/StaticFiles/pdf/HCEI_Summary-Final.pdf.

Hawaiian Electric Company. 2009. "Fuel Oil Use in Hawaii." www.heco.com/vcmcontent /StaticFiles/pdf/FuelOilUse_8-2009.pdf.

Hawaii Free Press. 2008. "Molokai Ranch: Protesters to Cash in with Takeover Plan." *Hawaii Free Press*, 22 March. www.hawaiifreepress.com/main/ArticlesMain/tabid/56/articleType /ArticleView/articleId/1711/Molokai-Ranch-Protesters-to-Cash-in-with-Takeover-Plan .aspx.

Hawaii Natural Energy Institute. 2008. "History of HNEI." www.hnei.hawaii.edu/history .aspat.

Hawaii State Constitution. No date. Art. XI, sec. 8. http://hawaii.gov/lrb/con/conart11.html.

Hawley, A. H. 1950. *Human Ecology: A Theory of Community Structure*. New York: Ronald Press Co.

Hawthorne, M. L. 2010. "Commentary: LEED Versus Passive House: What's the Difference?" *Daily Journal of Commerce*, 24 February 24. http://findarticles.com/p/articles/mi _qn4184/is_20100224/ai_n50447587/.

Hoene, C. W. 2009. "City Budget Shortfalls and Responses: Projections for 2010–2012." *Research Brief on America's Cities*. Washington, DC: National League of Cities, December. www.nlc.org/ASSETS/5A4EFB8CF1FE43AB88177C808815B63F/BudgetShortFalls _10.pdf.

Holling, C. S. 1994. "Buzz: New Science and New Investments for a Sustainable Biosphere." In *Investing in Natural Capital: The Ecological Economics Approach to Sustainability*, ed. A. M. Jansson, et al., 57–97. Washington, DC: Island Press.

Honolulu Civil Beat. 2010. "HECO to Offer Electric Car Owners Discounted Rates." *Honolulu Civil Beat*, 13 August 13. www.civilbeat.com/articles/2010/07/28/3143-heco-to -offer-electric-car-owners-discounted-rates/.

Honolulu Sea Water Air Conditioning LLC. 2008. "The Honolulu Sea Water Air Conditioning Project." 9 December. http://honoluluswac.com/.

Howrey, LLP. 2007. "Washington, D.C. Enacts Green Building Requirements for Private Projects." *Construction WebLinks*, 16 April. www.constructionweblinks.com/Resources /Industry_Reports__Newsletters/Apr_16_2007/wash.html.

ICLEI. No date. "Report Shows the Power of U.S. Cities to Mitigate Climate Change." www.icleiusa.org/news-events/press-room/press-releases/report-shows-the-power-of-u-s -cities-to-mitigate-climate-change2014and-the-steps-they-need-to-take-to-adapt.

Interstate Renewable Energy Council. 2010. "Hawaii PUC Approves Method of Electric Rate Decoupling." March. http://irecusa.org/2010/03/hawaii-puc-approves-method-of -electric-rate-decoupling/.

IPCC. 1990. *First Assessment Report*. Geneva: International Panel on Climate Change, World Meteorological Institute.

Jacobs, J. 1961. *The Death and Life of Great American Cities*. New York: Random House.

Jaquiss, N. 2010. "Power to the Pedal." *Willamette Week*, 17 February. www.wweek.com /editorial/3615/13701/.

Jepson, E. 2004. "The Adoption of Sustainable Development Policies and Techniques in U.S. Cities." *Journal of Planning Research and Education* 23 (3): 229–41.

Kalani, N. 2010. "Hawaii Electric Car Initiative Will Begin with Infrastructure." *Pacific Business News*, 10 January. http://pacific.bizjournals.com/pacific/stories/2010/01/25/focus2 .html.

Kampschroer, K. 2010. *Federal Green Buildings*. Statement before the Subcommittee on Government Management, Organization, and Procurement of the House Committee on Oversight and Government Reform, 21 July. U.S. General Services Administration, www .gsa.gov/portal/content/159125.

Karush, S. 2006. "D.C. Council Passes Green Building Rules." *Associated Press*, 6 December. www.washingtonpost.com/wp-dyn/content/article/2006/12/06/AR2006120600165.html.

Katzev, R. 2003. "Car Sharing: A New Approach to Urban Transportation Problems." *Analysis of Social Issues and Public Policy* 3: 65–86.

Keep Akron Beautiful. "The Greenprint for Akron." 2010. www.keepakronbeautiful.org /greenprint.

Kirchhoff, S. 2009. "Economic Downturn Pounds Commercial Real Estate Market." *USA Today*, 12 January. www.usatoday.com/money/economy/2009-01-11-commercial-real -estate_N.htm.

Kramek, N., and L. Loh. 2007. *The History of Philadelphia's Water Supply and Sanitation System: Lessons in Sustainability for Developing Urban Water Systems*. Philadelphia, PA: Philadelphia Global Water Initiative.

Kullman, J., and K. Leland. 2008. "New Lab Aims to Advance Solar Energy Industry." *Arizona State University News Service*. http://asunews.asu.edu/20080711_solarlab (1 July 2010).

Kurtz, K. 2008. "The Pragmatism and Charisma of Willie Brown." *The Thicket at State Legislatures*, 21 March. National Council of State Legislatures. http://ncsl.typepad.com/the _thicket/2008/03/by-karl-kurtz-w.html.

LaFond, M. 1995. "Cooperative Transport: Berlin's Stattauto (Instead of Cars)." *Rain Magazine*. http://afo.sandelman.ca/afz/issue9-II.html (20 June 2010).

Lambert, S., director, LEED-ND. 2010. Personal communication, August 31.

Law, S. 2010. "Next Big Thing: Green Neighborhoods." *Sustainable Life*, 11 March. Accessed from U.S. Green Building Council, *USGBC in the News*, www.usgbc.org/News /USGBCInTheNewsDetails.aspx?ID=4336 (21 September, 2010).

Lawson, L. J. 2005. *City Bountiful: A Century of Community Gardening in America*. Berkeley: University of California Press.

Ledger.com. No date. "Unemployment Rate: Hawaii." *Ledger.com*. www.ledgerdata.com /unemployment/hawaii/1982/august/.

Lefkowitz, M. 2007. "Akron Prepares Sustainability Plan." *GreenCityBlueLake*, 14 November. www.gcbl.org/blog/marc-lefkowitz/akron-launches-sustainability-plan.

Leland, K. 2008. "ASU to Deploy Largest University Solar Installation." *Arizona State University News Service*. http://asunews.asu.edu/20080617_solar (1 July 2010).

Leonard, T. 2009. "U.S. Cities May Have to be Bulldozed in Order to Survive." *Daily Telegraph*, 12 June. www.climateactionplans.com/2009/06/us-cities-may-have-to-shrink-to-survive/.

Lepain, K. 2010. "What's on Your Plate, ASU?" *Arizona State University State Press Magazine*. http://statepressmagazine.com/2010/01/18/whats-on-your-plate-asu/ (1 July 2010).

Lopez, R. 2004. "Measuring the Health Effects of Sprawl, a National Analysis of Physical Activity, Obesity and Chronic Disease." *American Journal of Public Health* 94, no. 9.

Lovely, L. No date. "Milwaukee's Old Sixth Street Viaduct Yields to Modern Cable-Stayed Spans." *Construction Equipment Guide*. www.constructionequipmentguide.com/Milwaukees-Old-Sixth-Street-Viaduct-Yields-to-Modern-Cable-Stayed-Spans/1384/ (2 May, 2010).

Lu, J. 2010. *Survival Rates of Young Street Trees in New York City*. New York: MillionTreesNYC, Green Infrastructure, and Urban Ecology Research Symposium. http://milliontreesnyc.org/downloads/pdf/symposium_research_abstracts.pdf.

Luniak, M., and B. Pisarski. 1994. "State of Research into the Fauna of Warsaw (Up to 1990)." *Memorabilia Zoologica* 49: 155–65.

Machlis, G. E., J. E. Force, and W. R. Burch, Jr. 1997. "The Human Ecosystem. 1. The Human Ecosystem as an Organizing Concept in Ecosystem Management." *Society and Natural Resources* 10: 347–67.

Mallach, A. 2010. "Facing the Urban Challenge: Reimagining Land Use in America's Distressed Older Cities—The Federal Policy Role." *Brookings*, 18 May. www.brookings.edu/papers/2010/0518_shrinking_cities_mallach.aspx.

Mandarano, L. A. 2000. *Office of Watersheds Strategic Plan*. Philadelphia, PA: Philadelphia Water Department Office of Watersheds.

Market Ventures, Inc. and Karp Resources. 2005. "New York City Wholesale Farmers' Market Study." *Market Ventures, Inc. and Karp Resources*: 8.

Marshall, J. D., and M. W. Toffler. 2005. "Framing the Elusive Concept of Sustainability: A Sustainability Hierarchy." *Environmental & Scientific Technology* 39, no 3.

Mapes, J. 2009. *Pedaling Revolution: How Cyclists are Changing American Cities*. Corvallis, OR: Oregon State University Press.

Martin, E., and S. Shaheen. 2010. *Greenhouse Gas Emission Impacts of Carsharing in North America. Final Report*. San Jose: Mineta Transportation Institute.

Martin, E., S. Shaheen, and J. Lidicker. 2010. "Carsharing's Impact on Household Vehicle Holdings: Results from a North American Shared-Use Vehicle Survey." Forthcoming in *Transportation Research Record: Journal of the Transportation Research Board*.

McCann, B. A., and R. Ludwig. 2003. "Measuring the Health Effects of Sprawl: A National Analysis of Physical Activity, Obesity, and Chronic Disease." Smart Growth America Surface Transportation Policy Project, September.

McDonnell, M. J., et al. 1997. "Ecosystem Processes Along an Urban-to-Rural Gradient." *Urban Ecosystems* 1: 21–36.

McDonnell, M. J., and S. T. A. Pickett. 1993. *Humans as Components of Ecosystems: The Ecology of Subtle Human Effects and Populated Areas.* New York: Springer-Verlag.

McDonnell, M. J., and S. T. A. Pickett. 1990. "Ecosystem Structure and Function along Urban-Rural Gradients: An Unexploited Opportunity for Ecology." *Ecology* 71: 1232–37.

McHarg, I. 1969. *Design with Nature.* New York: American Museum of Natural History.

McKinney, M. L. 2002. "Urbanization, Biodiversity, and Conservation." *BioScience* 52: 883–90.

Melnick, R., and J. S. Hall. 2009. "Regional Roles and Relationships: A Fifty-Year Evolution of Governance in Metropolitan Phoenix, 1960–2008." In *Governing Metropolitan Regions in the 21st Century*, ed. D. Phares, 154–74. Armonk, NY: M.E. Sharpe, Inc.

Menomonee Valley Benchmarking Initiative. 2005. *2005 State of the Valley: Evaluating Change in Milwaukee's Menomonee Valley.* Milwaukee, WI: Sixteenth Street Community Health Center, Department of Environmental Health and the University of Wisconsin-Milwaukee, Center for Urban Initiatives and Research.

Menomonee Valley Partners. 2010. *A Decade of Transformation, Momentum for the Future, 2009 Annual Report.* Milwaukee, WI: Menomonee Valley Partners Inc.

Menomonee Valley Partners. 2006. *Sustainable Design Guidelines for the Menomonee River Valley.* Milwaukee, WI: Menomonee Valley Partners, City of Milwaukee, and the Sixteenth Street Community Health Center.

Merchant, B. 2010. "It's Official: The Climate Bill Is Dead." *Treehugger*, 22 July. www.treehugger.com/files/2010/07/its-official-climate-bill-is-dead.php.

Metcalf, G. 2010. Personal interview with Gabriel Metcalf, cofounder of City Carshare. San Francisco, 20 June.

METRO. 2009. *Regional Population and Employment Range Forecasts.* (March draft, Metropolitan Service District, Portland, Oregon.) http://library.oregonmetro.gov/files/20-50_range_forecast.pdf .

Metropolitan Washington Council of Governments. No date. www.mwcog.org/.

Metropolitan Washington Council of Governments. No date. "Environment: Green Building." www.mwcog.org/environment/greenbuilding/.

Mikherji, N., and Morales, A. 2010. "Practice: Urban Agriculture." *Zoning Practice*, no. 3.

Millard-Ball, A., G. Murray, J. Ter Schure, C. Fox, and J. Burkhardt. 2005. *TCRP Report 108: Car-Sharing: Where and How It Succeeds.* Washington, DC: Transportation Research Board of the National Academies.

MillionTreesNYC, No date. "Trees for Public Health Neighborhoods." *MillionTreesNYC.* www.milliontreesnyc.org/html/million_trees/neighborhoods.shtml.

Misky, D., and C. Nemke. 2010. "From Blighted to Beautiful." *Government Engineering* May–June: 14–16.

Moore, L.V., and A. Diez Roux. 2006. "Associations of Neighborhood Characteristics with the Location and Type of Food Stores." *American Journal of Public Health.*

Morland, K., S. Wing, and A. D. Roux. 2002. "The Contextual Effect of the Local Food Environment on Residents' Diets." *American Journal of Public Health.*

Morrison Institute for Public Policy. No date. *The New Economy: Policy Choices for Arizona.*

Munsey & Suppes. 2007. *Milwaukee Brewers Miller Park.* www.ballparks.com/baseball/national/miller.htm (23 April, 2010).

Myers, P. 2008. "Investors Fund US $10.75 M for Honolulu Seawater Air Conditioning." *Renewable Energy World.com*, 9 July. www.renewableenergyworld.com/rea/news/article/2008/07/investors-fund-us-10-75-m-for-honolulu-seawater-air-conditioning-53000.

National Institute of Building Sciences. 2009. *Whole Building Design Guide*. www.wbdg.org/design/minimize_consumption.php.

National Renewable Energy Laboratory. 2009. *Hawaii Clean Energy Initiative Existing Building Energy Efficiency Analysis*. 17 November, 2009–30 June, 2010. NREL/SR-7A2-48318, June 2010. Golden, Colorado: U.S. Department of Energy, National Renewable Energy Laboratory.

Natural Resources Conservation Service. 2003. "FY-2003 New Jersey Farm and Ranch Lands Protection Program." *Natural Resources Conservation Service*. www.nrcs.usda.gov/programs/frpp/StateFacts/NJ2002.html (August 5, 2010).

Navigant Consulting, Inc. 2007. *Arizona Solar Electric Roadmap Study*. Burlington, VT: Navigant Consulting, Inc.

Neukrug, H. 2009. Testimony of Howard Neukrug to the U.S. House of Representative Transportation and Infrastructure Committee. Subcommittee on Water Resources and Environment. Washington, DC: U.S. House of Representatives Transportation and Infrastructure Committee. Subcommittee on Water Resources and Environment.

Neuman, W. 2010. "Second Iowa Producer Recalls 170 Million Eggs." *New York Times*, 20 August. www.nytimes.com/2010/08/21/business/21eggs.html.

New Jersey Department of Environmental Protection. No date. "Green Acres Program." *New Jersey Department of Environmental Protection*. www.state.nj.us/dep/greenacres/ (August 5, 2010).

Newman, P., T. Beatley, and H. Boyer. 2009. *Resilient Cities: Responding to Peak Oil and Climate Change*. Washington, DC: Island Press.

New York City Council Press Room. 2009. "Speaker Quinn Announces 'Food Works New York.'" The Council of the City of New York Office of Communications. http://council.nyc.gov/html/releases/foodworks_12_7_09.shtml (August 5, 2010).

New York City Department of City Planning. 2008. "Going to Market: New York City's Neighborhood Grocery Store and Supermarket Shortage." Department of City Planning. www.nyc.gov/html/dcp/html/supermarket/index.shtml (August 5, 2010).

New York City Department of Education. No date. "School Meals Program." New York City Department of Education. www.opt-osfns.org/osfns/meals/default.aspx (August 5, 2010).

New York City Department of Environmental Protection. No date. "Watershed Protection." New York City Department of Environmental Protection. www.nyc.gov/html/dep/html/watershed_protection/index.shtml (August 5, 2010).

New York City Department of Health and Mental Hygiene (NYCDHMH). 2010. *New York City Healthy Bodegas Initiative 2010 Report*. New York: NYCDHMH.

New York City Department of Health and Mental Hygiene. 2009. *Report to the New York City Council on Green Carts FY2008–2009*. http://nyc.gov/html/doh/downloads/pdf/cdp/GreenCartReport_FY08.pdf (September 2009).

New York City Department of Health and Mental Hygiene. No date. "Physical Activity and Nutrition." New York City Department of Health and Mental Hygiene. www.nyc.gov/html/doh/html/cdp/cdp_pan_hbi.shtml (August 5, 2010).

Nicol, G., acting associate director, Permits and Review Group, Department of Environmental Resources. 2010. Personal communication, 23 August.

Nowak, D. J., et al. 2007. *Assessing Urban Forest Effects and Values: New York City's Urban Forest*. Newtown Square, PA: U.S. Department of Agriculture, Forest Service, Northern Research Station.

NYC.gov. No date. "Food Retail to Support Health Initiative." *NYC.gov*. www.nyc.gov/html /misc/html/2009/fresh.shtml (August 5, 2010).

O'Connell, L. 2009. "Exploring the Roots of Smart Growth Policy Adoption by Cities." *Social Science Quarterly*, 89 (5): 1356–72.

Office of the Governor of Hawaii. 2008. "State and Hawaiian Electric Strike Sweeping Agreement for Hawaiian Energy Future." 20 October. www.heco.com/portal/site/heco /menuitem.508576f78baa14340b4c0610c510b1ca/?vgnextoid=195aca9d24c2d110Vgn VCM1000005c011bacRCRD&vgnextchannel=c6caf2b154da9010VgnVCM100000530 11bacRCRD&vgnextfmt=default&vgnextrefresh=1&level=0&ct=article.

Office of the Mayor, City and County of San Francisco. 2009. *Executive Directive 09-03. Healthy and Sustainable Food for San Francisco*. www.sfgov3.org/ftp/uploadedfiles /sffood/policy_reports/MayorNewsomExecutiveDirectiveonHealthySustainableFood.pdf.

Office of the Mayor, City of New York. 2008. *Executive Order No. 122. Food Policy Coordinator for the City of New York and City Agency Food Standards*. The City of New York, 19 September. www.cspinet.org/new/pdf/nyc_food_standards_executive_order.pdf (August 9, 2010).

Oregon Employment Department. 2009. *Unemployment in Oregon*. Salem, OR: Oregon Employment Department.

Osofsky, H. M., and J. K. Levit. 2008. "The Scale of Networks: Local Climate Change Coalitions." *Chicago Journal of International Law* 8, no. 2.

Owen, D. 2009. *Green Metropolis: Why Living Smaller, Living Closer, and Driving Less are the Keys to Sustainability*. New York: Riverhead Books.

Pacific Business Journals.com. 2009. "Revenue Bonds Go Unused as Credit Market Tightens in Hawaii." *Pacific Business Journals.com*, 20 February. http://pacific.bizjournals.com /pacific/stories/2009/02/23/story8.html.

Pearsall, H., and J. Pierce. 2010. "Urban Sustainability and Environmental Justice: Evaluating the Linkages in Public Planning/Policy Discourse." *Local Environment* 15 (6): 569–80.

Pew Charitable Trusts. 2009. "The Clean Energy Economy: Repowering Jobs, Businesses and Investments across America," June. www.pewtrusts.org/news_room_detail.aspx?id= 53254.

Philadelphia Water Department. 2010a. *Office of Watersheds*. Philadelphia, PA: Philadelphia Water Department. http://www.phillywatersheds.org (June 16 2010).

Philadelphia Water Department. 2010b. *Stormwater Management Guidance Manual*. Philadelphia, PA: Philadelphia Water Department.

Philadelphia Water Department. 2009a. *Green City Clean Waters: Long Term Control Plan Update*. Philadelphia, PA: Philadelphia Water Department.

Philadelphia Water Department. 2009b. *Green City Clean Waters: Long Term Control Plan Update. Vol 2: Triple Bottom Line Analysis*. Philadelphia, PA: Philadelphia Water Department.

Philadelphia Water Department. 2006. *Philadelphia Water Department Regulations*. In Chapter 6, "Stormwater Management," ed. City of Philadelphia. Philadelphia, PA: City of Philadelphia.

Philadelphia Water Department. 1997. *Long Term Control Plan*. Philadelphia, PA: Philadelphia Water Department.

Plumb, C. 2003. "U.S. Blasts Kyoto Pact as Straightjacket." *Reuters*. www.commondreams .org/headlines03/1201-01.htm.

Pickett, S. T. A., and J. M. Grove. 2009. "Urban ecosystems: What Would Tansley Do?" *Urban Ecosystems* 12: 1–8.

Pickett, S. T. A., et al. 2008. "Beyond Urban Legends: An Emerging Framework of Urban Ecology, as Illustrated by the Baltimore Ecosystem Study." *Bioscience* 58: 139–50.

Pickett, S. T. A., et al. 2001. "Urban Ecological Systems: Linking Terrestrial Ecological, Physical, and Socioeconomic Components of Metropolitan Areas." *Annual Review of Ecology and Systematics* 32: 127–57.

Platt, R. 2006. *The Human Metropolis*. Amherst: University of Massachusetts Press.

Platt, R., R. Rowntree, and P. Muick. 1994. *The Ecological City: Preserving and Restoring Urban Biodiversity*. Amherst: University of Massachusetts Press.

Pooley, E. 2010. "In Wreckage of Climate Bill, Some Clues for Moving Forward." *Yale Environment 360*, 29 July. www.energybulletin.net/node/53620.

Poppendieck, J. 2010. *Free For All: Fixing School Food in America*. Berkeley: University of California Press.

Population Research Center, Portland State University. 2009. *Portland Demographic Trends*. Updated 22 November. Available on compact disk.

Portland Development Commission. No date. *Economic Development Strategy: A Five-Year Plan for Promoting Job Creation and Economic Growth*. www.pdxeconomicdevelopment .com/docs/Portland-Ec-Dev-Strategy.pdf (26 June 26, 2010).

Portland Energy Office. 2000. *Carbon Dioxide Reduction Strategy: Success and Setbacks*. Portland, OR.

Portland General Electric. 2009. *The Electricity Sector's Role in Oregon Carbon Emissions*. Portland, OR.

Portland Sustainable Development Commission. 2005. "Summary of Energy Efficiency and Renewable Energy Committee Research and Recommendation to Adopt the Goal to Achieve a 100 Percent Renewable Energy Economy by 2040." 18 January.

Portney, K. 2003. *Taking Sustainable Cities Seriously: Economic Development, the Environment, and Quality of Life in American Cities*. Cambridge: MIT Press.

Portney, K. E., and J. M. Berry. 2010. "Participation and the Pursuit of Sustainability in U.S. Cities." *Urban Affairs Review* 46 (1): 119–39.

Portney, K. E., and Z. Cuttler. 2010. "The Local Nonprofit Sector and the Pursuit of Sustainability in American Cities: A Preliminary Exploration." *Local Environment* 15 (4): 323–39.

Pothukuchi, K., and J. L. Kaufman. 2000. "The Food System: A Stranger to the Planning Field." *Journal of the American Planning Association*, no. 2: 113.

Powell, L. M., et al. 2007. "Food Store Availability and Neighborhood Characteristics in the United States." *Preventive Medicine* 44, no. 3: 189–95.

Prince George's County Goes Green. 2009. *Goes Green Steering Committee's Annual*

Report to County Executive Jack B. Johnson. Spring. www.princegeorgescountymd.gov
/Government/AgencyIndex/GoingGreen/pdf/2009-annual-green-report.pdf.

Progressive Policy Institute. 2003. "Driving Down Carbon Dioxide." Washington,
DC, 14 November. www.ppionline.org/ppi_ci.cfm?knlgAreaID=116&subsecID=
900039&ccontentID=252224.

Pucher, J., and R. Buehler. 2008. "Making Cycling Irresistible: Lessons from the Netherlands, Denmark, and Germany." *Transport Reviews* 28, no. 4 (2008): 1–57.

Puna Geothermal Venture. 2009. "History of the Puna Geothermal Venture." www
.punageothermalventure.com/PGV/15/history.

Pyke, C. 2009. "Acknowledgements: From the Director of Research at USGBC." *The Journal of Sustainable Real Estate* 1, no. 1. www.costar.com/josre/JournalPdfs/00-Preface
-Contents-Board.pdf.

Raco, M. 2007. "Spatial Policy, Sustainability and State Restructuring: A Reassessment of
State Sustainable Community Building in England." In *The Sustainable Development
Paradox*, ed. R. Krueger and D. Gibbs. New York: Guilford Press.

Redclift, M. 2005. "Sustainable Development (1987–2005): An Oxymoron Comes of Age."
Sustainable Development 13, no. 4.

Redden, J. 2009. "Views Mixed on Climate Change Strategy." *Portland Tribune*, 9 July. www
.thetribonline.org/sustainable/print_story.php?story_id=124699156820032200.

Register, R. 2006. *Ecocities: Rebuilding Cities in Balance with Nature*. Gabriola Island, B.C.:
New Society Publishers.

Rosenzweig, C., et al. 2006. *Mitigating New York City's Heat Island with Urban Forestry, Living Roofs, and Light Surfaces*. Presentation at 86th American Meteorological Society Annual Meeting, Atlanta, GA. www.giss.nasa.gov/research/news/20060130/103341.pdf.

Sabatier, P. A., W. Focht, M. Lubell, Z. Trachtenberg, A. Vedlitz, and M. Matlock, eds. 2005.
Swimming Upstream: Collaborative Approaches to Watershed Management. Cambridge:
MIT Press.

Samuelsohn, D., and R. Bravender. 2009. "EPA Releases Bush-Era Endangerment Document." *New York Times*, 13 October. www.nytimes.com/gwire/2009/10/13/13greenwire
-epa-releases-bush-era-endangerment-document-47439.html.

Scheer, H. 2007. *Energy Autonomy*. London: Earthscan.

Science Foundation Arizona. No date. "History." www.sfaz.org/about-sfaz/our-history.aspx (1
July 2010).

Sentman, S., LEED AP, chair of the National Capital Region Chapter of the USGBC. 2010.
Personal communication, 2 September.

SFCriticalMass.org Blog. No date. www.sfcriticalmass.org/ (23 June 2010).

SFCTA (San Francisco County Transportation Authority). 2008. *Automobile Trips Generated: CEQA Impact Measure and Mitigation Program*. San Francisco: County of San
Francisco.

SFCTA (San Francisco County Transportation Authority). 2004. *Countywide Transportation
Plan*. San Francisco: County of San Francisco.

SFMTA (San Francisco Municipal Transportation Agency). 2010a. *2009 San Francisco State
of Cycling Report*. San Francisco: San Francisco Bicycle Program, Department of Parking
and Traffic, Municipal Transportation Agency.

SFMTA (San Francisco Municipal Transportation Agency). 2010b. *Pilot Study of Required Right Turns on Eastbound Market Street*. San Francisco: San Francisco Municipal Transportation Agency.

SFMTA (San Francisco Municipal Transportation Agency). 2009. *2008 San Francisco State of Cycling Report*. San Francisco: San Francisco Bicycle Program, Department of Parking and Traffic, Municipal Transportation Agency.

Shaheen, S., and A. Cohen. 2007. "Growth in Worldwide Carsharing: An International Comparison." *Transportation Research Record: Journal of the Transportation Research Board* 1992: 81–89.

Shaheen, S., A. Cohen, and M. Chung. 2009. "Carsharing in North America: A Ten-Year Retrospective." *Transportation Research Record: Journal of the Transportation Research Board* 2110: 35–44.

Shaheen, S., D. Sperling, and C. Wagner. 1998. "Carsharing in Europe and North America: Past, Present, and Future." *Transportation Quarterly* Summer: 35–52.

Sigma Group. 2004. *Locating in Milwaukee's Menomonee River Valley, an Impact Report*. Milwaukee, WI: Sigma Group and the Sixteenth Street Community Health Center.

Sixteenth Street Community Health Center. 2002. *Menomonee River Valley National Design Competition, Executive Summary*. Milwaukee, WI: Competition sponsored by the Sixteenth Street Community Health Center, Menomonee Valley Partners Inc., the City of Milwaukee, the Milwaukee Metropolitan Sewerage District, Wisconsin Department of Natural Resources, and Milwaukee County.

Sixteenth Street Community Health Center. 2000. *A Vision for Smart Growth: Sustainable Development Design Charrette Milwaukee's Menomonee River Valley 1999–2000*. Milwaukee, WI: Sixteenth Street Community Health Center, Department of Environmental Health.

Skyscraper City. 2009. "Longest Undersea Cable in the World." *Skyscraper City*, 9 July. www.skyscrapercity.com/showthread.php?t=975420.

Slavin, M. I. 2010. "Where the Wind Blows and Sun Shines: A Comparative Analysis of State Renewable Energy Standards." *Renewable Energy World North America* (May/June): 1–4.

Slavin, M. I. 1988. *Washington County Economic Base and Labor Market Analysis*. Hillsboro, OR: Washington County, Oregon, Department of Land Use and Planning.

Smith, J. 2008. "ASU Recycling Program Expands—and Compacts." *Arizona State University News Service*. http://asunews.asu.edu/20080814_recycling (1 July 2010).

Smith, L. C. 2010. "Unfreezing Arctic Assets." *Wall Street Journal*, 18 September. http://online.wsj.com/article/SB10001424052748703440604575496261529207620.html?mod=WSJ_hps_LEFTTopStories.

Snyder, D. 2008. *Interview with David Snyder, former executive director of SFBC*. San Francisco, 15 June.

Solar Energy Industries Association. 2010. "Solar Tax Policies Can Add 200,000 New Jobs, Nearly 10,000 Megawatts of Solar Installation." 19 May. www.seia.org/galleries/pdf/Solar_Factsheet_EUP_Full_Study.pdf.

Springside School. 2010. *Inside Springside School*. Springside School. www.springside.org.

State of Hawaii Department of Business, Economic Development and Tourism and U.S. Bureau of the Census. 2010. *2009 State of Hawaii Data Book*. http://hawaii.gov/dbedt/info /economic/databook/db2009/index_html.

State of Hawaii Department of Business, Economic Development and Tourism and U.S. Bureau of the Census. 2008. *State of Hawaii Energy Resources Coordinator Annual Report 2008*. http://hawaii.gov/dbedt/info/energy/publications/erc08.pdf.

State of Hawaii Department of Business, Economic Development and Tourism and U.S. Bureau of the Census. 2005. *Energy and Hawaii: The Need for Options, Strategic Integrated Policies, and Change*. Honolulu, HI.

State of the Air. 2010. "Most Polluted Cities" *American Lung Association*. www.stateoftheair .org/2010/city-rankings/most-polluted-cities.html.

Sterlicchi, J. 2010. "GM to Power Up Michigan Volt Battery Plant." *Business Green*, 6 January. www.businessgreen.com/business-green/news/2255661/gm-power-volt-battery-plant.

Story, M., et al. 2008. "Creating Healthy Food and Eating Environments: Policy and Environmental Approaches." *Annual Review of Public Health* 29: 253–72.

Stringer, S. M. 2010. "FoodNYC: A Blueprint for a Sustainable Food System." NY: *Office of the President of the Borough of Manhattan*. www.mbpo.org/release_details.asp?id=1496 (August 9, 2010).

Sukopp, H. 2002. "On the Early History of Urban Ecology in Europe." *Preslia Prahs*, 74: 373–93. In *Urban Ecology: An International Perspective on the Interaction Between Humans and Nature*, ed. J. M. Marzluff, et al. New York: Springer, 2008.

Svendsen, E. S., and L.K. Campbell. 2008. "Urban Ecological Stewardship: Understanding the Structure, Function and Network of Community-Based Urban Land Management." *Cities and the Environment* 1: 4.

Switzky, J. 2002. "Riding to See." In *Critical Mass: Bicycling's Defiant Celebration*, ed. C. Carlsson, 186–92. Oakland, CA: AK Press.

Temple-Villanova Sustainable Stormwater Initiative. 2010. Regional BMP Projects. Temple-Villanova Sustainable Stormwater Initiative 2009. www.csc.temple.edu/t-vssi /BMPSurvey/vacant_lands.htm (June 7 2010).

Thompson, E. Jr., A. E. Harper, and S. Kraus. 2008. "Think Globally—Eat Locally: San Francisco Foodshed Assessment." *American Farmland Trust*. www.farmland.org /programs/states/ca/Feature%20Stories/San-Francisco-Foodshed-Report.asp (August 5, 2010).

Treuhaft, S., M. J. Hamm, and C. Litjens. 2009. *Healthy Food for All: Building Equitable and Sustainable Food Systems in Detroit and Oakland*. MI: Michigan State University.

Tumber, C. 2009. "Small, Green and Good: The Role of Neglected Cities in a Sustainable Future." *Boston Review*, March/April. http://bostonreview.net/BR34.2/tumber.php.

Turner, W. R., N. Toshihiko, and M. Dinetti. 2004. "Global Urbanization and the Separation of Humans from Nature." *Bioscience* 54: 585–90.

Underwriters Laboratory. 2009. "UL Creates Largest Solar Testing Lab in North America." *Quality Digest*. www.qualitydigest.com/inside/quality-insider-news/ul-creates-largest -solar-testing-lab-north-america.html.

Union of Concerned Scientists. 2007. *Confronting Climate Change in the U.S. Northeast: New York*. Washington, DC: Northeast Climate Impacts Assessment. www .climatechoices.org/assets/documents/climatechoices/new-york_necia.pdf.

United Nations Environmental Program. 2000. Agenda 21: Section 28, Local Authorities. New York: United Nations.

United States Conference of Mayors. 2008. *U.S. Conference of Mayors Climate Protection Agreement*. www.usmayors.org/climateprotection/agreement.htm.

Ursery, S. 2003. "Miami-Dade Studying Climate Change." *American City & County*, 1 December. http://americancityandcounty.com/mag/government_miamidade_studying _climate/.

U.S. Census Bureau. 2010. "Honolulu CDP, Hawaii." *State & County QuickFacts*. http://quickfacts.census.gov/qfd/states/15/1517000.html.

U.S. Census Bureau. No date. *Density Using Land Area For States, Counties, Metropolitan Areas, and Places*. www.census.gov/population/www/censusdata/density.html.

U.S. Conference of Mayors. 1999. "U.S. Conference of Mayors Forms National Council for Resource Conservation." http://usmayors.org/pressreleases/documents/ncrc.htm (accessed August 12, 2009).

U.S. Conference of Mayors and the Mayors Climate Protection Center. 2008. "Current and Potential Green Jobs in the U.S. Economy." www.usmayors.org/climateprotection /surveys.htm.

U.S. Department of Energy. No date. "Memorandum of Understanding Between the State of Hawaii and the U.S. Department of Energy." n.d. http://apps1.eere.energy.gov/news/pdfs /hawaii_mou.pdf.

U.S. Department of Energy, Energy Information Administration. 2010a. "Crude Oil and Total Petroleum Imports." 29 July. www.eia.doe.gov/pub/oil_gas/petroleum/data _publications/company_level_imports/current/import.html.

U.S. Department of Energy, Energy Information Administration. 2010b. "Estimated Levelized Cost of New Generation Resources, 2016." www.eia.doe.gov/oiaf/aeo/electricity _generation.html.

U.S. Department of Energy, Energy Information Administration. 2010c. "Independent Statistics and Analysis." www.eia.doe.gov/.

U.S. Department of Energy, Office of Energy Efficiency and Renewable Energy. 2010. "Wind Powering America." www.windpoweringamerica.gov/wind_installed_capacity .asp.

U.S. Department of Energy, National Renewable Energy Laboratory. 2010a. "Hawaii Clean Energy Initiative Existing Building Energy Efficiency Analysis, November 17, 2009–June 30, 2010." NREL/SR-7A2-48318.

U.S. Department of Energy, National Renewable Energy Laboratory. 2010b. "Hawaii, 50 meter Wind Power." 26 March. www.windpoweringamerica.gov/images/windmaps/hi_50m _800.jpg.

U.S. Department of Energy, National Renewable Energy Laboratory. 2008. "Energy Imports and High Rates Squeeze the State." 5 September. www.nrel.gov/features/20080905 _islands_initiative.html.

U.S. Department of Labor. Bureau of Labor Statistics. 2010a. www.bls.gov/home.htm.

U.S. Department of Labor. Bureau of Labor Statistics. 2010b. "Unemployment Rates for Metropolitan Areas." www.bls.gov/web/metro/laummtrk.htm.

USDOT (United States Department of Transportation). 2010. *The National Bicycling and Walking Study: 15-year Status Report*. Washington, DC: USDOT.

U.S. Environmental Protection Agency. 2010. *Watershed Management Approach*. U.S. Environmental Protection Agency, September 12, 2008, 1994. www.epa.gov/owow/watershed/framework/ (20 May, 2010).

U.S. Environmental Protection Agency. 2008. *Managing Wet Weather with Green Infrastructure. Action Strategy*, edited by Office of Water. Washington DC: U.S. Environmental Protection Agency.

U.S. Environmental Protection Agency. 2007 "New York City Filtration Avoidance Determination. Surface Water Treatment Rule Determination for New York City's Catskill/Delaware Water Supply System." www.epa.gov/region2/water/nycshed/doc_links.html (August 5, 2010).

U.S. Environmental Protection Agency. 2004. *Report to Congress: Impacts and Control of CSOs and SSOs*, edited by Office of Water. Washington DC: U.S. Environmental Protection Agency.

U.S. Environmental Protection Agency. 2001. *Report to Congress: Implementation and Enforcement of Combined Sewer Overflow Control Policy*, edited by Office of Water. Washington DC: U.S. Environmental Protection Agency.

U.S. Environmental Protection Agency. 1994. *Combined Sewer Overflow Control Policy*, edited by Office of Water. Washington DC: Federal Register.

U.S. Environmental Protection Agency. No date. *Heat Island Effect*. www.epa.gov/heatisld/.

U.S. Environmental Protection Agency. No date. "Heat Island Effect Research." www.epa.gov/heatisland/research/index.html (August 5, 2010).

U.S. General Services Administration. No date. *Sustainable Design Program*. www.gsa.gov/portal/category/21083.

U.S. Geological Survey. No date. *The Water Cycle: Evapotranspiration*. http://ga.water.usgs.gov/edu/watercycleevapotranspiration.html.

U.S. Green Building Council. 2009a. "Foundations of LEED." www.usgbc.org/ShowFile.aspx?DocumentID=6103.

U.S. Green Building Council. 2009b. "Summary of Government LEED Incentives." www.usgbc.org/ShowFile.aspx?DocumentID=2021.

U.S. Green Building Council. No date. "Green Building Facts." www.usgbc.org/DisplayPage.aspx?cmspageID=1718.

U.S. Green Building Council. No date. "Public Policy Search." www.usgbc.org/PublicPolicy/SearchPublicPolicies.aspx?PageID=1776.

Veslany, K. 2002. *Purchase of Development Rights: Conserving Lands, Preserving Western Livelihoods*. San Francisco: Trust for Public Land.

Vitiello, D., and Nairn, M. 2009. *Community Gardening in Philadelphia 2008 Harvest Report*. PA: University of Pennsylvania.

Vitiello, D., and Nairn, M. 2008. *Community Gardening in Philadelphia*. PA: University of Pennsylvania.

Voicu, I., and Been, V. 2007. *The Effects of Community Gardens on Neighboring Property Values*. New York: New York University.

Vorhees, J. 2009. "EPA Unveils New Emissions Standards for Cars." *Scientific American*, 15 September. www.scientificamerican.com/article.cfm?id=auto-standards-cafe-rules-green-house-gas-epa.

Wachs, M. 1998. "Creating Political Pressure for Cycling." *Transportation Quarterly* 52, no. 1: 6–8.

Weinberg, H. 1995. *Do All Trails Lead to Oregon? An Analysis of the Characteristics of People Moving to and From Oregon 1985–1990.* Center for Population Research and Census, Portland State University.

Weiss, J. D. 2002. "Local Government and Sustainability: Major Progress, Significant Challenges." In *Stumbling Toward Sustainability*, ed. J. Dernbach. Washington, DC: Environmental Law Institute.

Whatcomcounts.org. 2009. "Portland's Local Action Plan to Reduce Carbon Dioxide Emissions." www.whatcomcounts.org/whatcom/modules.php?op=modload&name=PromisePractice&file=promisePractice&pid=155.

White, S., et al. 1988. *The Changing Milwaukee Industrial Structure, 1979–1988.* Milwaukee, WI: The Urban Research Center, University of Wisconsin–Milwaukee.

Whyte , W. 1958. *The Exploding Metropolis.* New York: Doubleday.

Wildermuth, J. 2010. "City Working to Make Car-Sharing More Popular." *San Francisco Chronicle*, 6 August.

Wisconsin Department of Natural Resources. 1996. *Henry Aaron State Trail, Feasibility Study Master Plan and Environmental Assessment.* Madison, WI: Menomonee Valley Greenway Advisory Committee, National Park Service, and Wisconsin Department of Natural Resources.

Wittig, R., et al. 1995. "What Should an Ideal City Look Like from and Ecological View? Ecological Demands on the Future City." *Ökologie und Naturschuz*, 4: 157–61, in *Urban Ecology: An International Perspective on the Interaction Between Humans and Nature*, ed. J. M. Marzluff, et al. New York: Springer, 2008.

World Commission on Environment and Development. 1987. *Our Common Future: Report of the World Commission on Environment and Development.* New York: Oxford University Press. Published as Annex to General Assembly document A/42/427, Development and International Co-operation: Environment, August 2, 1987.

World Wildlife Fund. 2001. "Nike Partners with WWF and Center for Energy and Climate Solutions to Reduce Greenhouse Gas Emissions." www.worldwildlife.org/who/media/press/2001/WWFPresitem10798.html (accessed March 23, 2010).

Wray, H. J. 2008. *Pedal Power: The Quiet Rise of the Bicycle in American Public Life.* Boulder: Paradigm Publishers.

Zeemering, E. 2009. "What Does Sustainability Mean to City Officials?" *Urban Affairs Review*, 45 (2): 247–73.

Zenk, S. N., et al. 2005. "Fruit and Vegetable Intake in African Americans Income and Store Characteristics." *American Journal of Preventive Medicine.*

Ralph Bennett, AIA, LEED-AP, is president of Bennett Frank McCarthy Architects of Silver Spring, Maryland. The firm specializes in residential architecture from single-family homes and renovations for institutional housing, to master planning and urban design. The firm's work has won a number local and national design awards and competitions. Bennett is professor emeritus in the School of Architecture Planning and Preservation at the University of Maryland where he taught in the design studio program at all levels, graduate and undergraduate, for thirty-one years. Bennett is a former commissioner and chair of the Montgomery County Housing Opportunities Commission where he served for thirteen years, and he is a former president of the Potomac Valley Chapter of the American Institute of Architects. In the spring of 2010, he devised and taught a course called "Measuring Sustainability" in which eleven students became accredited as LEED Green Associates.

Douglas A. Codiga is an energy and environmental attorney in Honolulu, Hawaii. Codiga regularly advises clients in a wide range of environmental matters with an emphasis on emerging clean energy, climate change, and green building law and policy. In 2007, he founded Hawaii's first climate and sustainability law practice group at the law firm of Schlack Ito, LLC. With graduate law degrees from the University of Hawaii and Yale Law School, Mr. Codiga frequently publishes and lectures on clean energy, climate change, and environmental law and policy in Hawaii and the Asia Pacific region, including Singapore, China, and Japan. His publications include environmental law treatises and feature articles on Hawaii's climate change, clean energy, and green building laws and policies. He is an affiliate of the U.S. Sea Grant Center for Island Climate Adaptation and Policy and has lectured at the University of Hawaii law school on environmental law since 1996.

Nevin Cohen is assistant professor of environmental studies at the New School, where he teaches courses in urban planning and food systems. He serves as chair of the Tishman Environment and Design Center, the university's interdisciplinary environmental research and education center and home to its undergraduate program in environmental studies. Dr. Cohen's current research focuses on urban food policy, particularly innovative planning strategies to support food production in the urban and peri-urban landscape, public policies to engage citizens in sustainable food production, planning and food access, and civic agriculture in cities and suburbs. He has a PhD in urban planning from Rutgers University, a master's in city and regional planning from Berkeley, and a BA from Cornell.

Christopher De Sousa is associate professor and chair of urban planning at the University of Wisconsin–Milwaukee. He is also a faculty member in the Department of Geography and the Urban Studies program, as well as founding co-director of the Brownfields Research Consortium. Dr. De Sousa received his MSc in planning and PhD in geography from the University of Toronto. His research activities focus on various aspects of brownfields redevelopment, urban environmental management, and sustainability reporting in the United States and Canada. He is currently involved in a collaborative research project examining best management practices in sustainable brownfields redevelopment funded by the U.S. Environmental Protection Agency. His recent book entitled *Brownfields Redevelopment and the Quest for Sustainability* is published by Elsevier/Emerald Group.

Jonathan Fink is vice president for research and strategic partnerships at Portland State University. Previously, Dr. Fink developed and led institution-wide approaches to sustainability research, teaching, and business operations as sustainability officer at Arizona State University and director, respectively, of the University's Center for Sustainability Science Applications and Global Institute of Sustainability. He has worked with the staff of the National Academy of Sciences to promote enhanced funding of urban systems research by federal mission agencies. He is a fellow of the Geological Society of America and the American Association for the Advancement of Science, a trustee of the Arizona Chapter of the Nature Conservancy, and a member of the board of advisors of the Smithsonian Institution's National Museum of Natural History and the National Advisory Board for KB Homes.

Amy E. Gardner, AIA LEED-AP, is a faculty member at the University of Maryland School of Architecture, Planning, and Preservation, and director of the Center for the Use of Sustainable Practices. With a focus is on academic-industrial partnerships, and on developing design and research practices necessary for creating enduring ecological design, she is principal investigator for UMD's entry to the 2011 Department of Energy Solar Decathlon, as well as University of Maryland's LEAFHouse entry to the 2007 Solar Decathlon. As a principal in the firm Gardner Mohr Architects LLC, Professor Gardner is also committed to environmental stewardship through integrated, inventive design and professional leadership. Her work has been recognized with many design honors; published in the *Washington Post, Builder, Dream Homes of Greater Washington DC, ArchitectureDC*; televised on HGTV and the Learning Channel; and exhibited at the National Building Museum, and the Baltimore and D.C. chapters of the AIA.

Aaron Golub is assistant professor in the School of Geographical Sciences and Urban Planning and School of Sustainability at Arizona State University. His teaching and research interests include planning for alternative transportation modes, the social and environmental impacts of transportation, and the history of urban transportation in the United States. He has worked on numerous research projects related to public transportation planning and policy, car sharing, and environmental justice issues in transportation. He is also an avid bicycle commuter and has been a car-share user for more than eight years. Dr. Golub received his doctorate in civil engineering from the University of California at Berkeley in 2003.

Jason Henderson is professor of geography at San Francisco State University. His research interests include the politics of transportation (including bicycle advocacy), debates over parking, and the relationship between transportation policy and political ideology. Henderson is currently writing a book on the politics of mobility in San Francisco and has published scholarly papers on transportation politics in Atlanta and San Francisco. He teaches courses on urban transportation and land use at SFSU, and serves on various community boards and committees involving transportation and planning in San Francisco.

Gerrit Knaap is professor of urban studies and planning at the University of Maryland and executive director of the National Center for Smart Growth Research and Education. He is the author of more than fifty articles and five books on state and local land use planning and economics. His research interests include the economics and politics of land use planning, the efficacy of economic development instruments, and impacts of environmental policy. Knaap is recipient of the Chester Rapkin award. With Greg Lindsey, he shared the 1998 best of the Association of Collegiate Schools of Planning award. In 2006, he received the Outstanding Planner Award from the Maryland chapter of the American Planning Association. Gerrit serves on the Science and Technical Advisory Committee to the Chesapeake Bay Commission. As executive director of the National Center for Smart Growth Research and Education, he is a member of the Maryland Governor's Smart Growth sub-cabinet.

Lynn Mandarano is assistant professor at the Department of Community and Regional Planning and research fellow at the Center of Sustainable Communities at Temple University. Her research focuses on understanding the influences planning innovations such as collaborative processes and sustainable development practices have had on our natural resources and governance capacity in local to regional environmental planning contexts. Her work has been published in the *Journal of Planning, Education and Research, Society and Natural Resources, Journal of Environmental Planning and Management*, and *Journal of the American Water Resources Association*. Dr. Mandarano worked for more than twenty years as a professional consultant in environmental planning and public policy for U.S. municipal, county, and state governments, private business, and international clients.

P. Timon McPhearson is assistant professor of urban ecology at the New School's Tishman Environment and Design Center in New York City, where he teaches undergraduate ecology and environmental science and coordinates the Environmental Studies program for the university. He earned his PhD in ecology, evolution, and natural resources from Rutgers University, is a former National Science Foundation Fellow, and was a scientist at the Center for Biodiversity and Conservation at the American Museum of Natural History. Dr. McPhearson was awarded a Columbia Science Fellowship (postdoctoral) with Columbia University's Earth Institute where he helped create the university's first required undergraduate science course, Frontiers of Science. Dr. McPhearson's current research is focused on understanding the socio-ecology of urban systems, including an interdisciplinary, long-term study of the relationship between urban land management practices and ecosystem structure and functioning in New York City.

Jennifer Obadia is a doctoral candidate in the Agriculture, Food, and Environment program at the Friedman School of Nutrition Science and Policy at Tufts University. Her research focuses on the viability of farmers' markets in Massachusetts. Outside the classroom, Jennifer works on farmers' market nutrition programs at the Massachusetts Department of Agricultural Resources. She is also actively involved in nutrition and agriculture education. Jennifer has developed a school garden program at a Boston elementary school and a nutrition program at an area high school. Before enrolling at Tufts, Jennifer spent two years working on an organic vegetable farm and two years teaching sustainable agriculture and environmental science. She has an MS in sustainable development and conservation biology from the University of Maryland, College Park, in 2003 and a BA from New York University's Gallatin School in 1999.

Kent E. Portney is professor of political science at Tufts University. He has published widely on issues of sustainable cities in the United States, including his 2003 book *Taking Sustainable Cities Seriously: Economic Development, the Environment, and Quality of Life in American Cities,* and recent articles in *Public Administration Review, Urban Affairs Review* and *Local Environment.* His work currently focuses on how local and regional governance systems affect the "political will" for local public officials to embrace sustainability policies and related programs.

Madlen Simon is an experienced architect, educator, and scholar dedicated to preparing students for professional careers in architecture. During thirty years in professional practice, Professor Simon developed a keen interest in innovative education for the next generation of architects. She brings to architectural education both design expertise and scholarly reflection on practice. Professor Simon entered academia in 1991 after fourteen years practicing architecture in two world-renowned architecture firms—Skidmore, Owings & Merrill and Edward Larrabee Barnes Associates—as well as leading her own firm, Simon Design. Professor Simon directs the Architecture Program at University of Maryland and teaches seminars and architectural design studios including the comprehensive studio, sustainable skins studio, solar decathlon studio, and building culture seminar. She is coprincipal investigator on the University of Maryland's Solar Decathlon 2011.

Matthew I. Slavin is founder and principal of Sustaingrüp, a Washington, D.C., based consultancy helping business and government to embrace a culture of sustainable business practices, develop and adopt clean-tech energy innovation, and craft climate change strategies. Slavin's work on aligning business and government leadership, goals, and resources to address the challenge of creating a cleaner environment, fostering energy security and strengthening economic competitiveness began in the 1980s and his work has taken him both to a number of states and cities in the United States as well as overseas. Matt is a frequent contributor to publications on clean energy, climate change and sustainability and his writing has been featured in leading professional journals and metropolitan newspapers. He holds a PhD from the School of Urban and Public Affairs, Portland State University.

Kent Snyder is a sustainability consultant and attorney in Portland, Oregon. He received his BS cum laude in 1975 in environmental biology from Kansas State University and his JD in 1978 from Lewis & Clark Law School. Kent served for ten years on the Sustainable Development Commission of Portland and Multnomah County including three years as cochair. During his tenure, Kent helped steer launch of Portland's Green Building Initiative, various sustainable procurement policies, Toxics Reduction Strategy, Sustainable Economic Development Plan, and the city's Climate Action initiatives. He is a member of the board of directors of the International Sustainable Development Foundation, the board of councilors of the China–U.S. Center for Sustainable Development and is chair of the board of directors of EPEAT, Inc. Kent also chairs the national board of trustees of the American Leadership Forum. Kent is an attorney and a nationally recognized expert in bankruptcy law.

Cari Varner is a PhD student in urban and regional planning at the University of Maryland. In 2009, the Design Futures Council selected Cari as an emerging leader in sustainable design. Between 2007 and 2010, she was assistant director of the Carl Small Town Center, a nonprofit community design center at Mississippi State University. She holds a bachelor of science degree in design and environmental analysis from Cornell University and a master of science in environmental psychology and a master of urban planning from the University of Michigan. Cari's research interests focus upon human-environmental relations and the way the built environment contains clues to understanding our own culture and values.

Jason Zeller has more than thirty years of professional experience in the public utilities and energy field. He was the coauthor of a groundbreaking study in 1979 that examined opportunities for saving energy in New York City. He is a licensed attorney in California, Oregon, and Washington and currently is an assistant chief counsel with the California Public Utilities Commission. He has worked as both a technical analyst and attorney in all aspects of public utility regulation and most recently has concentrated on energy conservation opportunities with water utilities. From 1990–1997 Mr. Zeller served as the Manager of the Washington State Energy Facility Site Evaluation Council and was involved in the environmental review of numerous proposed power plants and oil pipelines. Mr. Zeller is a magna cum laude graduate of Claremont McKenna College, has a master of arts in urban affairs and policy analysis from the New School University and a juris doctor degree from New York Law School.